The Crisis of
Catiline

REACTING TO THE PAST is an award-winning series of immersive role-playing games that actively engage students in their own learning. Students assume the roles of historical characters and practice critical thinking, primary source analysis, and argument, both written and spoken. Reacting games are flexible enough to be used across the curriculum, from first-year general education classes and discussion sections of lecture classes to capstone experiences, intersession courses, and honors programs.

Reacting to the Past was originally developed under the auspices of Barnard College and is sustained by the Reacting Consortium of colleges and universities. The Consortium hosts a regular series of conferences and events to support faculty and administrators.

NOTE TO INSTRUCTORS: Before beginning the game you must download the game materials, including an instructor's manual containing a detailed schedule of class sessions, role sheets for students, and handouts.

To download these essential resources, visit https://reactingconsortium.org/games, click on the page for this title, then click "Game Materials."

The Crisis of Catiline

ROME, 63 BCE

BRET MULLIGAN

BARNARD

The University of North Carolina Press

Chapel Hill

Cover art: Caesare Maccari, *Cicero Denounces Catiline* (1888).

ISBN 978-1-4696-6413-2 (pbk.: alk. paper)

ISBN 978-1-4696-6414-9 (e-book)

Contents

Illustrations

The Crisis of Catiline

1

Introduction

Rome, 63 BCE: a chaotic year of urban and rural unrest, economic instability, sensational trials, and electoral misconduct. You are a Roman senator. Can you save the Republic . . . and yourself?

The Crisis of Catiline begins in 63 BCE.[1] If you are playing the multisession version of the game, it begins in the sweltering summer, just after a controversial election. Lucius Sergius Catilina (or Catiline), a charismatic (and scandal-plagued) noble, has just lost his second election for the consulship.

Consuls were the most influential and powerful **magistrates** in the Roman Republic. There were always two co-equal consuls, elected to one year in office, who could check each other's power. When within Rome, they functioned as the heads-of-state; outside of the city, they served as commanders-in-chief of the military.

Dissatisfaction with the current system made Catiline popular among the urban and rural poor and with many disaffected members of the nobility whose careers were thwarted by the wealthy and insular faction that dominated Roman politics. During the most recent campaign, Catiline proposed significant reforms to address the hardships facing poor Roman citizens, whose livelihoods had been undermined by the social and economic changes caused by Rome's emergence as a commercial and military superpower. Could these reforms rebalance power between the **senate** and the Roman people—the twin pillars of the Roman Republic (*senatus populusque Romanus*, or *SPQR*)—or will it lead, as Catiline's opponents claim, to chaos and a revolution that will destroy the most successful and durable form of government the world had ever known?

Fear of Catiline has led the entrenched elites to support an unlikely champion: Marcus Tullius Cicero, a brilliant orator and savvy politician. The son of a well-off businessman from the small town of Arpinum, sixty miles southeast of Rome, Cicero is an outsider, a "new man" (***novus homo***)—the first member of his family to be elected as a Roman magistrate and so join the Roman senate. Cicero and some of Rome's more perceptive leaders acknowledge that cautious reform is necessary, but they also believe that Catiline's reckless promises and rumored plans for violence pose a threat to public order. Other senators remain unsure about whether Catiline or Cicero can be trusted to set the best course for Rome.

Your instructor will set the moment in 63 BCE when your version of *The Crisis of Catiline* will begin. Your game may address multiple issues confronting Rome in the summer of 63 or dive straight into the depths of the crisis in the fall of that year. But eventually the game (and Rome) will arrive at November 8, 63 BCE, when you and your fellow senators must decide whether you will issue the final decree of the senate (***senatus consultum ultimum***, or ***SCU***), which authorizes the consuls to "take any measure necessary that the state suffer no harm."

Have Catiline's enemies conspired to thwart desperately needed social and economic reforms by slandering Catiline and his followers? What proposals will Catiline and his supporters make, and what actions will they take? And what will other Romans do about (or to) Catiline and those who support him and his policies? Now, Roman, is your time to decide.

Once the game arrives at November 8, Cicero, as consul, may act against his opponents even without senatorial authorization. Uncertainty about what authority the consul possesses will be untenable to the senators who support Catiline but also to many other senators who fear the unchecked power of the state, a faction, or Cicero himself. Cicero and his supporters, therefore, should strongly want to pass a decree that supports their authority. In the absence of this support, how can they be sure that their actions to safeguard the Republic have support? Will they be legally culpable for actions they take in defense of the state? A failure to support the consuls might even call into question actions taken by senators and consuls during previous moments of unrest. A strong show of support for the consul might just pull Rome back from the brink.

Economic turmoil contributed to the unstable conditions that threaten Rome in 63 BCE. But *The Crisis of Catiline* will eventually require you to act to solve a *political* crisis. If the senate is unable to find a legislative solution to this crisis, instability will increase and events will spin out of control. In short, all senators—of every faction—have a vested interest that the senate take some action that reduces the chances of complete chaos. The results of the earlier debates (in the multisession version of the game) shape the ground on which the debate over the *SCU* will be waged. Every speech, every decision matters—just as it did in 63 BCE.

Your role sheet will reveal whether you support Catiline, oppose him, or remain undecided about which path to take; you may even have your own agenda. But as a senator, your goal will be to lead Rome out of this crisis by persuading the senate to adopt decrees (*consulta*) consistent with the goals of your character or faction. You will do this by persuading your fellow senators through one or more short speeches that propose solutions to the crises that confront Rome—or by supporting or condemning the proposals made by other senators. Crafting a persuasive speech will require you to reflect on how Rome arrived at this point of crisis. You will also have to consider the viewpoints of your friends and enemies, which you can discover by listening carefully to their speeches and speaking with them outside of the senate. Some Romans will oppose your opinions to their dying breath—but others are persuadable by the right argument, if it is well-presented.

The fate of Rome (and quite possibly your own life) is in your hands. Take care, Roman, that you prosper!

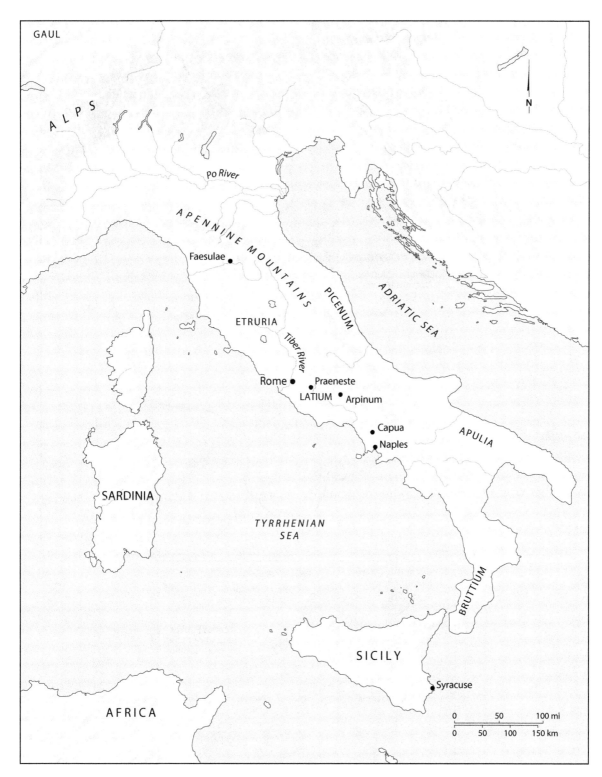

MAP 1.1 Roman Italy in 63 BCE.

Source: Ancient World Mapping Center (awmc.unc.edu).

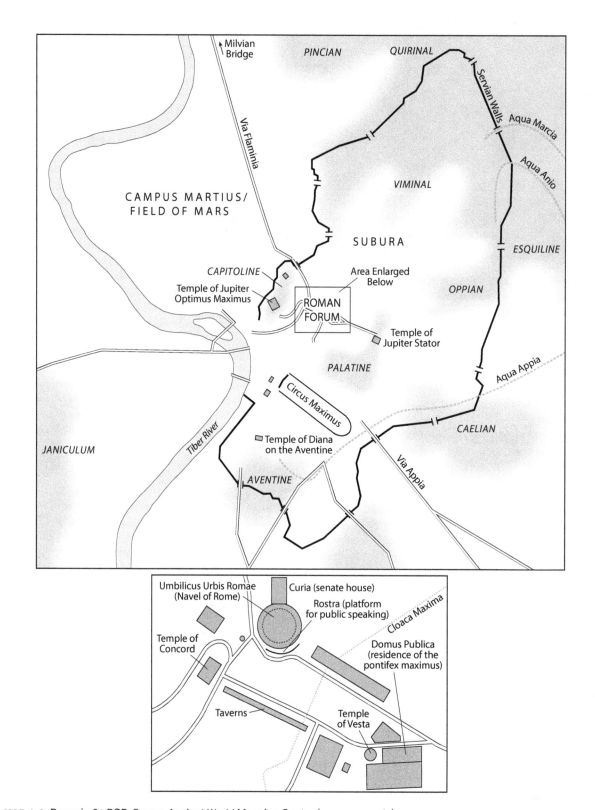

MAP 1.2 Rome in 63 BCE. *Source:* Ancient World Mapping Center (awmc.unc.edu).

PROLOGUE: QUINTUS'S FINAL MISSION

It was still dark as Quintus stalked up Rome's Flaminian Way. A passerby might detect his slight limp, an enemy's gift during the Battle of Neae. Through a break in the temples crowding the Field of Mars, he caught a glimpse of his **patron**'s estate on the Pincian Hill, backlit by the coming dawn. At first light, his patron—the great Lucius Licinius Lucullus, conqueror of King Tigranes of Armenia—would appear at the threshold of his house.[2] There he would be greeted by his **clients**: Romans and foreigners, common soldiers, gossips, merchants, tradesmen, bankers, and even other senators. Some of these clients would come to ask Lucullus's advice, others to seek his assistance in a legal matter or a business venture; some, like Quintus, would come only to show their continued loyalty to Lucullus and their willingness to help their patron.[3] Even as a civilian, Quintus maintained his military discipline and was never late to this ritual greeting—the salutation—not once in the three years since Lucullus and his army had returned victorious from the East.

Quintus blended into the crowd outside Lucullus's gate just as a brilliant dawn broke across the Pincian. The doorman threw open the gates, and Lucullus appeared at the threshold dressed in an impeccably white toga. As his clients shouted *"Ave, Domine!"* (Hail, Master!), Lucullus stood motionless and impassive, the expected response of a great patron. Those who had business with Lucullus jostled into a queue; the rest moved to collect their daily treat from large baskets dropped outside the doors by four of Lucullus's slaves. Quintus peered into a basket and snorted: a large bunch of some strange vegetable.[4] He began to stoop down but then stopped and caught his breath: Lucullus had fixed his gaze on him and slowly gestured for *him* to come inside. There were senators waiting! Ambassadors! Wealthy and important men. Quintus avoided their glares and tried in vain to smooth his rumpled, grimy tunic as he slid past them.

Quintus walked across Lucullus's magnificent atrium—awash in colorful marble and packed with Greek statues—and into the tablinum, his patron's office at the very center of his house. Lucullus sat reading at his large desk, a pile of scrolls on one corner, an oil lamp flickering on another. After what seemed like an eternity, Lucullus put aside the scroll and looked up. "Quintus Sextilius, my brother-in-arms. I hope you have been well. When we fought in Pontus and Armenia, you were a man I trusted to discover the enemy's plans and report them to me honestly. Are you still an honest man, now that we are back in Rome?"

"Of course, General."

Lucullus stared at Quintus, inhaled sharply, and slowly exhaled, saying:

Good. I have a final mission for you. Perhaps the most important I have ever assigned you. You have heard the rumors. While the senate debates amnesty and reform, storm clouds gather.[5] Murder. Treachery. Plots against the consuls. Threats to our liberties—and the Republic. What do the reformers have planned? Is Catiline plotting a revolution? Or has my friend Cicero fabricated these charges to thwart the reformers? Manlius is said to be raising an army in the North, or so Cicero tells me. I need to know that is really happening and what the various factions in the city have planned. Go to the house of Scribonius Curio, the orator and a leader of the ***Boni***, "the good, loyal men," as they call themselves. I've already sent a letter announcing your visit. Beyond that, I leave it to your skills to find out what is really happening in Rome. I need not remind you to be skeptical of these politicians: each will only give you a piece of the truth. Can I count on you today, Quintus, as I did beneath the walls of Artaxata?"

"Of course, General," Quintus replied, perhaps a little too loudly. Immediately, a young slave escorted him outside, past the long queue of jealous, impatient clients. The heat and smell of the city assaulted him as he retraced his steps toward the Forum and then the house of Curio.

Quintus was lost in thought when, over the rising din of the city, he heard his name. "Quintus! Quintus Sextilius, wait!" It was Marcus Antonius, walking with a few friends. Antonius was young but already infamous. Antonius's grandfather had been murdered during the Sullan terror two decades ago, but Antonius was daring and brilliant. He seemed poised to climb the treacherous ladder of Roman politics.[6] A whiff of scandal already hung around Antonius, but Quintus knew he had friends in every faction—the *Populares* (like Crassus and Caesar), who cultivated the support of the people; followers of Catiline (like Lentulus Sura); the Boni, led by Cicero and Murena; and even staunch defenders of the traditional order, the *Optimates* (like Catulus).

"Quintus Sextilius," Antonius said, "I hope you are well. What brings you into the Forum at such a dangerous time?" Quintus replied that he was doing a favor for Lucullus. "Of course you are," smiled Antonius, grasping at once what a man like Lucullus would want with an old veteran like Quintus. "Come," Antonius said, "I'm on my way to the house of Scribonius Curio to learn more about yesterday's events in the senate. Perhaps you'll find our conversation interesting . . ."

Populares Position

As Quintus walked across the Forum, Marcus Antonius spoke about Cicero and Catiline and the legislation before the senate:

My friends find themselves in a most awkward position. The Optimates, who support the prerogatives of the senate above all else, suspect that those who support the people, the Populares they call them, are conspiring with Catiline. Personally, and I am not ashamed to say it, I think that Catiline makes a great deal of sense. The Optimates, tucked away in their posh villas with their retinues of lackeys and slaves, do not realize how Rome has changed. Rome is no longer a city of shepherd huts and she-wolf lairs! Romans rule the world, and the world has come to our seven hills. But Rome is dangerous for the poor. Food is scarce. Apartments are ramshackle. Quintus, you live in the Subura.[7] You know that a poor person is more likely to die in the collapse or burning of his home than of old age! Rome can only be strong when her people are strong.

Yet, earlier this year, when the **tribune** Rullus proposed first the abolition of debts and then real land reform, Cicero and his allies, the Boni, aligned with the Optimates to thwart the passage of these laws.[8] I grant that canceling debts might be controversial. But how could anyone object to the land bill? Land would have been purchased at a fair price using treasure from Pompey's conquests in the East. And public lands in Campania, all now unoccupied, would have been distributed to the urban and rural poor. But Cicero spoke vigorously against it, citing its costs and claiming that land would be no benefit to the poor.[9] No benefit to the poor!? No wonder there is such desperation here and throughout Italy, when a consul can forget that Rome's empire was won by its landowning farmers.[10] Emotions were raw. As a gesture of conciliation, the Populares thought, "Surely, we can at least have amnesty for the sons of men proscribed and condemned by that tyrant Sulla." But no! Even this basic recognition of the rights of Roman citizenship was blocked by Cicero and his henchmen.[11] No wonder so many now, in desperation, turn to Catiline.

As if this insult to the people were not enough, Cicero then defended Gaius Rabirius, a man who slaughtered fellow Romans without trial. He did this not because he thought Rabirius was innocent —no man could!—but all to blunt any challenge to the authority of their precious *consultum ultimum*.[12] Should justice care that Rabirius committed his crimes almost forty years ago? Cicero claims that the *consultum ultimum* is needed to prevent the chaos of mob rule. Rabirius and the other murderers had climbed on the roof of the senate house, torn off its tiles, and stoned to death Saturninus (a tribune of the plebs!) and his followers! Rabirius did this after they had surrendered to the consul and were awaiting lawful trial. Where was the imminent threat to public order? Even if you grant the authority of the decree, as soon as the threat had passed, surely the decree has run its course. Or, does the *consultum ultimum* allow anyone with the senate's favor to resort to violence with impunity whenever the mood strikes? *That* is mob rule! Rabirius's conviction shows that the people believe that their tribunes should be protected and that the rights of Roman citizens are inviolate. Cicero will risk everything if he rests his authority on the illegal and discredited authority of the *consultum ultimum*. A mob in fine togas is still a mob.

So Rabirius was defended—because of compassion, they said. Yet when my friends proposed an amnesty for those unjustly convicted and those unfairly driven from the senate, where was Cicero and his compassion then? If we are to avoid open conflict, an amnesty might show the downtrodden and the people that the Optimates and Boni are willing to be reasonable and to work so that the law is just and not a weapon to be wielded against their political and personal enemies.

But this business of Catiline raising an army? If it is true, then Catiline is less clever than I suspected. What folly! First, the threat of insurrection gives a pretext to move against those who seek reform. They have been itching for any excuse to curtail the tribunes since Pompey and Crassus restored their powers.[13] We must preserve and strengthen the powers of the tribunate. It is our best check on the abuse of the people by the powerful. But just as Cicero should not act outside the law, neither should Catiline, no matter how necessary his reforms.

Many of my friends will be on the Aventine today, listening to Catiline and his associates rallying the people. But let's not forget who Catiline is. Need I mention Catiline's "service" to Sulla during his reign of terror?[14] How many **knights** met their fate because of Catiline's tongue and Catiline's blade?[15] He even arranged for his own brother-in-law to be added to list of the proscribed and tortured to death Marius's nephew on the tomb of

Lutatius Catulus! Catiline says he is a friend of the people—and maybe now he is. But when he had the chance to resist tyranny, he put citizens' necks to the sword in the name of the dictator. I cannot shake the feeling that he cares more for the consulship of Catiline than the welfare of the people.

But no matter what happens, the Populares will never support a *consultum ultimum*. Unless, of course, we can find advantage in lying with strange bedfellows!

Their arrival at Curio's house spared Quintus the raunchy joke he was sure would follow Antonius's mention of "bedfellows." Curio had gone to visit Cicero, but Curio's wife, Memmia, showed them into the modest atrium, where they waited, quietly joking about a ridiculous sculpture of a drunken Bacchus. Curio soon arrived, huffing and puffing in his heavy toga. Curio greeted Antonius warmly: "Marcus Antonius, my good friend! And look, you've brought a new friend." Antonius introduced Quintus, and Curio replied, "Quintus Sextilius. Excellent. I've heard of your bravery at Themiscyra. Lucullus said to expect you!" (Antonius shot Quintus a surprised look.)

Boni Position

Curio continued:

I just returned from a meeting with Cicero, who plans to deliver a blistering indictment of Catiline in the senate. Soon there will be no turning back. It will be one or the other.

I know that Lucullus has doubts about Cicero. But he truly is our best hope to restore Rome's stability and to reunite all Romans in pursuit of the common good—senators, knights, the poor in Rome and the countryside. No good can come from antagonizing the Optimates. Land reform? Distributing free grain? I know the poor suffer. I am not blind. But we must also not be fools. Free grain would fill bellies, yes. But free citizens must be able to support themselves or else they will be become dependent on the giver. And dependent men cannot be free; they are slaves in all but name. They will support their benefactor at the expense of liberty. Soon they will tolerate and even demand a tyrant.

We can only improve the lot of the poor and reduce corruption if we all work together to find a path that is agreeable to all the actors in this great play. Rome has been strong because, as other cities careened from despot to despot and government to government, Rome was stable, secure, and prosperous. No foreign enemy ever made us doubt ourselves. You, Quintus Sextilius, have stood victorious on the very edge of the world! Why should we do to ourselves what Hannibal or the Cimbri could not?[16] For 446 years the Republic has stood. We must preserve and reform our government: the senate and people of Rome. Together. This is what Cicero, I, and the other Boni want. We are loyal to the Republic.

Yes, I suppose that we could see a limited amnesty as a way to temper passions and bring Rome together. But only if the amnestied had been unjustly convicted or expelled from the senate. Perhaps the sons of the expelled could be readmitted, if they could prove their virtue? But we must never forgive those who would corrupt our state for their own selfish ends. One does not let the wolf back among the sheep.

And, of course, we can give no quarter to revolutionaries. I believe what Cicero has said about Catiline. Chaos will reign if he and his henchmen are not called to answer for their actions. Attempting to kill the consuls? Overturning the election? Burning the city?! We must unite against this threat to our very existence. Only then can Rome address her real and dire challenges.

Antonius began to debate Curio on various points but eventually moved toward the door. He shouted over his shoulder: "Quintus, if you wish to know what the people really think, I promised I would visit a friend on the Aventine.[17] Join me if you want to learn the true opinion of the people." Quintus followed, but he soon lost track of Antonius in the press of the Aventine crowd. "It's probably for the best," Quintus thought; there was much more to learn if he were to fulfill Lucullus's directive. He made his way instead toward the Palatine, where he hoped to learn more about the motives of the Optimates.

The shadows were lengthening as Quintus walked up the Via Triumphalis. Suddenly, he heard shouts behind him. Turning, he saw three men attacking a fourth, who gasped for help. Before Quintus could reach them, the three men saw him and raced off toward the Subura. The other man scrambled up, blood running down his face, and staggered away in the other direction. On the ground, Quintus noticed a small wooden tablet. It was sealed with the mark of the **praetor** Quintus Metellus Celer![18] He tucked it into his tunic and walked briskly to a tavern a few blocks away.

Optimates Position

Once safely inside and with a sausage and a cup of wine on his table, Quintus carefully examined the tablet. His eyes grew wide when he saw its addressee: Quintus Caecilius Metellus Nepos, one of the tribunes-elect and a leader of the Optimates! He cracked the seal, opened the tablet, and read:

Gaius Quinto fratre s.d.p. (Gaius warmly greets Quintus, his brother.)[19]

I just returned from the house of Tullius Cicero, where we discussed how best to approach the matters that will soon come before the senate. It would be far better for the ship of state to be guided by a more experienced pilot from a more experienced family. But fate is what we must endure, not what we choose.

We must not underestimate Sergius Catiline. Enmeshed in vice and swimming in perversion but dangerously clever. The man is a paradox. A slave to every urge, every unclean impulse, yet capable of great physical courage. A hard man with a soft spirit. A monstrous and dangerous combination—a tyrannical combination!—but only if we, who now as ever safeguard the best interests of the Republic, are not prudent.

No one should doubt Catiline's charisma. And now he has the attention of the mob with his calls for land reform, free grain, amnesty, and the forgiveness of debt. We must thwart every thrust by this pimp of the people's passions. Land reform? A fancy word for theft. They will take land that we have cultivated and improved for generations and give it to some drunken fool who knows as much about farming as I do about what lies beyond the Atlantic. Free grain? Not free to those who will have to buy it! And a man who does not earn his bread is no more free than the dog who steals scraps from my table. Amnesty? Forgiveness of crime and immorality! They will say they want justice—but service in the senate is the greatest responsibility in the world. Those men have neglected that duty, or sold it for a piece of dirty silver. They have no virtue. True justice would be their perpetual banishment. In our mercy we allowed them to live among us after betraying the Republic. Forgiveness of debt? *Tabulae novae*! Clean slates," they shout! More words to disguise more theft! How can they speak of justice with one side of their mouth, while with the other they try to steal from the prudent? Remember the fable of the diligent ants and the lazy grasshopper.[20] These "reformers" would take what prudent men have stored and give it to men who think of nothing but their immediate pleasure. To cancel debts will destroy credit! Honest, prudent men, who have and will repay their debts, will have to pay a crushing premium to offset the losses the lenders know they will suffer because of the profligate and dishonest. How is that just?

We have seen this play before and know how it ends. You remember the glorious defense of liberty by Gaius Servilius Ahala when our Republic was still young. During a famine, Spurius Maelius had sold grain at a steep discount to the people, corrupted the market, stashed weapons, and refused the summons of the dictator Cincinnatus![21] Ahala slew this would-be tyrant by concealing his dagger in his armpit (*ahala*). Tiberius and Gaius Gracchus attempted Maelius's same strategy on an even grander scale: revolution under the guise of

reform.[22] Again the best men united to stop their legislation, which would have utterly undermined the Republic's foundations. But Catiline is more ruthless than the Gracchi and more dangerous than Maelius. Maelius had boldness but was a **plebeian**. Catiline is a **patrician**, from a family as ancient as our own.

The people have again rejected Catiline—for a second time, mind you! Has any "people's champion" ever been so hated by the people? Yet still he refuses to accept defeat. Even as he attempts to push his discredited reforms on the senate, he begins to raise an army against the senate and people of Rome. And again he conspires to assassinate a consul! Vile, villainous treason! Tell me, brother, what course of action should be barred to Cicero now that he must grapple with this hydra of villainy? The enemy is among us! Catiline sits in the senate. His creatures prowl the streets, no doubt hoping to find good men like us or our clients and catch them unawares.

Everything flows toward Sergius Catiline—but don't underestimate Licinius Crassus or his puppet Julius Caesar. I thought we were rid of Sergius Catiline three years ago, when he was banned from running for office because of his corruption. But no, the following year, there was Sergius Catiline again, with Crassus supporting him from the shadows. Plots against the leading senators! What treachery!

It will all be settled soon. The traditional defenders of Rome must again answer the call to arms. We must block every insane "reform" pushed by the Populares. To allow even one will begin the slide to tyranny. If Catiline—or Crassus—has more revolutionary thoughts, we will stop them as well, just as we have every would-be tyrant who sought to destroy liberty for the last 446 years. If we falter, the city will lie exposed to destruction, as surely as when Tarpeia opened the gates to the Sabines or when the Gauls were scaling the Capitoline.[23] When Hannibal was at the gates, our ancestors showed what greatness true Romans possessed. When threatened with torture Scaevola willingly thrust his hand into the fire—courageous testimony of our relentless hostility to tyranny.[24] I vow that this Republic will not die as long as a single member of our illustrious family, the Caecilii Metelli, draws breath. May the gods nod their heads in support of our defense of liberty and the Republic.

    s.t.v.b.e.e.v. (If you are well, I too am well.)

As Quintus sat swirling his cup of wine and contemplating Metellus's letter, he heard more shouting and saw Antonius staggering down the street, singing loudly. "Quintus Sextilius!" he hollered. "You survived the Aventine! Bravo! Join me at the house of Titus Pomponius Atticus, the philosopher. He's holding a dinner for all who are tired of talking politics. I believe my good friend Cornelius Nepos, the historian, will be there. You can tell him about Lucullus's campaign in the East!"

Quintus and Antonius trudged up the Esquiline Hill to the house of Atticus. As they entered the dining room, conversation had turned to Nepos's desire to write a world history. Nepos was debating some obscure point concerning the geography of Gaul with Posidonius, the Greek historian, and Sempronia, the wife of Decimus Junius Brutus. Two young poets, Licinius Macer Calvus and Valerius Catullus, were there too, both amused and bored by the academic debate.

Indeterminates Position

Atticus welcomed the new arrivals:

Marcus Antonius, welcome! And who is your friend? Ah, Quintus Sextilius! The hero of Nisibis! You are, of course, welcome as well. You just missed our friend Helvius Cinna. He wanted to rest before the important debate in the senate tomorrow. Imagine! Cinna the poet taking an interest in faction, law, and politics. I regret to say that before he left, Cinna made it clear that he is no sure vote for my dear friend Cicero. Cicero, you remember, had some pointed criticism for Cinna's *Zmyrna*,

that learned and challenging poem. And Cinna, like all poets, can hold a grudge.

There are several senators who would just as soon rid themselves of both Catiline and Cicero as see either of them victorious. One of the many reasons why politics, as you know, holds no interest for me. But even a philosopher does not wish to see blood run in the streets. I was in Athens the year after Sulla's siege, you know. There I learned in no uncertain terms that although one may ignore politics, politics does not always return the favor. It would be better if a solution could be found without the need for bloodshed . . .

Atticus paused, a horrible memory seemed to flash across his face: "Well . . . these are not the topics for which my meals are famous, now are they? Let us turn to happier pursuits. Catullus, I believe you have a new poem about my dear friend Marcus Tullius Cicero, do you not?"

Catullus grinned and responded, "Indeed I do, my dear Titus, one that bears directly on Cicero":

O most learned of the descendants of Romulus, as many as there are and were, Marcus Tullius, and will be in later years. Catullus gives great thanks to you, Catullus the worst poet of all. As he is the worst poet of all, just so you are the best patron of all.[25]

Atticus cheered in the Greek style—"*sophos* (bravo), *sophos*, three times *sophos*!"—thinking that a humble Catullus had praised Cicero's support of his friends and the arts. But Quintus noticed that Nepos seemed confused about whether the poem was sincere. Antonius was about to burst out laughing at what he perceived to be a riotous insult of Cicero when he realized that his interpretation differed from that of his host and quickly muted his laugh with a long gulp of wine.

Quintus thought to himself: "Catullus has hit the mark, hasn't he? What kind of man is Cicero? Does he have the interests of Rome foremost in this heart, as he claims, or is it ambition that drives him and us toward the rocks of civil strife?" After a day trying to find the truth, Quintus remained as uncertain about what was really happening in the city as he was about the meaning of Catullus's poem. Tomorrow at dawn he will stand before Lucullus. What will he report? What *is* really happening in Rome?

BASIC FEATURES OF REACTING TO THE PAST

This is a historical role-playing game set in a moment of heightened historical tension; it places you in the role of a person from the period. After a few preparatory lectures, the game begins and the students are in charge. By reading the game book and your individual role sheet, you will find out more about your objectives, worldview, allies, and opponents. You must then attempt to achieve victory through formal speeches, informal debate, negotiations, and conspiracy. Outcomes sometimes differ from actual history; a debriefing session sets the record straight. What follows is an outline of what you will encounter in Reacting and what you will be expected to do.

Game Setup

Your instructor will spend some time before the beginning of the game helping you understand the historical background. During the setup period, you will read several different kinds of materials:

- The game book (what you are reading now), which includes historical information, rules and elements of the game, and essential historical documents.
- A role sheet, which provides a short biography of the historical person you will model in the game as well as that person's ideology, objectives, responsibilities, and resources. Some roles are based on historical figures. Others are "composites," which draw elements from a number of individuals. You will receive your role sheet from your instructor.

Familiarize yourself with the documents before the game begins and return to them once you are in role. They contain information and arguments that will be useful as the game unfolds. A second reading while *in role* will deepen your understanding and alter your perspective. Once the game is in motion, your perspectives may change. Some ideas may begin to look quite different. Those who have carefully read the materials and who know the rules of the game will invariably do better than those who rely on general impressions and uncertain memories.

Game Play

Once the game begins, class sessions are presided over by students. In most cases, a single student serves as some sort of presiding officer. The instructor then becomes the game manager (GM) and takes a seat in the back of the room. Though they do not lead the class sessions, GMs may do any of the following:

- Pass notes
- Announce important events
- Redirect proceedings that have gone off track

Instructors are, of course, available for consultations before and after game sessions. Although they will not let you in on any of the secrets of the game, they can be invaluable in terms of sharpening your arguments or finding key historical resources.

The presiding officer is expected to observe basic standards of fairness, but as a fail-safe device, most games employ the "podium rule," which allows a student who has not been recognized to approach the podium and wait for a chance to speak. Once at the podium, the student has the floor and must be heard.

Role sheets contain private, secret information that you must guard. Exercise caution when discussing your role with others. Your role sheet probably identifies likely allies, but even they may not always be trustworthy. However, keeping your own counsel and saying nothing to anyone is not an option. In order to achieve your objectives, you *must* speak with others. You will never muster the voting strength to prevail without allies. Collaboration and coalition building are at the heart of every game.

Some games feature strong alliances called *factions*. As a counterbalance, these games include roles called *Indeterminates*. They operate outside of the established factions and while some are entirely neutral, most possess their own idiosyncratic objec-

tives. If you are in a faction, cultivating Indeterminates is in your interest, since they can be persuaded to support your position. If you are lucky enough to have drawn the role of an Indeterminate, you should be pleased; you will likely play a pivotal role in the outcome of the game.

Game Requirements

Students playing Reacting games practice persuasive writing, public speaking, critical thinking, teamwork, negotiation, problem solving, collaboration, adapting to changing circumstances, and working under pressure to meet deadlines. Your instructor will explain the specific requirements for your class. In general, though, a Reacting game asks you to perform three distinct activities:

Reading and writing. What you read can often be put to immediate use, and what you write is meant to persuade others to act the way you want them to. The reading load may have slight variations from role to role; the writing requirement depends on your particular course. Papers are often policy statements, but they can also be autobiographies, battle plans, newspapers articles, poems, or after-game reflections. Papers provide the foundation for the speeches delivered in class.

Public speaking and debate. In the course of a game, almost everyone is expected to deliver at least one formal speech from the podium (the length of the game and the size of the class will determine the number of speeches). Debate follows. It can be impromptu, raucous, and fast paced. At some point, discussion must lead to action, which often means proposing, debating, and passing a variety of resolutions. GMs may stipulate that students must deliver their papers from memory when at the podium, or they may insist that students wean themselves from dependency on written notes as the game progresses.

Wherever the game imaginatively puts you, it will surely not put you in the present. Accordingly, the colloquialisms and familiarities of today's college life are out of place. Never open your speech with a salutation like "Hi guys" when something like "Fellow citizens!" would be more appropriate.

Always seek allies to back up your points when you are speaking at the podium. Do your best to have at least one supporter second your proposal, come to your defense, or admonish inattentive members of the body. Note-passing and side conversations, while common occurrences, will likely spoil the effect of your speech, so you and your supporters should insist upon order before such behavior becomes too disruptive. Ask the presiding officer to assist you. Appeal to the GM as a last resort.

Strategizing. Communication among students is an essential feature of Reacting games. You will find yourself writing emails, texting, attending out-of-class meetings, or gathering for meals. The purpose of frequent communication is to lay out a strategy for achieving your objectives, thwarting your opponents, and hatching plots. When communicating with fellow students in or out of class, always assume that he or she is speaking to you in role. If you want to talk about the "real world," make that clear.

CONTROVERSY

Most Reacting to the Past games take place at moments of conflict in the past and therefore are likely to address difficult, even painful, issues that we continue to grapple with today. Consequently, this game may contain controversial subject matter. You may need to represent ideas with which you personally disagree or that you even find repugnant. When speaking about these ideas, make it clear that you are speaking *in role*. Furthermore, if other people say things that offend you, recognize that they, too, are playing roles. If you decide to respond to them, do so using the voice of your role and make this clear. If these efforts are insufficient, or the ideas associated with your particular role seem potentially overwhelming, talk to your GM.

When playing your role, rely on your role sheet and the other game materials rather than drawing upon caricature or stereotype. Do not use racial and ethnic slurs even if they are historically appropriate. If you are concerned about the potential for cultural appropriation or the use of demeaning language in your game, talk to your GM.

Amid the plotting, debating, and voting, always remember that this is an immersive role-playing game. Other players may resist your efforts, attack your ideas, and even betray a confidence. They take these actions because they are playing their roles. If you become concerned about the potential for game-based conflict to bleed out into the real world, take a step back and reflect on the situation. If your concerns persist, talk to your GM.

COUNTERFACTUALS

In a few respects, *The Crisis of Catiline* departs from the actual history of ancient Rome. These intentional departures are "counterfactual"—they do not accord with history. The following counterfactual elements enhance game play and introduce additional sources to support your debates.

Historical moment. The setting of *The Crisis of Catiline* follows the historical events until the point in 63 BCE when the game begins (the summer in the multisession version of the game, November 8 in the shorter version). But significantly, the debate on the authorization of the *SCU* is shifted from October 21 to November 8. This allows you to reference the events in Cicero's speeches against Catiline, with the exception of the passage of the *SCU*. To preserve the contingency of history, a few actions taken between October 21 and November 8 are left ambiguous in the historical context and timelines.

Use of sources. The game also allows you to use ancient Greek and Roman texts written after 63 BCE as though they were contemporary sources for the key ideas and arguments in play during the game. Some of Cicero's works (*Laws* and *On Duties*), as well as those of Sallust, Livy, Valerius Maximus, Seneca the Younger, Appian, Plutarch, and Juvenal, were written decades or centuries after 63 BCE. When you quote these in the senate, you should omit reference to the author, but you could say something like "As a wise/foolish Roman said/wrote . . ." or "I once heard Cicero say" when referring to passages in *Laws* and *On Duties* (you can assume that Cicero does believe these things, even if he hasn't written them yet in 63 BCE). In your written speeches, you should include the complete citations.

In the senate. The meeting of the senate largely follows Roman practice, although in reality only the most prestigious senators would have the opportunity to speak. Younger or less powerful senators, including many of the characters in the game, would be expected to support their powerful patrons. But to give voice to as many viewpoints as possible in the game, all senators have a right—indeed a duty—to speak during the debates. Romans only very rarely extended debate beyond a single day, voting on the topic after the most senior of the senators had spoken or once night was beginning to fall. But if you are playing the game in a large class, sessions may stretch over more than one "day" within the game.

Passage of legislation. In the late Republic, the senate only had the power to recommend laws that were passed by the Popular Assembly. The passage of a law by the people might be highly contested, as the experience of the Gracchi and other reformers proved. For the purposes of the game, however, you can assume that a ***consultum*** passed by the senate will be ratified by the people.

Passage of time. If you are playing the multisession game, the passage of time between each session is elastic. But unless the GM signals otherwise, assume that about a month passes between each meeting of the senate. This is enough time to exchange multiple letters within Italy or Gaul or send and receive a single message from the East. The GM will decide how much time has elapsed in all instances.

Anachronism. Remember: although Reacting time is elastic, it is not reversible. The game takes place in the summer and/or fall of 63 BCE. With the exception of the use of ancient but anachronistic sources (see above), no one can refer to "facts" that have not yet occurred, people who have not lived, or (modern) texts that have not been written. The success of Reacting depends on you immersing yourself in the historical moment and tackling these problems with the tools and ideas available to Romans at that time. If you make comments that would be meaningless to Romans in 63 BCE, your supporters may well think you've lost your mental faculties and you may lose influence in the senate (and so *pedarii*)—the censor might even strike you from the ***Album Senatorum***.

2

Historical Background

133 BCE	Tiberius Gracchus forces passage of a controversial land reform program; he and his followers are murdered by senators and knights; riots convulse Rome.
122–121 BCE	Gaius Gracchus passes a more radical land reform law, including subsidized food for the poor. After the senate passes a *senatus consultum ultimum* (*SCU*), Gracchus is killed (or commits suicide). Treason trials and executions rock Rome.
100 BCE	The tribune Saturninus and the praetor Glaucia attempt to force passage of a radical legislative program. Saturninus and Glaucia are lynched after the senate passes an *SCU*.
91–90 BCE	Drusus, a democratic and pro-Italian politician, is murdered, touching off the revolt of the Italian allies in the Social War (91–87 BCE).
89 BCE	The urban praetor, Aulus Sempronius Asellio, is murdered by a mob of creditors when he attempts to reduce debts caused by the disruptions of the Social War.
88 BCE	The tribune Publius Sulpicius Rufus is killed after he passes legislation diluting the power of the aristocracy over voting. Sulla marches on Rome and then heads east to attack Mithridates.
84 BCE	Cinna, consul for the fourth consecutive year, is murdered by his troops.
83–82 BCE	Sulla's second march on Rome. The Capitoline Temple of Jupiter Optimus Maximus and the Sibylline Oracles burn in the chaos.
81–79 BCE	Sulla, as dictator, unleashes **proscriptions** on opponents and wealthy Romans and confiscates land for his

veterans. Reforms limit the power of tribunes and ambitious politicians. Sulla dies in retirement.

77 BCE	The proconsul Lepidus revolts in Etruria, but his army defects to Pompey.
73–71 BCE	The third, and last, of the great slave revolts begins under Spartacus, who is eventually defeated by the praetor Marcus Crassus. Six thousand slaves are crucified.
67–66 BCE	Pompey quickly defeats the pirates threatening Rome's food supply and is sent east against Mithridates. Catiline is governor of Africa and marries Aurelia Orestilla, daughter of the consul of 71 BCE.
65 BCE	The consular elections are overturned because of corruption. Leading senators exonerate Catiline of a plot to kill the new consuls after he is banned from running because of a looming corruption trial. Foreigners are expelled from Rome for appropriating citizenship rights.
64 BCE	Cicero is the first "new man" (*novus homo*) elected consul in thirty years, defeating Catiline.
Jan. 63 BCE	Cicero leads the opposition to the Rullan agrarian reforms.
Mid-63 BCE	Rabirius is found guilty for his part in the killing of Saturninus and his supporters in 100 BCE. A technicality allows him to avoid execution.
July 63 BCE	Catiline is defeated again for the consulship, running on a radical platform of debt cancellation, wealth redistribution, and other popular measures. Impoverished Sullan veterans revolt in Etruria. Disturbances occur throughout Italy.

THE GROWTH OF ROME AND ITS EMPIRE

Founding of Rome. According to myth, Rome was founded on April 21, 753 BCE by Romulus and Remus, twin sons of Mars, the Roman god of war, and Rhea Silvia, a descendant of the Trojan hero Aeneas. Romulus, however, soon killed his brother in a quarrel over the right to name their settlement. Romulus became Rome's first king and opened his city as an asylum to men who were outcast from other cities. After abducting women from their neighbors, the Sabines, the Romans united with the Sabines and Rome began to prosper. Early Rome was ruled by kings. Although the king's power was great, a council of wealthy elders, called the senate, advised the king. All male citizens capable of military service met in the Popular Assembly to ratify the decisions of the king. This assembly, which represented the Roman people, or the *populus Romanus*, theoretically possessed ultimate political authority. In time, the Roman people would demand that their theoretical power gain the force of law.

Origin of the Republic. Exactly when and how Rome transitioned from a monarchy to a republic is among the most disputed questions in Roman history. At the time of the transition, Rome was controlled by the Etruscans, a cosmopolitan people whose homeland was to the north of Rome. The traditional story held that in 509 BCE an Etruscan prince raped a Roman noblewoman named Lucretia. When Lucretia committed suicide rather than endure the abuses of tyranny, she emboldened other Roman nobles to overthrow the monarchy, expel the Etruscan royal family, and establish the Republic. Forever after, the word *rex*, or "king," was cursed in Rome and there was no greater charge against a Roman than that he was aiming to establish himself as king. Although Romans came to see the establishment of the Republic as a singular event, the overthrow of the Etruscan monarchy was in fact part of a long-term trend throughout central Italy as towns reasserted their independence against an Etruscan state weakened by war and famine. The collapse of Etruscan hegemony in central Italy led to a prolonged struggle for supremacy among the settlements and tribes of the region. After nearly a century of conflict with its neighboring towns, Rome established its dominance in central Italy, setting the stage for its explosive expansion throughout Italy and the Mediterranean in the following centuries.

Basic institutions. It was during this period of conflict with its neighbors that Rome developed its republican political system. To avoid the possibility of any single man seizing power, two important controls were established:

term limits: most of the higher offices (magistracies) were held for only one year; and
collegiality: most magistracies were held by two or more individuals who had the right to veto actions by their co-officeholders that they felt were harmful to the state.

The upper reaches of Roman political authority were shared among several interlocking groups and individuals, as follows:

The SENATE comprised around 300 men at the time of the crisis of Catiline. Because it could initiate legislation, control expenditures, oversee foreign policy, and supervise most aspects of public administration, it had practical control over the government. The senate was the only political body in which public debate was permitted. Together, senators were called the *patres conscripti*, or "the enrolled fathers." Senators were wealthy and needed to possess a large amount of property. Politicians were enrolled in the senate after serving as a quaestor (see below). Senators served for life, unless they were removed by the censors for corruption or failing to maintain their property.

The CONSUL was the highest and most prestigious regular political official. When consuls were in Rome, they were responsible for the legal, political, and diplomatic apparatus of the Roman state; outside of Rome they served as supreme commanders of the military. There were always two consuls, each with the power to block the decisions of the other, an effective check against the ability of a consul to become a tyrant. Consuls were accompanied by a bodyguard of twelve lictors, who carried the fasces, a double-headed axe in a bundle of rods that symbolized the consul's *imperium*, or his "power to command" the obedience of Roman citizens in military operations and to punish malefactors. Throughout the history of the Republic, election to the consulship was almost always dominated by a small group of noble families, although occasionally a talented "new man," or *novus homo*, from a non-consular family was able to win election to the office. Drawn from a slate of candidates proposed by the senate, consuls were elected to one-year terms by the Centuriate Assembly.

All male Roman citizens of military age participated in one or more of the following assemblies:

The CENTURIATE ASSEMBLY (*comitia centuriata*) elected consuls, praetors, censors, aediles, and quaestors; declared war; and served as a court of appeal for citizens sentenced to death. Because the wealthy dominated a majority of voting cohorts, while most citizens were assigned to comparatively few cohorts, nobles controlled an effective majority despite their small numbers.
The TRIBAL ASSEMBLY (*comitia tributa*) elected all other magistrates and ratified laws.
The PLEBEIAN ASSEMBLY, a subgroup of the Tribal Assembly, elected tribunes and plebeian aediles, offices open only to plebeians. Eventually the decrees of the Plebeian Assembly acquired the full force of law. This is the origin of the term "plebiscite".

Other magistracies developed to administer Rome's increasingly large and complex society:

- A DICTATOR could be appointed by the consuls during times of severe crisis to take control of the entire apparatus of the Roman state. The dictator possessed superior authority (*imperium maius*) over all magistrates but was limited to a single six-month term. The dictatorship was common in the early Republic but eventually fell into disuse and was further stigmatized by the abuses of Sulla (see below, "Sulla's second march on Rome and the Sullan terror").
- The PONTIFEX MAXIMUS (chief pontiff) oversaw public sacrifices, regulated the calendar, and supervised the priests who conducted all public religious activities in the shrines and temples of Rome. The Romans did not have a hereditary class of religious officials. The offices of the priests were instead filled by lay citizens. The *pontifex maximus* was an elected position and one of the few elected for life.
- CENSORS in 443 BCE began to compile the official lists of senators and knights (the next highest property class), to maintain the roll of citizens, to set property taxes, and to contract for major public projects. Unique among magistrates, censors were elected every five years to eighteen-month terms and possessed the power to expel members of the senate for moral transgressions. A censor's decisions were final and could only be overturned by the other censor.
- PRAETORS oversaw the foreign and citizen law courts and assumed the administrative duties of consuls when they were absent from Rome.
- AEDILES supervised public places, public games, economic regulation, and Rome's grain supply.
- QUAESTORS assisted the consuls, generals, and kept public records.
- PROMAGISTRATES like proconsuls and propraetors governed provinces after their year in elected office in Rome.

The most distinguished magistrates (consuls, praetors, some aediles, and censors, as well as dictators) and some priests were permitted the honor of sitting on a distinctive, backless, ivory-legged "curule seat" and so were known as "curule magistracies."

Over time a standard sequence of political offices developed. Known as the *cursus honorum*, it began with election to the quaestorship at around the age of thirty and progressed through the aedileship and praetorship to the ultimate prize: the consulship.

After serving in a magistracy, a Roman was usually required to wait at least two years before becoming eligible for another office. Reelection to the same office, especially the consulship, was exceedingly rare. In this way, political power was spread among the Roman political elite, who were thus encouraged to maintain the stability of the system. This constant turnover, however, assured that most magistrates had little or no direct experience in their offices at the time of their elections. Because most magistrates were elected to single, annual terms, there was a tendency for magistrates to focus more on their own short-term advantage than the longer-term concerns of the Roman people. As a result, the advisory role of the senate took on added significance.

Unlike the federal and state governments in the United States of America, Rome did not have a written constitution that delineated the political and legal framework of the state. Rather, Rome's political system developed over centuries through a combination of legislation and custom, known as the *mos maiorum* (the way of the ancestors). As a result, precedent was an essential factor in determining whether political actions were acceptable. By the time of the crisis of Catiline, however, generations of bad precedents had revealed that there were few limitations to constrain a politician who was cunning, daring, and shameless enough to seize an advantage.

Roman patronage. Relationships outside of the family were defined in part by the system of **patronage,** or *clientela*, which established a complex set of mutual obligations between a patron and his many

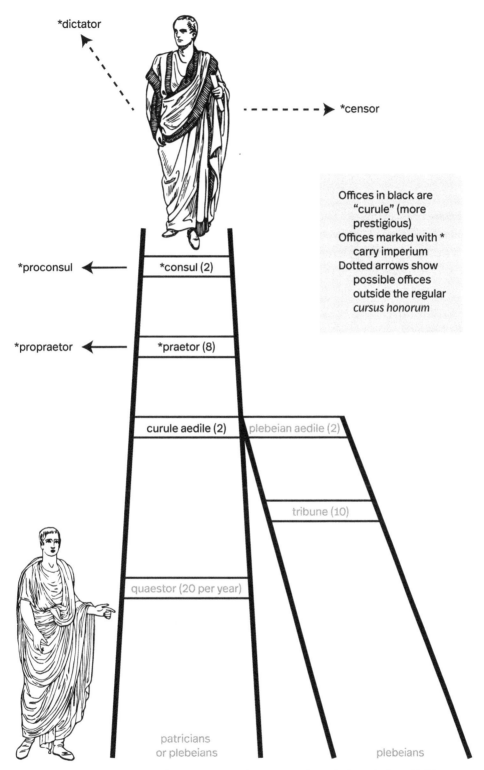

*dictator

*censor

*proconsul ← *consul (2)

Offices in black are
"curule" (more
prestigious)
Offices marked with *
carry imperium
Dotted arrows show
possible offices
outside the regular
cursus honorum

*propraetor ← *praetor (8)

curule aedile (2)   plebeian aedile (2)

tribune (10)

quaestor (20 per year)

patricians
or plebeians

plebeians

FIGURE 2.1 The *cursus honorum* (the sequence of Roman magistracies), by Barbara McManus. Used with permission.

clients. A patron was expected to protect, mentor, and support his clients. The client was expected to support the patron to the best of his abilities, often by voting for him and his friends. Powerful Romans typically had many clients in inferior classes, but more prominent nobles could also serve as the patrons of other nobles, who would have their own clients in turn. The number of clients a patron had was one manifestation of the social authority, or *dignitas*, wielded by powerful Romans.

Patricians and plebeians. Before the end of the monarchy, Roman society had become stratified into two distinct classes: the noble patricians and the common plebeians, also called the plebs. Patricians belonged to a few ancient families that dominated the political and religious life of the city. The more numerous plebeians tended to be poor, although even in the early period there were some wealthy plebeian families. The origin of the distinction between patrician and plebian is uncertain, but it seems likely that these classifications were rooted in an early manifestation of the Roman system of patronage and that at some point the social stratification into patricians and plebeians became hereditary.

Struggle of the Orders and secession. Both patricians and plebeians enjoyed basic civic rights, but in the early years of the Republic, patricians possessed an almost exclusive claim to the senate and religious offices. Eventually, the distinction was formalized and plebeians were prevented from holding many political offices. Excluded from political power, they were often subjected to harsh treatment by patrician magistrates. This state of civic affairs led to the **Struggle of the Orders**, a centuries-long conflict to secure political and legal rights for the plebs.

The main weapon of the plebeians in pressing for more equitable treatment was secession, a kind of general strike in which the plebs withdrew from civic and military participation until their demands were met. Because Rome was constantly at war during this period, secession posed a serious threat to the interests of the landowning political elite. In 494 BCE, the plebeians first seceded to the "Sacred Mountain" outside of Rome, refusing to fight even while Rome was under attack by several neighboring tribes.[1]

Tribunes of the plebs. As part of the settlement of 494, the plebs won the right to elect ten tribunes of the plebs. Tribunes were empowered to protect the life and property of all plebeians against arbitrary abuses by patrician magistrates. The bodies of tribunes were declared sacrosanct, making it a religious offense to harm a tribune when they exercised their power of ***intercessio***, or interposition, by standing between the magistrate and the pleb and saying "I forbid this" (*veto*). Plebeians took an oath to consider cursed anyone who violated the sacrosanctity of a tribune.

The Decemvirate and the Concord of the Orders. Because laws during this period were passed down orally and controlled by the patrician pontifex maximus, plebs were often subjected to arbitrary justice, including enslavement for debt. In 451 BCE, another secession, this time to the Aventine Hill within Rome, forced the senate to establish a commission of ten men, known as the Decemvirate, to codify existing laws. In 449, they published the Law of the Twelve Tables, but only after a scandal led to the overthrow of the commission. When one of the commissioners, the cruel Appius Claudius, had lusted after Verginia, her father killed her rather than see her abused by the power-crazed Appius. The Roman people, repulsed by Appius's behavior, overthrew the commissioners after first compelling them to promulgate laws more favorable to the plebeians, including the abolition of debt-slavery for citizens. The expansion of plebeian rights continued in 445 when they gained the right to marry into patrician families. In 367, plebeians were permitted to seek election as consul. By 338, the senate could no longer override votes by the Plebeian Assembly and plebeians were eligible for election to all magistracies. In 287, another plebeian succession gave the laws passed by the Plebeian Assembly, known as plebiscites, the full force of law.

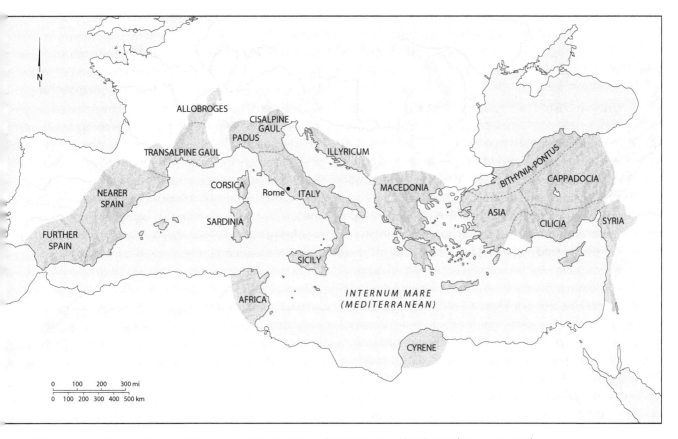

MAP 2.1 Rome's empire in the first century BCE. *Source:* Ancient World Mapping Center (awmc.unc.edu).

The peaceful resolution of the struggle for plebeian rights was recognized as the Concord of the Orders. The classes of patricians and plebeians continued to exist and remained socially, if no longer legally, important.

Territorial expansion. The internal Struggle of the Orders played out against a period of Roman expansion in Italy. In 396 BCE, Rome conquered the nearby city of Veii after a protracted struggle. In the early third century BCE, Rome gained control over all of central Italy. By 201 BCE, following the second of three Punic Wars against Carthage, Rome dominated the western Mediterranean. In 146, Carthage lay in ruins and Greece was conquered. Rome was master of the Mediterranean, although independent kingdoms in Asia Minor and Egypt would finally be conquered only in the first century BCE. Rome's rapid

expansion throughout the Mediterranean and contact with the cultures of the East revolutionized the social and economic lives of the Romans. Yet Rome's success had sown the seeds of the Republic's destruction and its eventual transformation into a dictatorship similar to the Hellenistic (or Greek) monarchies it had conquered.

Before the destruction of Carthage, the people and the senate managed the Republic together. . . . The fear of the enemy focused the community on good pursuits. But when that dread was lost, prosperity cultivated the usual vices: wantonness and arrogance. Thus, the peace they craved in adversity proved to be more cruel and bitter than adversity itself. For the nobles began to abuse their prestige and the people to abuse their liberty and every man took, pillaged, and plundered for himself.

So everything was split into two rival groups, and the Republic, which had formerly been shared, was torn to pieces.—Sallust, *The Jugurthine War* 41.

Agrarian crisis. The infusion of wealth from Rome's victories transformed it into one of the most important commercial hubs in the Mediterranean. For those Romans who earned their livelihood through small-scale farming and crafts, however, the "globalizing" economy and the almost constant military service caused great hardships. Participation in the Roman army during this period was limited to citizens who owned property. The vast majority of these were farmers who worked small plots of land ranging from seven to twenty acres (an acre is about three-quarters the area of a football field). To supplement their meager harvests, many worked as day laborers on larger farms and grazed livestock on public land, the *ager publicus*, which had been seized during Rome's earlier wars of expansion. The almost continual warfare in Italy during the late third and early second centuries BCE took an enormous toll on these farmers, causing the number of Roman citizens to plummet from 285,000 before the First Punic War (264–241 BCE) to only 144,000 by 193 BCE. The foreign wars fought in the second century required these farmers to be abroad for years at a time, during which their farms suffered from a lack of labor and often fell into disrepair, debt, and foreclosure. The decline in the number of landowners reduced the number of citizens eligible for military service. The burden of military service thus fell more heavily on the remaining citizen farmers, who were compelled to spend even more time away from their farms—thus accelerating the downward cycle. The military and strategic success of Rome, which garnered enormous wealth for Rome's elite, paradoxically undermined Rome's traditional economy and the source of Roman military power.

How Rome's Empire Changed Rome

Elite landlords, often using the wealth generated by Rome's wars of conquest, purchased the indebted farms and combined them into large commercial estates known as *latifundia*. *Latifundia* often specialized in a single crop and were worked by enslaved laborers. Small farmers were unable to compete with the efficient, export-oriented *latifundia*. The size of these farms grew as many of the elite began to rent additional plots of public land. Often, these estates rented more public land than was permissible under the law, further threatening the communal resources needed to sustain the smaller farms. Moreover, the influx of enslaved laborers from Rome's foreign wars depressed the economic prospects of free citizens, who could no longer work as day-laborers. Meanwhile, the concentration of brutalized slaves on massive farms resulted in a series of large-scale uprisings known as the Servile Wars. The first two Servile Wars occurred in Sicily (135–132 and 104–100 BCE). The last, led by the gladiator Spartacus, would threaten the Roman heartland of Italy (73–71 BCE). As the agrarian crisis accelerated, many of the rural poor flocked to Rome in search of employment. High rents from the swelling urban population forced the poor into overcrowded, poorly constructed apartment buildings (*insulae*, or "islands") where they lived at continual risk of building collapse, disease, and fire.

THE CRISES OF THE REPUBLIC

Rome's explosive conquest of the Mediterranean exposed a critical weakness in the Roman political system. The republican system was constructed to avoid the accumulation of power by one person or family. Magistrates were thus limited to short terms in office, generally a single year, after which they could be held accountable for their actions while in office. The powers of a magistracy were also usually apportioned among several coequal colleagues (for example, the two consuls and two censors). When Rome's population and territory were small and its wars were waged against relatively poor towns of tribes in Italy, no single military command provided enough wealth to overwhelm the ability of the Roman nobility to check the wealth and prestige won by a victorious general. Nor could a reformer acquire enough new clients to destabilize the balance of political power. But as Rome's population grew and Rome fought wars against larger, wealthier, more distant foes, the power attained by generals who conquered new territory and by politicians who passed popular reforms threatened the balance of power within the senatorial aristocracy. A single campaign against a wealthy power in the East could bring the victorious general enough wealth to upend the political status quo. A political or economic reform could generate thousands or even tens of thousands of clients, loyal to the reformers and ready to support them in subsequent elections.

Optimates and Populares (and Boni)

Beginning in the mid-second century BCE, some senators worked to check the concentration of political power that would diminish the traditional prerogatives and authority of the senatorial aristocracy. Such conservative senators are referred to as Optimates, or "the best men." Because of their opposition, beloved generals often returned from successful and lucrative campaigns only to find themselves political pariahs at their moment of triumph. Likewise, reformers saw sensible and necessary legislation defeated by senators who feared destabilizing the increasingly precarious balance of power. Finding their ambitions thwarted by the Optimates, another group of Roman politicians began to seek alternative sources of power among the Roman people and also Rome's Italian allies. Because they looked to the people as the source of their power, these politicians are often called Populares, or "men of the people." Between these two groups were the Boni, a group that favored moderate, incremental reform to restore the harmony between the senate and the people.

Populares and Optimates were not permanent political parties in the modern sense. Nor were their members drawn from different social classes. Rather these terms represent different approaches to politics within the Roman elite. Populares utilized the power of the tribunate to press for social, economic, and political reforms, because these were the measures that were most likely to garner the support of the poor. Optimates sought to limit the power of the tribunes, to preserve the dominance of the aristocracy in the political assemblies, and to maintain the balance of power within the aristocracy. Although certain families became associated with each approach, lineage was not a guarantee of how a Roman would seek or wield political power. Cicero, an outsider to Rome's aristocracy, began his career by allying himself with Populares, attacking the corruption of the well-connected senator Verres and supporting Pompey's extraordinary commands in the East, before moving decisively toward an alliance with the Optimates during the crisis of Catiline. Pompey himself began his career as another outsider who used appeals to the people to further his political agenda, only to find himself, in the 50s and 40s BCE, the last protector of the senate against Julius Caesar. Claudius Pulcher was from one of the oldest and most decorated families in Rome yet would renounce his patrician status in order to be elected tribune. Most Populares and Optimates believed they were working in the best interests of the Republic; both engaged in unscrupulous behavior, the manipulation of the system, and political violence. Although neither actively sought the Republic's destruction, their exploitation of a faltering political system hastened its collapse.

The Reforms of the Gracchi and the Collapse of Civil Peace

In 137 BCE a young Roman noble by the name of Tiberius Sempronius Gracchus traveled through northern Italy. There, he observed firsthand the devastating consequences of the agrarian crisis. He resolved to support agrarian reform to address the misery he witnessed. The actions by Tiberius and his brother Gaius demonstrate the political power available to politicians who could muster the support of the urban and rural poor. But his attempts to arrest the continued decline of citizen manpower by reestablishing small family farms in Italy would provoke a violent backlash. Although these events occurred seventy years before the crisis of Catiline, the reform attempts of Tiberius and his brother reveal many of the same social, economic, and political problems that enflamed subsequent political crises in Rome, including the crisis of Catiline.

When Tiberius was elected tribune in 133 BCE, he proposed that a special commission should be established to redistribute to the poor the public lands that had been illegally occupied by large landowners. The three commissioners would also establish colonies of Roman citizens in recently conquered provinces outside of Italy. There was broad agreement among the Roman elite that land reform was needed. Tiberius himself was from a powerful family—his father had twice been consul and his mother was the daughter of Scipio Africanus, who had defeated Hannibal in the Second Punic War. The consul for 133 assisted in drafting the bill, and it had the support of the pontifex maximus and also the ***princeps senatus***, who happened to be Tiberius's father-in-law. Nevertheless, economic and political factors hampered the legislation. The same senators who had to approve the agrarian reforms were in many cases the landowners whose land would be confiscated. To gain the support of these senators, Tiberius proposed a com-

promise: landowners who had illegally occupied public land would gain legal title, rent-free, to a substantial portion of the occupied land. But the rest would have to be restored to the state for distribution to landless citizens.

On its own, this reasonable and generous compromise might have succeeded. But any substantial reform also posed a political challenge to the nobility, since the commissioners who enacted this program would gain the loyalty of thousands of settlers. They would also have the unchecked power to survey the land and determine which land was public and which private, a power open to abuse. When Tiberius's proposal met with vehement opposition in the senate, Tiberius bypassed the senate and took his bill directly to the people in the Plebeian Assembly. Tiberius summarized the moral case for reform in an address to the Roman poor:

> Even the wild beasts that roam over Italy have a cave or lair to settle down in; but the men who fight and die for Italy have air and sunlight—but nothing else. Homeless, they wander about with their wives and children. Their generals lie to them and exhort them to defend their tombs and shrines from the enemy. But not a one has even a family altar. None of this multitude has an ancestral tomb. They fight and die to support others in wealth and luxury. Although they are called "masters of the world," they have not a single lump of earth to call their own (Plutarch, *Life of Tiberius Gracchus* 9).

It was not illegal for Tiberius to take his bill directly to the people, but it did violate the long-established practice that granted the senate the right to advise on legislation. Provoked by this affront, opposition to Tiberius's bill stiffened. When the tribune Octavius, encouraged by the senatorial opposition, vetoed the law, Tiberius took the unprecedented step of having the assembly vote to depose Octavius, reasoning that Octavius was acting not in the interest of the plebs but at the behest of the nobles whose power Octavius was duty-bound to check. Once Octavius was removed, the law was passed. Tiberius did nothing to reduce the fears of the opposition when he had himself, his brother Gaius, and his father-in-law Appius Claudius appointed as commissioners.

The senatorial opposition, led by the new pontifex maximus, Scipio Nasica, refused to fund Tiberius's Agrarian Commission. At this moment of impasse, news arrived that King Attalus III of Pergamon, a wealthy Hellenistic kingdom in Asia Minor, had died, bequeathing his land and wealth to the Roman people. Tiberius proposed that the Plebeian Assembly oversee the distribution of the inheritance, part of which would be used to fund his commission. This proposal provoked intense opposition by the senate, which had traditionally directed Rome's foreign policy and managed its finances. In the face of rising senatorial hostility, Tiberius decided to take another unprecedented step and stand for reelection, which would allow him to safeguard his legislation and prevent his enemies from prosecuting him for the removal of Octavius. Tiberius's actions can be viewed from two opposing perspectives:

Tiberius and his supporters. Tiberius was attempting to strengthen Rome by addressing a pressing economic and social problem. It would have been legal and ethical to confiscate the public land, which was illegally occupied by the large landowners, without any compensation. Tiberius's proposal was generous to these illegal occupiers of public land. Since the tribune Octavius was bound by oath to defend the Roman people, when he failed to do so, the people had the right—indeed, obligation—to depose him. Tiberius's opponents among the Optimates did not really care about the prerogatives of the plebeian tribunes, and at any rate they could not trump the judgment of the Plebeian Assembly. Since these nobles were planning legal action against Tiberius, who had only sought to defend the integrity of the tribunate, he reasonably sought to remain in office. Reelection as tribune would also permit Tiberius to staff the Agrarian Commission and ensure the fair redistribution of land. If unusual steps had been taken, it was only because the crisis was so dire and the opposition so unreasonable.

Senatorial opposition. Tiberius was attempting to consolidate power for himself and his family. Tiberius's failure to secure the approval of the senate for his legislation revealed that he would overturn precedent to achieve his personal political goals, even if it risked undoing the Concord of the Orders. His removal of Octavius was an attack on the rights of the tribunes that threatened the system of checks and balances that defined Rome's republican mode of government. If elections were no longer binding, then politics would devolve to the fickle whim of the mob. Such anarchy was antithetical to Rome's republican order and would inevitably result in the rise of a tyrant when a charismatic figure realized he could take advantage of the unchecked power of the majority. Tiberius's intention to run for consecutive reelection, which was traditionally granted only to essential leaders during times of crisis in war, was an attempt to avoid responsibility for his reckless behavior. Tiberius, therefore, had all the hallmarks of an aspiring tyrant: a noble who sought the support of the people to establish his power outside of the limitations imposed by law and tradition. Rome could tolerate neither a king nor a demagogue. The balance of power had to be restored by any means necessary.

The election soon turned violent. The senate, fearful of revolution, condemned Tiberius as a tyrant and authorized the consul Publius Mucius Scaevola to safeguard the Republic. When Scaevola refused to act against Tiberius and his supporters, Scipio Nasica, although only a private citizen, proclaimed, "Let any who wish to save the Republic follow me," the formal phrase spoken by consuls when they mobilized the people against an imminent threat to Rome. A group of senators led by Nasica marched to the Capitoline Hill, where the Plebeian Assembly was meeting. There, the senators clubbed to death Tiberius and hundreds of his supporters. That night their bodies were thrown into the Tiber. For the first time in centuries, violence had settled a political dispute among Romans. Nasica was quickly dispatched on a diplomatic mission to Asia, lest the people attempt to avenge Tiberius. The following year a special commission headed by the consul Popillius Laenas condemned to exile or death many who were thought to have supported Tiberius.[2]

For Rome, this was the beginning of civil bloodshed and the free rein of swords. Thereafter right was overthrown by might and the strongest took control.
—Velleius Paterculus, *Roman History* 2.3.3–4

Although the senate had mobilized to prevent Tiberius from gaining authority and prestige through the Agrarian Commission, once the political value of the commission was neutralized, the senate allowed it to proceed with the needed land reform. The commission, however, encountered resistance from Italian landowners, who were required to return large tracts of public land but who, as noncitizens, were ineligible for compensation. Partially in response to the growing resentment among the Italian allies, the consul Fulvius Flaccus proposed a law in 125 that would grant citizenship to the allies but he refused to debate the matter in the senate and the reform stalled. In the same year, the Latin town of Fregellae revolted. Although it was quickly suppressed, this revolt by an old ally of Rome revealed the growing animosity of the Italians, who were shouldering an ever-larger share of the burdens of military service, while reaping little of the rewards of empire. Unable to overcome resistance by both the senate and the local elites throughout Italy, the Agrarian Commission failed to resolve the land crisis.

In 123, Tiberius's younger brother, Gaius, was elected tribune. Assembling a broad coalition of the discontented middle class, urban poor, and small farmers, he sought to revive and expand Tiberius's reform agenda. Among his first acts, Gaius passed the *lex Sempronia*, which banned extraordinary tribunals like the one that had condemned the followers of Tiberius. In theory, a Roman citizen could no longer be declared an enemy of the state (**hostis**) and deprived of his legal rights before being convicted in a trial. To ease the plight of the urban poor, he proposed the establishment of numerous colonies, including the first outside of Italy. The urban poor also benefited from the first grain dole, in which the state sold wheat at fixed low prices to Roman citizens. He also ordered the construction of large grain warehouses in the city to prevent shortages and price fluctuations. The minimum age for military service was set at seventeen years old, and the basic equipment for Roman legionaries was to be provided by the state at no cost to the soldier, although property requirements for serving in the army were maintained.

Gaius was reelected tribune with the plan of tackling land reform. In the face of growing opposition, Gaius proposed two significant reforms in an attempt to gain political support. First, he cultivated the support of the **equites**, or knights, the Roman commercial class, who were wealthy but had little political power. For some time, provincial subjects had been entitled to sue a governor who extorted money during his term under the *quaestio de pecuniis repetundis* (an inquiry for recovering money). But these extortion trials were judged by senators, who had close familial and political associations with the senatorial governors. Indeed, many senators no doubt hoped to profit by serving as a governor of a wealthy province themselves someday. As a result, although the law had been in effect for the nearly thirty years, not a single conviction had been won. Because equites, many of whom were involved with trade with the provinces, would be more concerned about the long-term financial stability of the provinces, Gaius reasoned that they would be more diligent in prosecuting corruption by magistrates. The senate viewed this change as a threat to its traditional prerogatives, but the change did provide a more effective check on provincial corruption: nearly half of the extortion cases brought under the revised law resulted in a conviction. Indeed, two generations later, a trial under this law would launch Cicero's political career, and an indictment under this law would derail the career of Catiline.

Gaius also sought support outside of Rome by attempting to extend full citizenship to the Latins and granting additional rights to all of the peoples of Italy. The Latins were Rome's oldest and closest allies. They shared a language and culture with the Romans and they provided a growing share of Rome's troops. Granting these allies benefits from Rome's lucrative conquests would help solidify Rome's military advantage while also binding the still diverse peoples of Italy to Rome. But this farsighted proposal proved too much for many Romans, in particular the poor Romans who feared that their hard-won rights would be diluted by a mob of new citizens. Even when it became clear that Gaius lacked the support to pass this law, he persisted in attempting to force the law's passage. Gaius's support waned.

Even before Gaius's citizenship law foundered, his position among the people was being actively undermined by the tribune Livius Drusus, who would present more generous versions of Gaius's proposals. For example, when Gaius proposed two small colonies in which settlers would pay a small rent, Drusus proposed twelve large colonies, which settlers could hold for free. Drusus's proposals were so generous that it seems likely that they were never intended to be implemented but used only to undermine support for Gaius's more modest reforms. Drusus also assailed the character of Gaius's ally Fulvius Flaccus, the consul of 125 BCE who was elected as one of Gaius's fellow tribunes in 122. Drusus even suggested that Flaccus was inciting the Italian allies to revolt. The suspicions raised against Flaccus inevitably transferred to his ally Gaius. Gaius's plan to found a colony at the site of Carthage in Africa stoked further controversy. When the ceremonies that accompanied the founding of the new colony were marked by bad omens (unnatural winds, failed sacrifices, boundary stones pulled out by wolves), Gaius's opponents claimed that the gods opposed his plan to settle Romans on the land once occupied by Rome's greatest enemy.

The First *Senatus Consultum Ultimum*

In 121 BCE, as Gaius's popularity continued to erode, his opponents finally moved against him. An assembly was called to repeal the bill that had established the colony at Carthage. During the tense meeting, Quintus Antyllius, a client of the consul Lucius Opimius, pushed his way through a crowd of Gaius's supporters. When he impugned their honesty and made an obscene gesture, Gaius's supporters stabbed him to death with their pens. The next day, Opimius paraded Antyllius's corpse through the city, stirring more animosity against Gaius and his supporters. The senate, fearful of mass demonstrations and riots, took the unprecedented step of issuing a *senatus consultum ultimum* (*SCU*), or final decree of the senate. This decree authorized the magistrates to "take any measure necessary that the state suffer no harm." Normally, no Roman citizen could be executed without trial and appeal of the conviction to the people. The recent *lex Sempronia* had specifically forbidden the senate from voiding the rights of citizens without trial. Magistrates were also limited in the powers they could exercise within the city. The decree was, in effect, a declaration of a state of emergency in which civil rights were suspended. Supporters of the decree would argue that desperate times called for desperate measures; opponents would claim that the Senate lacked the authority to suspend the law or grant unlimited powers to any magistrate and undermine the traditional rights of citizens. Gaius and his followers retreated to the Aventine Hill. Attempts to negotiate a resolution failed. Opimius led senators, equites, and a force of Cretan archers to the Aventine and slaughtered Gaius and his followers after a brief battle. Thousands more were arrested and executed without trial in the aftermath. A few months later Opimius was indicted under the *lex Sempronia* for killing Roman citizens without trial. Opimius defended himself by claiming that his actions were authorized by the Senate and that no action could be illegal if it was done to preserve the state. The acquittal of Opimius seemed to legitimize the *SCU* as a legal response to a crisis. But the *SCU* remained a highly contentious action whenever it was deployed.[3]

Meanwhile a dynastic dispute in North Africa drew Rome into an unpopular war against Jugurtha, the king of Numidia. After corrupt and incompetent generals failed to subdue Jugurtha, Quintus Marcellus at last put Jugurtha on the defensive in 109 BCE but failed to capture him. Gaius Marius, a *novus homo* and Metellus's client, exploited Metellus's failure to win popular support for his own election to the consulship.

The Storm before the Storm

Reforms by Marius. As consul, Marius solved Rome's manpower crisis by abolishing the property requirement for serving in the army. On the one hand, this was a commonsense solution that recognized the shortage of Roman citizens eligible for military service. Their equipment was already paid for by the state and property requirements had already been lowered to the point that even citizens with only the smallest amount of land could serve in the army. Moreover, during times of emergency, Rome often waived this meager requirement. Nevertheless, the elimination of property qualifications had profound consequences for Roman politics and society. Soldiers became dependent on their general for their livelihood once they were discharged because the victorious general often gave them land from the conquered territories to support them in their retirement. The potential to gain thousands of clients increased the value of military commands dramatically. To provide for their new soldier-clients, generals gained an additional incentive to seek new (and lucrative) conflicts. They were also compelled to find land on which to settle their soldier-clients when their legions were demobilized. Although few at the time recognized its significance, Marius's reform irrevocably transformed the relationship between the Roman state, its generals, and its army.

Fresh from victory over Jugurtha in 104 BCE, Marius returned to Rome to find it gripped with fear of invasion by the Teutons and Cimbri, Germanic tribes that had won a series of victories against Rome, culminating in the Battle of Arausio in which over 80,000 legionaries were killed. To deal with the "Cimbric Terror," Marius was reelected to an unprecedented five consecutive consulships. Hailed as "another Camillus," after the illustrious general who had defeated an earlier invasion of Gauls in 390 BCE, Marius routed the tribes and preserved Rome. But his unrivaled prestige and status as a *novus homo* generated resentment among the aristocracy. With the military threat passed, Marius sought land for his triumphant veterans, many of whom were from long-standing allies of Rome in Italy. The Roman urban poor resented the prospect of non-Romans receiving land, but their support was courted with another bill that promised that grain would be sold at a heavily subsidized price. When the tribune Saturninus, Marius's ally, brought the measures to a vote, a group of senators claimed that they heard thunder, a bad omen that required the vote to be postponed. Saturninus, however, pressed ahead, threatening the senators that "hail often followed thunder." A fellow tribune vetoed the legislation, but still Saturninus ordered the voting to continue. A quaestor named Caepio used violence to attempt to dissolve the assembly. Marius's veterans, who were watching nearby, then interceded and forced the passage of the bill, which also required all senators to swear allegiance to the bill within five days of its passage. The pledge was another affront to the senate's prestige and powers, although only one senator (Quintus Caecilius Metellus Numidicus) elected exile over swearing the oath. Although Marius now faced opposition by the senate and the people, he managed to be elected consul for the sixth time in 100 BCE. When Gaius Memmius, one of the candidates for the consulship in the next election, was beaten to death by Saturninus's mob, the senate issued an *SCU*. Marius attempted to protect his supporters by locking them in the senate house under his custody while they awaited charges. But a mob of senators, including Gaius Rabirius, scaled the senate house, tore through the roof, and stoned Saturninus and his supporters with roofing tiles. Marius, his prestige diminished, went into voluntary exile in the East for more than a year. His land bill was never implemented, feeding the resentment among Rome's Latin and Italian allies.

The Social War. Animosity between the Romans and their allies continued to grow. In 95 BCE, Italians were expelled from the city of Rome. In 91, Livius Drusus, the son of Gaius Gracchus's opponent, sought to resolve the rift between Rome and Italy by incorporating the knights into the senate and enfranchising the Italian allies, giving them a stake in the success of the empire. As with Marius's reforms, Drusus's bill faced opposition from conservative senators and the urban poor. When Drusus was assassinated, revolts erupted throughout Italy, leading to the Italian, or Social (after the Latin word for "ally," *socius*), War (91–87 BCE). The war exacted a terrible human and economic toll throughout Italy and Rome was eventually forced to enfranchise all free persons south of the Po River. After the war's end, 500,000 Italians gained Roman citizenship. At an appalling cost, Rome and Italy were finally unified. In the crisis, Marius again displayed his military talent, as did one of his former officers, a noble named Lucius Cornelius Sulla.

Sulla heads east. Meanwhile, Rome's position in the eastern Mediterranean was deteriorating. Roman preoccupation with the Cimbric and Social Wars and discontent with corrupt Roman governors allowed Mithridates VI of Pontus to occupy most of Asia Minor and southern Greece. The command against Mithridates promised immense wealth and prestige to the victorious general. Violence erupted in 88 when the tribune Publius Sulpicius Rufus sought to grant the command to Marius instead of Sulla, who as proconsul was entitled to lead the campaign. Rufus's bill was resisted by the senate, who believed it usurped the senate's traditional authority over foreign policy. To block the passage of the bill, the consuls declared a *iustitium*, or a suspension of official business. Rufus surrounded himself with bodyguards and attempted to force the consuls to call a vote on the bill. When they refused, violence erupted throughout the city. In the ensuing chaos, Sulla sought refuge in the nearest house, which happened to be that of his former mentor and now bitter rival, Marius. Marius agreed to allow Sulla to leave the city

into exile, provided that he not try to stop Rufus's bill. Sulla agreed.

Sulla's march on Rome. Sulla instead fled south to Campania, where six legions that had served under him during the Social War were besieging the city of Capua. The soldiers enthusiastically endorsed Sulla's right to campaign against Mithridates (a campaign that promised rich plunder for his soldiers). Sulla marched into Rome, and for the first time a Roman army led by a Roman general slaughtered Roman citizens in Rome. Facing fierce resistance from the Roman people, Sulla burned rebellious neighborhoods. He defeated a hastily organized militia led by Marius and Rufus, whom the senate then declared *hostes*, or outlawed enemies of the state. Marius fled to Africa, but Sulla massacred Rufus and his supporters, repealed his laws, and strengthened the authority of the senate. Sulla then marched to the East to confront Mithridates.

Cinna's time. In Sulla's absence, Lucius Cornelius Cinna, consul of 87, attempted to repeal Sulla's laws. The other consul, Gaius Octavius, drove Cinna from the city and declared him a *hostis*. Cinna rallied the support of newly minted Italian citizens, recalled Marius, and quickly starved Rome into submission. Returning to Rome, Marius and his supporters—including the Bardyiae, Marius's personal bodyguard—roamed the streets, slaughtering their adversaries and confiscating their property. In 86, Marius attained a seventh consulship (with Cinna) but died soon thereafter. Cinna took control and appointed the consuls without elections in 85 and 84. His attempts to enroll the Italians and restore financial stability were unsuccessful. The economic crisis deepened as the counterfeiting of currency became so widespread that coin-testing stations were set up in the marketplace.

Sulla's second march on Rome and the Sullan terror. Meanwhile, Sulla, having learned of the situation in Rome, negotiated a generous peace with Mithridates and hastened back to Rome. The city was defended only by Cinna's inexperienced troops, who mutinied and killed Cinna. In 82 Sulla decisively defeated one army; another defected to Sulla. Marcus Crassus and Gnaeus Pompey raised a private army in the North and marched toward Rome to support Sulla. The combined army engaged and defeated a force of recently enfranchised Samnites outside of Rome's Colline Gate. Sulla used the captured Samnite rebels to make a grim point about the new political order. While Sulla calmly presided over a meeting of the senate on the day after the battle, 6,000 Samnites were tortured to death in the Circus Maximus—"only some criminals being punished," he calmly remarked to the horrified senators. To finance the settlement of his veterans, Sulla posted lists of persons who were declared outlaws. Many were political opponents or relatives of opponents, but others were the wealthy or personal targets of men who had Sulla's ear. These "proscribed" individuals could be hunted down, killed with impunity, and their property seized by the killer—with a share being paid to the treasury. During Sulla's proscriptions, 90 senators and 2,600 equites lost their lives and property. Some cities were fined; others were destroyed. Farmers were driven from their land throughout Italy to make room for Sulla's veterans.

Sullan reforms. Now dictator, Sulla broke the power of the Populares by forbidding tribunes from holding higher offices and restricting their veto to the personal protection of plebeian citizens. To limit the power of any one noble, he increased the number of magistracies and limited the terms of provincial governors to one year. He expanded the size of the senate to 600, filling its ranks with grateful equites. The prestige of the senate was restored and juries were to be composed entirely of senators. He discouraged the concentration of the poor in Rome by eliminating the grain dole. He also forbade generals from leaving their province without the permission of the senate. In short, Sulla undid every popular reform of the past few generations, while also trying to prevent another general from exploiting the same systemic weaknesses that had brought him to power.

Sulla then retired to his country estate in 79, believing that he had restored balance to the Roman state. His death the following year saved him from witnessing the quick demise of his new constitution. By failing to address the discontents of the populace that fueled the power of the Populares and championing a system that tempted generals with unlimited power, Sulla had only laid the foundation for further civil trauma.

Revolts of the 70s

Lepidus in Italy. The power vacuum caused by the civil wars and the opposition to Sulla's vicious reprisals spawned two rebellions: one in Italy by Marcus Aemilius Lepidus and one in Spain by Quintus Sertorius. Lepidus was a member of the Roman aristocracy who as consul in 78 sought to undo a number of Sulla's reforms. He attempted to restore the grain subsidy, distribute land in Etruria to the dispossessed, and restore the powers of the tribunes. When a group of Italian farmers sought to force Sulla's veterans off their land, the consuls were sent to quell the violence. Lepidus instead enlisted the discontented farmers in his private army and marched on Rome. The senate issued an *SCU* authorizing the other consul, Quintus Lutatius Catulus, to preserve the Republic. Gnaeus Pompey, who was in his late twenties at the time, raised a private army to support Catulus and defeated Lepidus at the Milvian Bridge outside of Rome.

Sertorius in Spain. After Lepidus died, his lieutenant, Perperna, took his remaining 20,000 men in the army and joined forces with Sertorius, who was leading a revolt against Sulla's regime in Spain. Pompey, fresh from his defeat of Lepidus, demanded the command against Sertorius. The senate, however, fearing the ambitions of the young, popular, and wealthy general, rejected his request. But Pompey simply refused to disband his legions and reiterated his demand. With the bloody examples of Marius, Cinna, and Sulla fresh in their minds, the senate acquiesced and dispatched Pompey to Spain. There, he and Quintus Caecilius Metellus Pius wore down the army of Sertorius. After Perperna assassinated Sertorius in 73 BCE, Pompey quickly dispatched the overmatched Perperna and returned to Rome. In Rome, Sulla's reforms continued to unravel. The distribution of subsidized grain resumed in the same year.

Spartacus and the Last Great Slave Revolt. In 73 BCE, a small band of gladiators under the leadership of Spartacus escaped from their barracks in Capua (near Naples, south of Rome). They defeated a small force of Romans and withdrew to Mount Vesuvius, where they raided the local countryside. After defeating a force of several thousand Roman troops, the numbers of the rebels swelled to over 70,000 men, women, and children. The next year the slaves annihilated a large army. Rome, in a panic, turned to Marcus Licinius Crassus, who drove Spartacus's forces to the toe of the Italian "boot." Crassus then destroyed Spartacus's army, while Pompey, returning from Spain, captured and executed the few rebels who had escaped, earning him a share of the honor—and Crassus's enmity. As a sign of his victory and a warning to other slaves, Crassus crucified 6,000 of Spartacus's followers along the Appian Way. The crosses stretched all the way from Rome to Capua, where the rebellion had begun. Pompey, although only thirty-five years old, was granted a **triumph** for his victory in Spain and, against custom (and Sulla's reforms), was elected consul with Crassus for 70 BCE, despite having never held public office.

Domestic Politics on the Eve of the Crisis

The consulship of Pompey and Crassus. Despite its tumultuous beginning, the consulship of Pompey and Crassus was relatively harmonious. The wounds of civil wars were soothed by a general amnesty that allowed even those who had rebelled against Rome, like the followers of Lepidus, to regain their citizen rights, provided they swore an oath of loyalty to the state. Pompey and Crassus then set their sights on reform. Concerned that their fellow senators would seek to check their ascendancy, they moved to restore the powers of the tribunate. The failure of

Sulla's reforms was now complete. Meanwhile, another crisis was coming to a head.

Pompey defeats the pirates. By 67 BCE, with Rome too consumed by its civil turmoil to police the seas, piracy had become an endemic problem, one threatening to severely disrupt Roman trade. Previous attempts to curtail piracy had proven ineffective. As the crisis grew acute, the tribune Aulus Gabinius proposed the *lex Gabinia*, which granted Pompey authority (*imperium*) over all territory within fifty miles of the sea, as well a massive force of 500 warships, 120,000 infantry, and 5,000 cavalry troops. In effect, Pompey was given extraordinary command over the entirety of Rome's empire. The law passed despite vehement opposition from conservative senators, who feared that the concentration of such power in the hands of a single magistrate would lead to tyranny. Although Pompey was allotted three years to defeat the pirates, he resolved the crisis in only eighty days. Most of the pirates he resettled (and bribed); some he defeated in action.

Pompey heads east. In recognition of his incredible success, Pompey was nominated to succeed Lucius Licinius Lucullus as commander against Mithridates. The law to give Pompey the command was supported by both Gaius Julius Caesar and Cicero, but most in the conservative faction of the senate opposed it. Once in the East, Pompey displayed the same daring and efficiency as he had with the pirates. By 65 BCE he had decisively defeated Mithridates in Pontus, which he annexed as a Roman province. The following year, he marched into Syria, deposed its king, Antiochus XIII Asiaticus, and made this, too, a Roman province. In 63, he moved south and established Roman supremacy in Phoenicia, Coele-Syria, and Judea. Pompey had conquered or made alliances with every notable kingdom in the East. In the process, Pompey acquired unprecedented power and prestige. He prepared to return to Rome in triumph. Meanwhile, back in Rome, the state was teetering on the brink of chaos as the crisis of Catiline came to a head.

Corruption and contested elections in the 60s.

In 66 BCE, the consuls-elect, Publius Autronius Paetus and Publius Cornelius Sulla (nephew of the dictator), were charged with electoral corruption (*ambitus*) by the very politicians they had defeated in the election, Lucius Manlius Torquatus and Lucius Aurelius Cotta, although it was widely thought that they had spent just as much, if not more, on bribes during the campaign as Autronius and Sulla! Bribery was a perennial problem, and it was a rare politician during this period who did not spread around money to win office. But some were more flagrant about it than others, and some lacked the political support to avoid prosecution. That is, the prohibition on bribery, which was supposed to level the playing field, instead became another way that political connections could be weaponized against one's opponents. When Autronius and Sulla were convicted, their election was annulled, and they were removed from the senate and then banned from seeking office. Torquatus and Cotta were elected consuls in a hastily organized second election. Catiline had been barred from running in the second election after a delegation from the province of Africa accused him of corruption when serving as governor. There were rumors that disgruntled senators—perhaps including Catiline, Gaius Julius Caesar, or even Marcus Licinius Crassus—were plotting to assassinate Torquatus and Cotta during their inauguration on January 1, 65 BCE. But the day passed without incident. Catiline stood trial for abuse of power as governor but was exonerated with the broad support of leading senators (including the consul Torquatus and others whom he had supposedly conspired to kill; Catiline refused Cicero's help during the trial). Later that same year, worsening economic conditions in Rome prompted the senate to expel all foreigners because they were said to be appropriating the rights of citizens.

The Catilinarian Crisis

In 64 BCE, Catiline, Antonius Hybrida, Cicero, and three other candidates ran for the consulship. Cicero vilified Antonius Hybrida and Catiline, who were supported by Crassus and Caesar. The Optimates, although hostile to Cicero, threw their support behind him to block Catiline. Cicero won the most votes and was elected consul with Antonius Hybrida. Cicero was the first *novus homo* elected consul in thirty years.

Rullan land reform. By 63 BCE, Rome seemed poised to explode. The economic situation continued to worsen in Rome and in the countryside. Another attempt was made at land reform, when Servilius Rullus proposed to establish a ten-man commission to purchase and distribute land south of Rome in Campania.[4] It was widely believed at the time that Rullus was a front for Caesar's anti-Pompeian efforts on behalf of Crassus. Cicero and the Optimates vehemently resisted the legislation. Passions rose yet further and the senate seemed poised to take dramatic action to maintain public order. Rumors of another *SCU* were in the air.

At this fraught moment, Caesar persuaded a tribune, Titus Labienus, to bring charges against Gaius Rabirius for his role in killing Saturninus and his followers thirty-six years before. Rabirius was by now an old man but one who was known to glory in his role in Saturninus's death (some even said he desecrated Saturninus's grave and would display his head during parties). The actual fate of Rabirius was incidental: the true question was the legality of actions taken under the authority of an *SCU* and whether these actions violated the fundamental legal protections of Roman citizenship. In effect, at precisely a moment when it looked like that turmoil over the Rullan land bill was going to cause the senate to issue an *SCU*, Caesar and Crassus engineered a direct attack on the authority of the senate and sought to reassert the sovereignty of the people and the protections of Roman citizenship, even—or especially—during a crisis.

The trial of Rabirius. In the summer of 63 BCE Rabirius was arraigned under an archaic law against sacrilegious treason, ***perduellio***, which was not tried in the permanent courts but by commissioners specially appointed by the praetor. Conveniently (and suspiciously) Caesar and his cousin Lucius Julius Caesar, were selected. Cicero spoke in Rabirius's defense, and the Optimates were able to force Caesar to accept that Rabirius would be exiled if found guilty (the law was ambiguous on this point). But when Rabirius was convicted, he appealed the judgment to the people, where he would face the death penalty if convicted. Now Rabirius's prosecutor, the tribune Labienus, presided over the appeal in the Centuriate Assembly! Cicero denounced the proceeding, but his attempts to justify Rabirius's killing of Saturninus alienated the crowd, who began to turn violently against him. Just as it seemed certain that Rabirius would be condemned, the praetor Metellus Celer hauled down the red flag that was flown from the Janiculum Hill during meetings of the assembly, the signal that all citizens had to muster to defend Rome from an attack by Etruscans (something that had not happened for hundreds of years). The assembly dissolved in chaos. Rabirius's trial, however, was not resumed, since both sides believed they had won the political battle. Because Rabirius had been convicted, Caesar and the Populares believed they had reestablished the inviolability of tribunes, demonstrated the sovereignty of the people over the consuls and senate in judicial and political matters, and showed that the *SCU* did not offer legal protection for those who would deprive a Roman citizen of his rights—and life—without trial. Because Rabirius still lived, Cicero and the Optimates believed that they had proven that they could—and would—take all steps necessary to preserve the authority of the senate and consuls during times of crisis.

Events would soon put these beliefs to the test. In this chaotic summer, Catiline again ran for the consulship, this time on a radical platform that called for cancellation of debts (*tabulae novae*), the redistribution of land, and other popular measures. Cicero attempted to postpone the elections, but the senate agreed to only a few days' delay. Cicero ran the election while wearing armor under his toga and surrounded by a personal bodyguard (to his supporters this proved the danger; to his opponents it was theatrics at best or the actions of a tyrant at worst). After

Catiline and other supporters of radical reform were defeated, reports begin to stream into Rome of disturbances throughout Italy. Of particular concern, Gaius Manlius began to gather troops in Etruria, drawing especially on impoverished veterans of the last civil war. The crisis of Catiline, so long developing, had begun.

A NOTE ON THE CRISIS OF 64–63 BCE

In retrospect, it is tempting to see the events of the late second and early first centuries BCE as a continuous sequence of political unrest that eventually undid the republican order of the Roman state. While the escalating stresses to the political system and the inadequacy of the reforms seem self-evident in hindsight, it is important to remember that Romans in 63 BCE did not realize that in less than a generation the Republic would be irrevocably lost, replaced by tyranny under a different name (the *principate*). Despite the recent turmoil, few Romans, even in the midst of the crisis of Catiline, doubted the long-term sustainability of Rome's republican system, which had survived in roughly the same form for over 400 years and which the Romans believed was the longest-lasting and most successful government the world had ever seen.

We might think that the emergence of tyranny was the inevitable result of Rome's territorial growth and the bureaucratic and military apparatus necessary to maintain its hegemony. But even "radicals" like Catiline were seeking to gain power within the existing system. Catiline sought to be consul, not king or a leader of a radical democracy. Indeed, the political elite's faith in the sustainability of the republican system is one of the factors that led to its fracturing, as the elite failed to enact necessary reforms and took expedient shortcuts that hollowed out the traditions that made possible the consensual model of Roman politics.

HISTORY OF THE *SENATUS CONSULTUM ULTIMUM*

When crisis struck the early Republic, Romans would routinely grant extraordinary powers to a dictator. Unlike the modern use of the word, an early Roman dictator was a constitutional officer who served as supreme political and military leader for a single term of six months with complete immunity for actions taken while in office. The dictatorship, however, fell into disuse after the conclusion of the Second Punic War in 201 BCE, as Rome experienced a period of political stability and its rapid growth in the second century BCE pushed wars ever farther from Rome. The office was revived during the chaos of the civil wars between Marius and Sulla (82 BCE). But Sulla's bloody dictatorship tainted the office in the eyes of the senate and the people of Rome.

In the late second and early first centuries BCE, however, the senate devised an alternative when renewed civil conflict often required swift and decisive action. Instead of creating a dictator, the senate issued the *SCU*: "Let the consuls see to it that the state suffer no harm."[5]

This simple decree empowered the consuls to take whatever steps they considered necessary to preserve the Republic, including actions that would violate the rights and privileges of Roman citizens. In normal times, Roman citizens were immune to mistreatment by magistrates by a set of hard-won legal protections. Often known collectively as the Valerian, Porcian, and Sempronian Laws, they stipulated that (1) citizens were immune from physical harm and coercion without trial; (2) if convicted, they could appeal to the people (*provocatio*); (3) they could seek the protection of a tribune (*intercessio*); and (4) if condemned, they could choose exile instead of death.

Because the actions a consul took under an *SCU* generally included extralegal acts that violated the traditional rights of Roman citizens, the legality of this final decree was highly contested. Did a magistrate have the ability—or indeed the obligation—to protect the state from suffering irreparable harm by taking actions that would otherwise be illegal? What, exactly, did the decree authorize the magistrates to do? Were there limits to its scope? When did its sanction expire?

Supporters of the decree argued that once Roman citizens constituted themselves as a private army and attempted to overthrow the state, they were no longer citizens (*cives*) but enemies of the state (*hostes*). *Hostes* could not logically enjoy the same legal protections as Roman citizens. In times of crisis, they said, an older law took precedence over whatever individual protections Roman citizens enjoyed: "Let the well-being of the people be the ultimate law" (*salus populi suprema lex esto*). Since magistrates were already sworn to protect the Republic, the decree did not grant them special powers or immunities; it was merely a signal by the senate that magistrates should deploy their inherent legal powers in defense of the Republic.

Opponents of the *SCU*, like Caesar, argued that the decree simply commanded the consul to act within Rome's traditional legal and political framework, not to violate the essential rights of Roman citizens. A magistrate, they argued, may take extraordinary action in stopping an ongoing insurrection, or apprehending riotous citizens, or striking down a tyrant. But once rebels or rioters were in custody, they no longer posed an immediate threat to the state or public order but were merely citizens who enjoyed their citizen rights until such time as a trial determined their guilt or innocence. They pointed out that the authority for the *SCU* rested on tradition (*mos*), a powerful foundation in Rome but one that lacked any legal support—indeed the *SCU* seemed expressly designed to circumvent uncircumventable laws. How can justice (*ius*) be based on violence (*vis*) without ceasing to be justice? Moreover, the entire apparatus of the Roman political order was designed to constrain the coercive power of magistrates. How, they asked, could a piece of that system override itself? If a magistrate were granted unchecked power, who or what could then limit his power?

The *Senatus Consultum Ultimum* before 63 BCE

121 BCE. For the consul Lucius Opimius against the ex-tribune Gaius Sempronius Gracchus and the tribune Marcus Fulvius Flaccus. Gracchus, out of office and so a private citizen, had assembled a personal bodyguard, which killed Opimius's client. Opimius, leading a group of senators and equites, killed Gracchus, Flaccus, and around 3,000 of their supporters on the Aventine. When Opimius was tried by a tribune "among the people" (*apud populum*), he claimed that he was justified in violating the law because he acted in accordance with the interests of the senate and the "well-being of the people" (*salus populi*). Opimius's acquittal set the precedent that a magistrate could take extralegal action when the senate so advised.

100 BCE. For the consul Gaius Marius against the tribune Lucius Appuleius Saturninus and the praetor Gaius Servilius Glaucia. Saturninus had fomented mob violence in an attempt to force passage of his legislative program. In 63 BCE Gaius Rabirius was prosecuted for treason and convicted for his role in killing Saturninus and Glaucia; Cicero's speech in his defense, *In Defense of Rabirius* (*Pro Rabirio*), survives.

77 BCE. For the consul Quintus Lutatius Catulus against the proconsul Marcus Aemilius Lepidus, who had raised a revolt in Etruria and was marching on Rome from his province of Cisalpine Gaul. When the bulk of his army defected to Pompey, Lepidus fled to Sardinia, where he died of natural causes.

3

The Game

The game begins in 63 BCE, either on November 8 (if you are playing the short version of the game) or a few months before (in the multisession version of the game). The core texts at the end of this book serve as the primary sources for the game. Your instructor may begin the game at a different point in the crisis and may suggest or require other readings.

Remember that the documents in the core texts are not sterile recitations of facts. They are passionate, clever, and biased testimonies composed by passionate partisans. Read the primary documents from the perspective of your character. Depending on who you are, Cicero's speech or Sallust's history may appear to be powerful indictments of a malignant threat to the senate and the people of Rome, or they may seem a tissue of lies spun by slanderous, megalomaniacal blowhards—or a little of both.

MAJOR ISSUES FOR DEBATE

The Crisis of Catiline requires you to act to solve a political crisis, albeit one entwined with social, economic, and legal factors. This game poses essential questions about how citizens and the government should react to a time of instability and about the relationship between the individual and the state:

> What constrains those in power or those seeking power?
>
> What do the wealthy owe to the poor? Or the state to marginalized citizens?
>
> What is the connection between personal behavior and that person's authority in public?
>
> How should a government react to a time of instability? How can an administration preserve stability after serious threats have been discovered?
>
> When does the preservation of civil order—or necessary change—justify the state to violate cherished rights? When does a threat to the state justify action that in "normal" times would be illegal?

When can the state use force against threatening (but not yet violent) citizens? What proof is needed to act against the disfavored, marginalized, or treasonous?

Issues like these—not the trustworthiness of evidence—are the core of what Romans are debating in 63 BCE. Since you are Roman, you will debate these via forceful rhetoric, savvy politicking, and salacious personal attacks, but the Republic lives or dies on these fundamental political questions.

RULES AND PROCEDURES: THE *MOS MAIORUM*

The presiding magistrate (typically Cicero at the start of the game) has almost total control over what happens during debate. This power, however, is constrained by decades of personal relationship with his fellow senators and hundreds of years of tradition: senators will not tolerate a presiding magistrate who abuses his power by behaving like a tyrant, gratuitously insults speakers, or prevents opposing viewpoints from being expressed. The point of senatorial debate, after all, is for the presiding magistrate to receive advice from each of his peers.

Objectives and Victory Conditions

Players typically win *The Crisis of Catiline* if, at the conclusion of the game, the historical characters they represent have accomplished their main objectives. Sometimes a single player or small group may be victorious, but typically, many characters can win the game. Most players are members of one of the three factions. Victory for one player in a faction usually means victory for all. For instance, if the Optimates have prevented debt reform and secured a *senatus consultum ultimum* (*SCU*) against those threatening the Republic, their vision of Rome is triumphant. But if the Populares pass comprehensive land reform and discredit the *SCU*, then they have likely won. Your individual objectives and those of your faction are found in your personal role sheets. Your instructor may assign a victory bonus for those of you who successfully navigate your way through this crisis.

In a sense, everyone who participates in the transformative educational experience that is *The Crisis of Catiline* is a winner—but in another, more accurate sense, some of your characters will be winners and others will be disgraced, exiled, or dead. If you achieve your political goals but find yourself on the losing side of a civil war (or an assassin's blade) your victory may be short-lived indeed. Nevertheless, to win you may not necessarily be alive or in Rome. As in life, success comes from playing the long game.

Some characters, especially the Indeterminates, have special or even unique victory objectives. For these players, defining "victory" may be more complicated; they should meet with the instructor if they have questions.

At the start of the game, no group has an overall advantage. The course of the debate will be determined by what proposals are made and how you support or criticize them.

Note: You may pretend to support one position to mask a secret goal that you work for behind the scenes. If this is the case, be sure to explain to the instructor that you are undertaking these actions and why; otherwise, the position you support publicly will be assumed to be your actual position.

The Setting

The Crisis of Catiline plays out against the backdrop of transformative changes to Roman society. Rome was founded as a small settlement at a bend in the Tiber River in Italy, but by the time of the crisis it had grown into the most powerful state in the ancient world, with subjects on three continents and an empire spanning nearly the entire Mediterranean. There was no longer any state that could pose a serious threat to Rome's dominance. Local potentates or Germanic tribes might raid across Rome's borders, kill Roman citizens, or even defeat a Roman army, but the resources available to Rome all but guaranteed its eventual victory over external foes.

Instead, the threats to Roman society were internal: corruption, economic disruption, mob violence, popular uprising, and civil war. During the early centuries of Rome's expansion, the foundation for Rome's unsurpassed military strength had been the small family farm, which provided the resources for nonelite Romans to purchase arms and serve in the army. But by the late second century, deteriorating economic conditions in the countryside forced many farmers to immigrate to Rome, where they joined the swelling ranks of the urban poor. Economic distress caused many who remained on their land to fall into debt. Attempts to resolve these and other crises in the generations before the crisis of Catiline led to a series of increasingly violent political conflicts between the Roman nobility and the poor—and within the nobility itself.

Competition among the Roman elites had always been ferocious. But beginning in 133 BCE, the wealth and power of Rome's expanding empire distorted a political system that had been optimized to balance the ambitions of aristocrats in central Italy. By 63 BCE the system of Roman governance, which had evolved and endured for over 400 years, was breaking—if it was not already broken. Romans had become the greatest threat to Rome.

Meetings in the Senate

Convening the senate. The presiding magistrate takes the auspices (looks to the sky for ill- or favorably-omened birds), then enters the senate house and offers a sacrifice. Since the senate always convenes in a space consecrated by the augurs as a temple, any senator may offer a small, bloodless sacrifice to the god at the altar (for example, valuable spices, a votive statuette). The presiding magistrate has the discretion to judge whether the meeting is sufficiently full for meaningful business to be done (that is, when a quorum has been reached).

Entry and departure of magistrates. When a magistrate with *imperium* (praetor, consul, or censor) enters or leaves the meeting, all in attendance should stand. Senators might also stand up on the arrival or departure of any individual to whom they wish to show particular respect.

Introducing the matter for discussion. The presiding magistrate does not propose a specific course of action but merely outlines the topic for discussion (the ***relatio***) before the senate. The *relatio* itself is always quite brief and in this form: "We ask you, conscript fathers, what will be good, favorable, and beneficial to the Roman people in the matter of . . . ?"

He then states succinctly the matter for discussion and concludes with these words: "About this matter, what action is pleasing?"[1]

Senatorial Debates

Having introduced the *relatio*, the presiding magistrate ordinarily opens the matter for debate. This is customarily done by calling each member of the senate to state his opinion on the matter. This invitation usually follows this simple formula:

"Speak, Decimus Junius (what you recommend)."[2]

Order of debate. Senators speak in the order they appear in the *Album Senatorum*, the list of senators maintained by the censors (see below). The most prestigious and experienced senators speak first; newly minted senators speak at the end of debate, after they have heard the opinions of their elders.

There are four important exceptions to this sequence of debate:

1) Current magistrates (that is, praetors, consuls, and censors) have an assigned position in the *Album Senatorum* but can deliver formal or informal speeches at any point in the debate.
   Magistrates who may speak at any time:
   - Marcus Tullius Cicero, consul, presiding magistrate
   - Lucius Aurelius Cotta, censor
   - Gaius Antonius Hybrida, consul
   - Publius Cornelius Lentulus Sura, praetor
   - Quintus Caecilius Metellus Celer, praetor
2) The presiding magistrate can call on senators to speak earlier in the debate if the matter directly concerns them or as a mark of special esteem, but this was unusual, since it could be perceived as a sign of disrespect to those senators who had been displaced.
3) The presiding magistrate will normally allow senators who are mentioned by name in the speech of another senator the privilege of making a brief reply.
4) The presiding magistrate may call on (senior) members of the senate to respond briefly to speeches made after they had delivered their formal speeches, especially if it touches on a proposal they made.

In Rome, this form of moderated debate happened organically, shaped by decades of participants' personal experiences and centuries of precedent. In *The Crisis of Catiline* senate, those senators who wish to ask a question or make a very brief retort should raise their hands after the speech. The presiding magistrate will call on as many as are feasible given the time constraints under which the debate is being run. The presiding magistrate would naturally give priority to those just mentioned by name and more senior senators in selecting respondents.

Delivering an opinion (*sententia*). When the presiding magistrate calls upon a senator by name, he is obliged to give some indication of his opinion, even if was simply agreeing with the position of a senator who has already spoken:

"I agree with Murena."[3]

If a senator plans to deliver a speech of any length, he should stand. Once on his feet, a member of the senate is entitled to speak for as long as he wishes without being stopped (although the presiding magistrate or another magistrate may make a brief interruption to ask a question or challenge a point). The only requirement is that he must, usually at the end of his speech, either make a specific proposal of what should be done about the *relatio* or express his agreement with the proposal of a previous speaker. Note that in the context of the game additional requirements (like a time limit) will likely be imposed.

Making a proposal (*consultum*). Remember that senators are always debating specific proposals (*consulta*). To propose a *consultum*, a senator must read it to the senate as part of his *sententia* and submit a copy, in writing, to the presiding magistrate (who will deliver it to the instructor at the end of the session).

To propose a *consultum*, the senator must say: "I propose the following be a ***senatus consultum*** . . ."

Any senator may offer an amendment to a *consultum* at any point before voting begins. The presiding magistrate will ask the original proposer if he accepts or rejects the amendment. If the amendment is accepted, the proposal will be changed. If the amendment is rejected, the other senator may submit it as his own separate proposal.

Responding to a *sententia*, or how to react like a Roman. Senators will react in some way to every speech with cheers, heckles, or grumbles.

Signaling agreement with your feet: If in agreement with a previous speaker, a member of the senate might immediately move near that speaker. He might also move away from a speaker to indicate his disapproval of that speaker's view. The conclusion of a speech might be followed by the quite extensive movement of people from one place to another.

Useful Latin phrases: If you wish to give the meeting of the senate a more authentically Roman feel, you might draw from this list of Latin expressions:

Mirábile!	Amazing!
Mirábile auditu!	Amazing to hear!
Mirábile dictu!	Amazing to say!
Sophós!	Brilliant!
Macte!	Well done!
Euge!	Yippee, wow!
Scílicet (ita res est).	Of course (it is true).
Babae!	Wow (amazing) or wow (disturbing)!
Pro dolor!	Alas! What a shame!
Eheu!	Oh, no!
Fufae!	Yuck!
Nefas!	Wicked!
Praedo! (or) Latro!	You pirate!
Sceleráte!	You criminal!
Mehércle!	Oh my Hercules, or OMG!
Di immortáles!	OMGs!

Speaking in the Senate

During debate you will typically be required by the traditions of the senate to state your opinion (*sententia*) about the topic (*relatio*) introduced by the presiding magistrate or about a proposal for action (*consultum*) introduced by another senator. You may make your own proposal for how to address the crisis

FIGURE 3.1 *The Orator* (*L'Arringatore*), ca. 100 BCE. Bronze statue from Sanguineto (Perugia). The statue, which resides at the National Archaeological Museum of Florence, depicts the Etruscan magistrate Aulus Metellus wearing Roman costume. Photo by Adam Eastland, Alamy Stock Photo.

that confronts Rome or comment on the wisdom or folly of a proposal that has already been made. Your instructor will inform you of exactly how you will be sharing your opinions during the game.

Legally, a senator may speak as long as he wishes, but debate will be limited to a duration determined by the instructor (likely between three and six minutes, or the equivalent of two to four pages of typed text). The order of speakers will follow standard senatorial practice (see "Order of debate" in the "Senatorial Debates" section above). With this in mind, you will be well served to discuss your ideas, concerns, fears, and/or plots with Romans who are likely to support (or oppose) your designs, especially if they will be speaking before you. Seek out allies, anticipate the arguments of your opponents, and find and court those senators who can be persuaded.

Since your goal is to persuade your fellow senators by means of a convincing speech in the Roman senate, you will need to conform to the expectations of a Roman audience. With this in mind, your speech must be:

Believable and consistent with the historical moment. You must avoid anachronism and may not allude to events or works that have yet to happen. Make no mention of any events after the day the senate is meeting. You must shun contemporary slang and allusions to pop or literary culture. During the game, you are a Roman: "to be or not to be" is just another antithesis (and a banal one at that); "I have a dream" has no historical-cultural significance for the Roman you (although Romans did often talk about dreams as signs from the gods). Instead quote at least one phrase or passage from one of the core texts or another primary source mentioned on your role sheet. Feel free to quote other *sententiae* by ancient Romans as well. Note: this is the one place where (slight) anachronism is permissible—you may secretly "quote" a Roman text written after 63 BCE. For example, you might pretend that you are the first person to claim that you are speaking "without anger or prejudice" (*sine ira et studio*), a notable phrase by the later Roman historian Tacitus (*Annales* 1.1).

Argued like a Roman. Romans rarely based their arguments on facts alone. Rather, they approached important decisions from the perspective of ethics and circumstance. Much more important than who did what when is the question of what kind of character would do what sort of thing in what kind of circumstance. For example, it matters less if you can prove Catiline really did sleep with his sister or if Cicero did bribe a witness than if you can show he was the kind of person who would engage in that activity. Refer early and often to the "Roman virtues" presented later in this chapter. Observe how your opponents lack these virtues and how your actions—and those of your friends—display them. But don't merely list virtues; explain their relevance by reminding your audience of at least one *exemplum*. That is, refer to the actions of a notable ancestor or, if you do not have an ancestor whose actions are relevant to the debate, a notable figure from Roman history: for example, Regulus, Coriolanus, Mucius Scaevola, Fabius Maximus, Brutus (the avenger of Lucretia, not Caesar's assassin two decades in the future!), etc.

Consistent with the practice of Roman oratory. Make the speech sound Roman by making frequent use of the rhetorical devices common in Latin oratory. Examples can be found in the section titled "Orating Like a Roman," below. Remember that Roman oratory is performance. You will gain the ear of the crowd through entertainment (supported by facts and reality, if possible). A dry rehearsal of law or facts will not persuade anyone. Be flamboyant, be funny, be over the top.

Consistent with your persona. Some of you are regal; some shady; some experienced; some young and excitable; some, frankly, a little unhinged.

Since Roman rhetorical training emphasized memory and improvisation, a Roman would never dream of reading a prepared speech. But, since you are unlikely to have the twenty years of rhetorical training and twenty or more years of practice at delivering speeches like the typical Roman senator, your instructor will let you know what, if any, supports you are allowed. Typically, however, you will not read your speech verbatim. If you anticipate this being a problem, please approach your instructor to discuss the situation.

If needed, your instructor will provide additional details about the expectations for your written speech(es).

Voting

Once the presiding magistrate has opened debate, he is obliged to continue calling for opinions (*sententiae*) until he has called on every member present at the meeting. Normally, if there is not enough time for this in a single day then he is obliged to renew the meeting on a subsequent day to continue the debate. In the game, however, junior senators may find their speeches shortened or skipped. If this happens, your instructor will consult with you.

If there are multiple proposals, the presiding magistrate has complete freedom in deciding how to handle competing proposals. He can put a proposal to a vote exactly as it had originally been suggested, or he can make changes to it, or he can refuse to put it to a vote at all. He can even create entirely new proposals that had not been discussed during the debate. But even senators who oppose a proposal will likely take offense if the magistrate refuses to bring a proposal to a vote, since gross alterations of *consulta* were at odds with the point of holding debate: to inform the actions of the consul.

The presiding magistrate also has freedom to decide the order in which he puts proposals to a vote. The result of one vote may influence his decision about which, if any, proposal to put forward next. If the presiding magistrate attempted to push through an unpopular proposal by including it in a single vote with a number of more popular items, members might protest by shouting "*Divide!*" (Split it up!). The presiding magistrate was not obliged to do so, but he would often bow to pressure. In the event that conflicting proposals are approved, the one approved last will have the force of the senate's recommendation.

Voting is always conducted by separation (*discessio*). The presiding magistrate reads the proposal and then says:

"Whoever agrees with this, move over there; those who think anything else, move over here."[4]

At the same time, he indicates where the first group should go and where the second. Those supporting the proposal are normally told to move to the person who had made the proposal. Since senators must either support the proposal or not support it, any senators who refuse to move are counted as votes against the proposal.

Voters

All members of the senate participate in the vote, with the exception of the presiding magistrate. As a prominent Roman, you also control the vote of a certain bloc of *pedarii*, nonspeaking senators who are your loyal clients and will vote with you. This models the influence of the patron-client system in ancient Rome, which exerted a profound influence over Roman politics. Note that although the presiding magistrate does not vote himself, he still controls the votes of his *pedarii*. The instructor will determine whether *pedarii* will be factored into voting.

The *Album Senatorum* lists how many votes each player controls at the beginning of the game (the senator plus his *pedarii*). But your *auctoritas* (influence) can be fleeting. Based on the strength (or weakness) of your speech and game play, you may gain (or lose) supporters. If you deliver a passionate, well-styled speech while someone else mutters incoherent nonsense, you may convince some additional *pedarii* to support you in the next debate.

Tallying the Votes

When the vote takes place, the presiding magistrate marks down each person's vote and, if *pedarii* are being used, how many total votes each has at the time of the vote (personal vote plus *pedarii*). The presiding magistrate calculates which group has a higher total number, and the majority will win the vote. The presiding magistrate may designate another member of the senate to assist in counting votes and maintaining order.

The presiding magistrate announces the vote by pointing to the side of the chamber with more votes and declaring: "This side seems greater."[5]

Settling Disputes

The presiding magistrate has latitude in determining how to interpret and follow procedure during a meeting of the senate. But if disputes about proper procedure arise, they will be decided by the princeps senatus (Catulus, if the character is in the game; the instructor, if not). A ruling by the princeps senatus has the weight of divine authority and cannot be appealed to another character in the game.

OUTLINE OF GAME SESSIONS AND READINGS

When you arrive in class for the game, you will be a Roman entering the Temple of Jupiter Stator ("Jupiter Who Upholds Order"). You will listen to and respond to speeches by your fellow Romans on issues of maximum importance to the survival of your country (and yourself).

Most games revolve around one or several topics of debate, and more issues will arise as the debates continue. Every character in *The Crisis of Catiline* has been formed with an opinion about (1) amnesty, (2) land reform, (3) debt reform, and (4) the *SCU*. Students will propose *consulta* (proposals) and debate these issues.

The game has three distinct phases: (1) setup, when the instructor introduces the mechanisms of the game, describes its historical context and primary texts, and assigns students to roles and factions; (2) game play, when the student players seek to win by debating and voting on major issues and policies; and (3) a debriefing, when the class discusses what happened, compares the events in the game to history, and ponders the major issues and texts from other perspectives.

Your instructor will reveal the schedule your game will follow.

Phase 1: Setup

Session 1: Introduction to Rome in 63 BCE

The instructor will explain the mechanics of the game and lead a discussion on Roman history.

REQUIRED READING

Game book: chapter 1, "Introduction," and chapter 2, "Historical Background"

SUGGESTED READING

You might also begin to familiarize yourself with the rules and procedures of the game: the *mos maiorum*.

Remaining Setup Sessions

Depending on your class schedule, one or more remaining setup sessions may include lecture and discussion about relevant aspects of Roman culture and history.

Players will receive their roles and learn about their Roman selves and the factions operating in 63 BCE Rome. They will meet with their factions or, if they are Indeterminates, meet privately with the game manager (GM).

Note: Depending on the number of students playing the game, there may be characters listed in the *Album Senatorum* who are not present in the game. The GM will post or distribute an accurate version of the album and notify players of any nonvoting roles involved in the game.

REQUIRED READING
- Personal role sheets
- Chapter 3, "The Game"
- Chapter 4, "Factions and Roles"

Phase 2: Game Play

This phase of the game will comprise one or more sessions devoted to the main issue(s) confronting Rome.

Game sessions will unfold in a predictable sequence: When players arrive in the senate, they will likely sit with their factions. Indeterminates will sit wherever they wish. The presiding magistrate will begin all sessions and introduce the topic(s) for the session. Players will propose *consulta* or express their support for or opposition to the *consulta* proposed by others. Every session will culminate in a vote on the *consulta*.

Debate will proceed in the order prescribed by the *Album Senatorum*. But members of factions should coordinate their approach to the topic(s). Every member of the faction is expected to participate in all sessions and debates, but particular players have special responsibilities (indicated in their personal role sheets).

The following provides an outline for a four-session version of the game. In the short version of *The Crisis*

of Catiline, your game play will focus on the question of the legitimacy of the *SCU* (Session 4); in the multi-session version of the game, you may play one or more of the other sessions (Sessions 1–4); and the game could be expanded with sessions devoted to other issues (for example, enfranchisement of new citizens, electoral or social reform, foreign policy). Your instructor will inform you of which sessions are being played in your game.

Session 1: Amnesty

A number of senatorial Romans have been convicted of crimes and expelled from the senate, forbidden from running for office, and compelled to go into exile—or have friends or family in this situation. Some have been convicted of electoral bribery, others have been removed from the senate for immorality, and still others have found themselves on the wrong side of past civil wars, especially those who dared resist Sulla. Recently, an increasing number have run afoul of the *lex Acilia Calpurnia*. Passed in 67 BCE by Gaius Calpurnius Piso and Manius Acilius Glabrio, it mandated that those convicted of electoral corruption "should neither hold office nor be a senator and should incur a fine besides." It has become common to exclude even the sons of those who have been expelled.

Those who have been unjustly accused in the past understand how terrible a false accusation can be, and many are still suffering from the repercussions of their trials and convictions. On the other hand, some of the men who have been convicted are untrustworthy at best and treasonous at worst. Would an amnesty be a show of goodwill from the senate that could reduce tensions in Rome, or would it eliminate consequences for bad acts and throw the government into chaos? The point of the debate is not to discuss a particular case—such concerns are beneath the dignity of the senate—but to discuss the wisdom of a general (or limited) amnesty during a time of political and moral crisis. In particular it should begin the debate about the value of citizenship and what it means if citizen rights can be revoked by a (possibly corrupt) court or a (panicked) majority.

MAIN AGENDA TOPICS

- Should former senators (and/or their sons) who have been expelled from the senate be readmitted?
- Should the amnesty be general or limited?

OTHER AGENDA TOPIC(S)

At the GM's discretion, *consulta* dealing directly with the underlying issues (for example, electoral bribery or other justifications for expulsion from the senate) may be introduced.

SUGGESTED CORE READINGS

- Cicero, *Laws* 2.7–14, 3.2–5
- Valerius Maximus, *Memorable Doings and Sayings* (Selections)
- Seneca the Younger, *On Mercy* 2.3–5, 2.7

Session 2: Land Reform

The Populares, a faction that claims to support the interests of the people, are pushing for the senate to be more responsive to the needs of the rural and urban poor by distributing some of the land held by the Roman state to its less fortunate citizens. Some senators support these measures because they believe in supporting the common people. There are rumors that others have been pushing for these reforms for more self-interested reasons.

A reform proposal introduced by Publius Servilius Rullus at the start of the year failed thanks to Cicero's intense opposition. In the light of the increasing desperation of the people, it seems opportune to launch another effort at reform. Should the senate pass a land reform? Will the measures actually help the common people, or will they just line the pockets of those in positions of power? What is the connection between material wealth and legal rights (and responsibilities)?

MAIN AGENDA TOPIC

- Should there be land reform?
- If yes, what form should it take?

OTHER AGENDA TOPIC(S)

At the GM's discretion, *consulta* dealing directly with other forms of social reform may be introduced.

SUGGESTED CORE READINGS

- Appian of Alexandria, *Civil Wars* 1.7–13
- Cicero, *On the Agrarian Law* 2 (Selections)
- Sallust, *Catiline's War* 37–39
- Juvenal, *Satire* 3 (Selections)

Session 3: Debt Reform

The Populares are pushing for the senate to be more responsive to the needs of the rural and urban poor by enacting some measure of debt relief. The more radical among them, like Catiline, have suggested a policy of debt cancellation (*tabulae novae*, or "new ledgers").

A generation before, there had been several attempts at debt reform. In 89 BCE, an attempt at reform ended in the assassination of the praetor Asellio (see core text Livy, *From the Founding of the City* 6.14–15, 6.31–32, 42.5); just three years later in 86 BCE there was widespread support for the *lex Valeria*, which allowed debtors to use bronze coinage to pay off debt denominated in silver (effectively reducing payments by 75 percent).

For Romans, debt reform was only partially a financial matter. It engaged directly with deeply held notions of personal and communal obligation and ethical behavior. What justifies the modification of a contract in a society in which the fulfillment of duty is a paramount virtue? What do the wealthy owe to the poor? Or the state to marginalized citizens? If a citizen is not responsible for his actions, does he continue to be free?

MAIN AGENDA TOPIC

- Should there be debt reform?
- If yes, what form should it take?

OTHER AGENDA TOPIC(S)

At the GM's discretion, *consulta* dealing directly with other forms of social or economic reform may be introduced.

SUGGESTED CORE READINGS

- Cicero, *Second Speech against Catiline* 7–11, 17–25
- Cicero, *On Duties* 2.80–84
- Plutarch, *Why We Ought Not Borrow*
- Livy, *From the Founding of the City* 6.14, 6.31–32, 42.5
- Appian of Alexandria, *Civil Wars* 1.54
- Juvenal, *Satire* 3 (Selections)

Session 4: Senatus Consultum Ultimum (SCU)

Before this session, the crisis escalates and violence seems imminent. The senate must decide whether it will pass an *SCU* to give the consuls the power to "take whatever action necessary to protect the safety of the Republic." Optimates believe that drastic action is necessary to prevent a total breakdown of public order—and maybe even civil war; Populares counter that the rights of Roman citizens must remain intact, *especially* during times of social and political unrest.

How should a government react to a time of instability? How can an administration preserve stability after serious threats have been discovered? When does a threat to the state justify action that in "normal" times would be illegal? When does the preservation of civil order—or necessary change—justify the state violating cherished rights? When can the state use force against threatening (but not yet violent) citizens? What proof is needed to act against the disfavored, marginalized, or treasonous?

MAIN AGENDA TOPIC

Should the senate authorize an *SCU*?

SUGGESTED CORE READINGS

- Cicero, *First Speech against Catiline*
- Cicero, *Second Speech against Catiline* 7–11, 17–25
- Sallust, *Catiline's War* 5–13
- Cicero, *Second Speech against Verres* 5.160–63

Note: Cicero's speeches against Catiline were delivered after the passage of the *SCU*, as Cicero sought to justify its authority. For the purposes of the game, whenever Cicero's texts claim that the *SCU* has

been passed against the Catilinarians, think of this as a statement of Cicero's conviction that it must be passed.

Session 5: Consequences

If Catiline and his followers have convinced the senate of the worthiness of their cause and avoided the passage of an *SCU*, what consequences should the current leaders face? If no *consulta* have been passed and the state seems unresponsive to the crisis, what is the response of desperate Romans? If the consuls-designate have been discredited, should elections be rerun? If the Optimates have proven themselves staunch leaders, what should be done about the reckless Catilinarians or all who support radical reform? Should they be put on trial? Does the state of emergency mean they can be condemned to exile—or even death—with trial or appeal to the people (as happened after previous *SCUs* in violation of the *lex Valeria* and *lex Porcia*)? Or, as some have started to suggest, is imprisonment an option? Are there other options? And there have been whispers that an army is on the move. . . .

AGENDA TOPIC

The presiding magistrate (in consultation with the GM) should determine the main issues being debated today.

SUGGESTED CORE READINGS

To be determined based on topic(s).

Phase 3: Debriefing

After the final game session, the GM will direct discussion during the final class(es) of the debriefing phase, indicating the victors and uncovering any secrets. The instructor will also relate the actual historical events of the period. If the game's outcomes differed from history, the class will discuss how and why. Finally, students will discuss their own views on the central issues and texts, especially the writings of Cicero.

Chance (Fortuna) *and Action Outside the Senate*

At any point in the debate, events may overtake the deliberations of the senate. You should be prepared for the unexpected (a riot caused by a particularly offensive speech, a sign from the gods, word that a prominent Roman has returned to Italy, etc.).

GAMBITS AND SPECIAL ACTIONS

Some versions of the game may permit gambits (actions that may be taken by any player) and special actions (available to specific characters, as listed on their role sheets).

Consult with the instructor if you are considering pursuing a gambit or special action. The instructor will provide you with additional information about the gambit / special action, if it is permitted in your version of the game. Beware: for all gambits / special actions (examples below), the risks of defeat are at least as high as the benefits of victory. Fortune, after all, favors the bold.

Dictatorship. In the storied past of the early Republic, dictators were elected for six-month terms to address a particular crisis (internal or external) or civil need. The dictator's power (*imperium*) is nearly absolute. Other magistrates remain in office, with their rights and privileges intact. But they are subordinate to the dictator. Within the city of Rome, the judgment of a dictator was subject to the "right of appeal to the people" (*provocatio*); outside the city, his word was final. He would usually appoint an assistant, a "master of the cavalry" (*magister equitum*). At the time of the crisis of Catiline, the office of dictator has been stained by the recent example of the Sullan terror. In the early Republic, however, the dictatorship was very frequently deployed, with more than a dozen in the fifth century and nearly fifty in the fourth century. The senate can pass a *consultum* instructing the consuls to appoint a dictator, whose selection is then ratified by the senate.

Ambassador of the Allobroges. The ambassador of the Allobroges, one of the Celtic tribes of Gaul, is one of the nonvoting roles that may be assigned by the instructor, but players may appeal to the ambassador even if he is not a played character. In that circumstance, the correspondence with the ambassador will occur through

TABLE 3.1 Legions available in the game

Legion	Location	Commander
First Legion	Rome	Hybrida (Celer in daily command)
Second Legion	Rome	Cicero (Celer in daily command)
Manlius's Legion	Etruria	Manlius
1 Veteran Legion	Southern Italy	Recruitable by Crassus, Glabrio, or Memmius
1 Legion of the Allobroges	Gaul	Ambassador of the Allobroges
Pompey's 10-plus legions	Asia (?)	Pompey Magnus

letters, and the instructor will write on behalf of the ambassador.

The Allobroges have significant resources, as well as a powerful army. Players may try to persuade the ambassador that supporting their cause will be beneficial to the interests of the tribe. A successful attempt to persuade the ambassador may lead to more power (if a senator can say he has the support of a Gallic tribe, his arguments may be much more persuasive), more *pedarii* (Romans will want to follow such a charismatic patron), or an army (see "Marching on Rome" below). A failed attempt may lead to a loss of *pedarii*, the Allobroges' giving support to the player's opponents, or even an uprising in Gaul and an attack on Rome. The instructor will decide (with the ambassador, if in play) what rewards or punishments should be dealt to a petitioner of the Allobroges.

Marching on Rome. Any character with control of an army may use that army to march on Rome. Players may also attempt to raise legions or draw on legions posted to the provinces to march on Rome. Whether an attempt to march on Rome is approved is entirely at the discretion of the instructor. While the rewards of a successful march are vast (victory!), the risks are great. In addition to defeat on the field of battle, a general who marches on Rome may also find his soldiers mutinying—or he may provoke the intervention of even more powerful forces. Note that the exact position of Pompey's legions is unknown at the start of the game, although the most recent report has him preparing to return to Rome from the East.

Mutiny. Roman commanders could, from time to time, lose the loyalty of their troops. If the senate has passed a *consultum* stating that more than one senator should accompany an army and there is a disagreement about the course of action that the army should take, the subordinate leader(s) (as determined by possession of *imperium*, *consultum* of the senate, and rank in the *Album Senatorum*) can attempt to gain control of the army.

Assassination. *The Crisis of Catiline* begins with (rumored) attempts on the lives of the consuls. It would not be surprising if prominent politicians found the end of a blade during these chaotic times. If you believe you can advance your interests or those of your faction by removing an opponent from the senate, you may wish to attempt an assassination—but only if your character is the kind of Roman who could engage in such action.

Trials. In general, *The Crisis of Catiline* should unfold in the political arena of the senate. But as the trial of Rabirius showed, sometimes political matters played out in Roman law courts. A senator who intends to prosecute another character for assassination, bribery, embezzlement, extortion while abroad, false witness, injury, treason, or violence should see the instructor for more information.

The Sibylline Books. The Sibylline Books are an ancient collection of sayings that Romans have consulted for guidance since before the birth of the Republic. In this game, consulting the Sibylline Books can cause a secret about another player to be revealed. However, there is no guarantee of success and it may even backfire, causing a secret to be revealed about the initiator or a member of his faction. A desire to consult the books must be passed by the senate like any other consultum, and it will be approved only if the Republic is judged to be in great crisis. The revealed secret (if one is revealed) is spoken aloud before the entire senate.

ORATING LIKE A ROMAN

Skill at speaking and debating was recognized as one of the most important skills a Roman could possess. It produced success in law, business, and politics. As a result, extensive training in rhetoric was the culmination of their formal education for most Roman men (and a few women). While Romans would take years learning the elements of successful oratory and honing their craft by delivering speeches in the persona of mythological and historical characters (like you in *The Crisis of Catiline*!), knowledge of the fundamental features of Roman rhetoric can help you better inhabit the historical moment—and be more persuasive and successful!

The act of orating begins with discovery (*inventio*). As you begin to craft your speech, you must first find the right subject matter and the right evidence and identify the best persuasive approach.

Once you have identified your subject, material, and general approach you can set to arranging and composing your speech. Speeches of the kind used by the characters in *The Crisis of Catiline* typically followed a five-part structure (below)—although experienced orators in such settings would sometimes vary their arrangement to better support their discovery.[6]

1. Introduction (*exordium*): Even in a continuous debate, it is important to cultivate the goodwill and sympathy of the audience and prepare them to receive the argument. As the rhetorician Aelius Theon advises, it is beneficial to make a personal connection: "One should also mention any previous relationship of the exhorter to the person being exhorted and if the latter at some time benefited by being persuaded. The same manner of treatment will be used if we are making some criticism, but if dissuading we shall use the opposite arguments."
2. Statement of the facts (*narratio*): This section should lay out the situation and what is known about it with brevity, clarity, and plausibility. Refer to the present, past, and future (in that

order): "The narration proceeds by the three times. Begin with the present, because it is difficult. Then run back to earlier times, because they have a large share of happiness. Then change to the future, because what is going to happen is much more dreadful. Let both figures and diction contribute to the portrayal" (Hermogenes 85).

3. Proof (*confirmatio*): This section "gains credit, authority, and support through the marshaling of arguments . . . in order to demonstrate your argument's plausibility or irrefutability" (Cicero, *On Invention* 1.34). Emphasize the positive and the precedented: "In exhorting then, we shall say that what we are urging is possible and easy and noble and appropriate; that it is beneficial, just, reverent (either toward the gods or toward the ancestors); that it is pleasant; that we are not the only ones doing it or the first; or that even if we are the first, it is much better to be the beginners of noble deeds; and that when done it brings no regret" (Aelius Theon).

Your proof may open with a partition (*partitio*), in which you list the points on which you and your opponent(s) agree and specify the points that remain in dispute. There are two kinds of proof: nonartistic proof (documents, witness testimony, etc.) and artistic proof, which depends on the reasoning and argumentation of the orator. These artistic proofs, which will be necessary for most of your speeches, are further classified into three modes: *Logos* (proving the truth of argument), *Ethos* (using the presentation of character to win the audience's approval), and *Pathos* (the arousal of the proper emotion in the audience). A successful speech will draw on all three modes.

4. Refutation (*refutatio*): What you try to prove in your proof you then attempt to disprove in the argument of your opponent by exposing the falsity of their assumptions, refuting a conclusion drawn from their assumptions, or by showing that the conclusion itself is false; if, however, your opponent's argument is strong, counter it with an even stronger argument (Cicero, *On Invention* 1.79).

5. Conclusion (*peroratio*): Refresh the memory of the audience with a brief recapitulation of the facts; or to do what is far more effective, stir their emotions through sympathy for yourself and indignation toward your opponents (Quintilian, preface to *Institutes of Oratory* 4).

Speak with style. Ancient rhetorical handbooks and treatises had boundless advice on style, but these all might be summarized as follows: the best style is the one most appropriate to the speaker and the speech and the audience. When considering your style, think of your character: "First of all, one should have in mind what the personality of the speaker is like and to whom the speech is addressed: the speaker's age, the occasion, the place, the social status of the speaker; also, the subject that the speeches are going to discuss. Then one is ready to try to say appropriate words. Different ways of speaking belong to different ages of life, not the same to an older man and a younger one; the speech of a younger man will be mingled with simplicity and modesty, that of an older man with knowledge and experience" (Aelius Theon). Beyond that you need a speech that is appropriate for the topic and the setting. In general, they thought a plain style was good for proving a point, a middle style for delighting your audience, and a grand style for swaying them. But however plain or grand or varied your style, you must always strive for clarity. And you should make judicious use of ornamentation—both the rhetorical devices that can make your thoughts memorable but also the perfect use of ornamentation (by which they meant metaphor). Examples of rhetorical devices can be found in a supplemental handout provided by your instructor.

Remember this! An ancient orator would memorize his speech—with more or less spontaneous modification depending on the circumstances and his skill. Your instructor will convey the exact expectations for your speech (should you memorize it? use notecards? an outline?). But although the ancients were masters at memory, they also recognized that it was a skill that took time and training to develop, and they created memory systems to help speakers improve their natural memory. They recommended that speakers use a sequence of memorable "images" (to represent key words, ideas, etc.) embedded in a familiar "background" (for example the houses on a familiar street, or the rooms as you progress through a building). As you moved through your speech, you moved through this mental space, using the memorable images to remind you of your key points, phrases, and ideas. This memory palace, or "method of loci," was at the heart of most Greco-Roman (and modern) methods of enhanced memory.[7]

Delivery. Delivery. Delivery. When Demosthenes, who was widely regarded in antiquity as the greatest orator, was asked about the considerations in speaking, he was said to have replied, "First, delivery; second, delivery; and third, delivery" (Cicero, *Brutus* 142). Quintilian says, "The rules for delivery are identical with those for the language of oratory itself. For, as our language must be correct, clear, ornate, and appropriate, so with our delivery; it will be correct—that is, free from fault—if our utterance is fluent, clear, pleasant, and smooth (*Institutes of Oratory* 11.3.30). He gives specific advice on how the body can be used to complement speech: the head can "indicate consent, refusal, and affirmation; there are positions expressive of modesty, hesitation, wonder, or indignation" (11.3.71); a glance can produce the greatest influence, expressing "supplication, threats, flattery, sorrow, joy, pride, or submission. It is on this that our audience hangs, on this that they rivet their attention and their gaze, even before we begin to speak. It is this that inspires the hearer with affection or dislike, this that conveys a world of meaning and is often more eloquent than all our words" (11.3.72). And, of course, gesture is essential but must be used sparingly:

"One of the commonest of all the gestures consists in placing the middle finger against the thumb and extending the remaining three: it is suitable to the *exordium*, the hand being moved forward with an easy motion a little distance both to right and left, while the head and shoulders gradually follow the direction of the gesture. It is also useful in the statement of facts, but in that case the hand must be moved with firmness and a little farther forward, while, if we are reproaching or refuting our adversary, the same movement may be employed with some vehemence and energy, since such passages permit greater freedom of extension" (11.3.92).

When it comes to dress, Quintilian says that "there is no special garb peculiar to the orator," but since all eyes are on the orator it should be "distinguished and manly" but without seeming to be the result of "excess care [which] is just as reprehensible as excessive carelessness" (11.3.137).

How does writing relate to speaking? Ancient orators never read their speeches (even notes), but they did recognize that the best path to giving a great speech was writing a great speech. One of the characters in Cicero's *On the Orator* says, "What is most fundamental, however, is something that, to be honest, we do least of all (for it involves a great deal of effort, which most of us try to avoid)—I mean writing as much as possible. It is the pen, the pen, that is the best and most eminent teacher and creator of speaking" (1.149).

ROMAN VIRTUES; OR, HOW TO BE A GOOD ROMAN

How should a Roman behave? To what standards was he held? What was a good life?

In ancient Rome, the perception of character mattered. You were the sum of your public manifestations—your actions, your words, your friends, your ancestors all contributed to your sense of your identity. A politician's every action—indeed, every word and gesture—mattered. In the competitive world of Roman politics, no opportunity could be wasted to show that you were a "good Roman." But what does this mean during the crisis of Catiline? The ideal Roman is successful across the full range of manly pursuits. More specifically, a good Roman will be an excellent soldier, an eloquent orator, and a courageous general in significant undertakings; lead the senate and the people with wisdom; gain honest wealth; have many children; and be distinguished among his peers.[8] Notice how many of these accomplishments are public rather than private. Good Romans strived to be recognized for displaying their accomplishments. Powering all of a good Roman's efforts were his pursuit, display, and upholding of the Roman virtues.

The degree to which a Roman attained these standards of virtue exerted enormous influence on his degree of excellence (*virtus*), his prestige (*dignitas*), his integrity (*integritas*), his influence (*auctoritas*), and his ability to forge lasting relationships with other Romans (*amicitia*). These general moral concepts, along with other more specific virtues, are described below. One's own behavior was paramount in determining one's social standing; but virtues were also thought to have a hereditary component. A good Roman built on the "virtue endowment" of his ancestors—and, if he faltered, he would damage the prestige of his ancestors and descendants.

Note: Each of the terms outlined below comprises a complex bundle of meanings and implications; the simple English translation given first might be the closest English analogue, but be sure to read the description to get a better sense of each virtue and how it functioned in Roman society and in concert with other virtues.

General Moral Concepts

Amicitia (friendship): Primarily referred to the network of relationships and obligations that bound together people outside the family. It includes both personal friendship and relationships like that between patron and client. During *The Crisis of Catiline*, such personal bonds can trump factional loyalty.

Auctoritas (influence): A Roman's ability to influence others and to direct the political process. It was the ability to put one's *dignitas* into action. One accumulated *auctoritas* through the standing of his family, his personal experiences, his material wealth, the strength of his *amicitia*, and the perception of his *virtus*. The historian Theodor Mommsen describes the "force" of *auctoritas* as "more than advice and less than command, an advice which one may not safely ignore"—or an offer you couldn't refuse. A character's *pedarii* could be thought of as a visible manifestation of his *auctoritas*.

Dignitas (prestige): The sum of a Roman's personal clout and influence because of his reputation, visual impressiveness or distinction, dignity of style and gesture, rank, moral standing, and achievement. *Dignitas* also incorporated the obligations that flow from these. It was the basis of one's *auctoritas*.

Integritas (integrity): A person who understood the virtues and who acted and judged others in accordance with these possessed *integritas*. He was complete (*integer*). One could think of *integritas* as the central point in a diagram where all the virtues intersect and overlap.

Virtus (excellence): A Roman valued dutifulness and courage in the public sphere. A man was thought to have *virtus* if he displayed *prudentia*, *iustitia*, *temperantia*, and *fortitudo* in his public dealings (see below). Although the highest female virtue was *pudicitia* (modesty or chastity), exceptional women, children, and even non-Romans could demonstrate *virtus*.

Roman Virtues

Aequitas (equitable conduct): A Roman should treat others justly and fairly in politics and personally.

Clementia (mercy): A Roman should grant tolerance, forbearance, and gentleness to the humbled weak. Its opposite was "savageness" (*saevitia*), the indiscriminate application of violence against the undeserving.

Comitas (appropriateness): A Roman should display good taste, decorum, and courtesy at all times when interacting with someone of lower social status. A Roman should never be boorish, crass, inconsiderate, or discourteous. His *comitas* was one of the aspects of *Romanitas* that distinguished him from the bestial barbarian and the obsequious Greek—although some more traditional Romans believed that *comitas* was a dangerous modern disposition and that social inferiors should be treated with *severitas*.

Constantia and *firmitas* (tenacity): A Roman should be confident in his positions. He should abhor fickleness. He possessed the strength of character to maintain one's convictions in the face of any challenge.

Fides (reliability): A Roman should be good to his word and undertake what was expected of him and trust that others would do the same. *Fides* was the reciprocal obligation—between a father and a son, a patron and his client, and a friend with a friend—that should underlay all Roman social, political, and financial transactions.

Fortitudo (courage): A Roman should be courageous in confronting dangers to himself, to his family, and to the state.

Frugalitas (frugality): A Roman should have simple tastes, be economical with his resources, and embrace a simplicity of style; but he should never be miserly, which would be a violation of *comitas*. Many thought this virtue was needed more than ever if the crisis of the Republic was to be resolved.

Gravitas (weight): The sense of responsibility, dignity, and earnestness that a Roman should project; his intellectual substance gained from years of experience and his depth of personality, austerity, and moral rectitude, requiring a harmony between one's actions and emotions. Closely related to *severitas*.

Humanitas (grace): The refined manners, tact, and style that a well-educated Roman aristocrat should have in his dealings with other members of the same social rank. Whereas *comitas* regulated relationships between social unequals, *humanitas* described proper behavior within the bounds of *amicitia*.

Industria (industriousness): A Roman should work hard for the betterment of the state and his family and friends. Even leisure should be productive, never lazy or idle.

Liberalitas (affable generosity): At its heart, *liberalitas* described the qualities of mind and character befitting a free person, and especially the generosity motivated by kindness or magnanimity more than by an explicit expectation of reciprocity (as was *amicitia*).

Pietas (dutifulness): A Roman should respect all his obligations: to the gods, to the state, to his parents, and to other blood relations.

Prudentia (discretion): A Roman should avoid unnecessary risk through judicious foresight and wisdom.

Salubritas (wholesomeness): It is no surprise that a Roman coined the phrase "sound mind in a sound body" (*mens sana in corpore sano*). Physical and mental health permitted the attainment of virtue and arose in turn from its cultivation.

Severitas (sternness): A Roman should discipline himself and exercise self-control in all areas of life. This extended to the strict regulation of his household, which should reflect his own virtues (or vices).

Temperantia (moderation): The balance in life and character that came when actions were guided by knowledge and wisdom. A Roman should resist the easy temptations of sensual pleasure.

Veritas (truthfulness): A Roman was as good as his word.

Convincing (and Being Convinced) via the Roman Virtues

Romans tended to argue as much or more on ethical grounds (that is, what was right for an individual or Rome) as on what was logical, practical, or plausible. But a Roman would never simply recite a list of relevant virtues. Instead, a Roman would argue about the practical implications of a virtue in the current situation through "exemplary ethics"—that is, he would make use of examples from Rome's vast treasury of myth and history to show how and why an action must be taken or shunned. As Fergus Millar has observed, "The most common vehicle for [Roman] debate . . . was not prediction about the future but reinterpretation of the past" (1998, 2). You will find this mode of argumentation in almost every Roman text you encounter.

Fortunately, for the time-constrained Roman orator (and the student coming fresh to ancient Roman culture), there were compendia of exemplary stories, grouped by the virtue (or vice) they illustrated. The most user-friendly of those that survives is Valerius Maximus's *Memorable Doings and Sayings*, which gathered anecdotes under headings like "Bravery" (3.2), "Justice" (6.5), "Why Ill-Famed Defendants Were Condemned or Acquitted" (8.1), and "Wise Sayings" (7.2). A selection of Valerius's writings on strictness, compassion, and reconciliation can be found in the core texts.

TOGA OR NOT TOGA? DRESS IN *THE CRISIS OF CATILINE*

Students often wonder if it is appropriate to try to dress like a Roman during the game. While there is no requirement to wear Roman dress, you may find that doing so lends a certain *gravitas* to your arguments. Below are some broad guidelines for dress and a resource for further information.

Contrary to many representations in popular culture, Romans were not naked under their togas. Men wore a tunic, a simple long shirt with cutoff sleeves that could be belted for further utility. The tunics of senators typically had two broad vertical red stripes that indicated their status. Tunics were typically made of coarse, undyed wool; so a gray, beige, or white tunic is reasonably accurate.

Only male citizens could wear a toga on top of their tunics. Most male citizens wore an off-white undyed wool toga, similar to the tunics described above. Candidates for political office would wear an artificially whitened toga to stand out. Individuals holding significant office (such as the consuls or tribunes) would add a broad red border to their toga to show their office.

Roman footwear was typically open-toed sandals.

For more details, which may spark ideas for you, see Barbara McManus's webpage on Roman dress: https://vroma.org/vromans/bmcmanus/clothing.html.

4

Factions and Roles

FACTIONS

In *The Crisis of Catiline*, most senators are aligned with one of three broad factions (outlined below), although the characters within those factions have their own specific political beliefs. Senators who do not align neatly with any of the three factions are called Indeterminates.

Populares: The Populares, or "men of the people," believe that the senate has a responsibility to protect and serve the people and therefore advocate for measures that help the common people and decrease the power of the senate and magistrates. They appeal to the disgruntled and disaffected Romans and Italians, especially the impoverished urban poor (the plebs), indebted aristocrats and farmers, and veterans who have failed as farmers. To ameliorate the financial pressures on the people, some (but not all) Populares advocate a radical program of debt forgiveness, land reform (redistribution of property), the curtailing of the prerogatives of the senate, the empowerment of popular assemblies, and the opening of magistracies and priesthoods to all, regardless of wealth or status. Some Populares deeply believe in the necessity of reform; others more cynically seek alternate modes of advancement after being marginalized by Optimates.

Boni: The Boni aim to restore stability through compromise but do not support radical policies. They are sympathetic to the concerns of the people, but they dread the instability that they believe will follow too hasty reform. Whereas the Populares argue that the senate should appease the people by adopting revolutionary policies like subsidizing grain, broadening the electorate, or increasing the power of the tribunes, and the Optimates try to address problems by adopting ever-more-conservative positions and consolidating power within the senate, the Boni believe fully in the governing ideal of *SPQR* (*senatus* *populusque Romanus*, "the senate and Roman people"): Rome is strongest when there is harmony between the senate and the people. They believe the senate should be more accountable to the people and address their legitimate concerns, but they will usually oppose a reform if it is unprecedented or threatens Rome's stability, which will lead the Republic to fall into another tyranny.

Optimates: Optimates oppose almost all reform because they believe that putting more power in the hands of the people will disrupt the stability of the Republic and lead to chaos. They work toward preserving or expanding the political prerogatives of the senate, which includes its ability to act to protect civic peace under the *senatus consultum ultimum* (*SCU*). Optimates oppose the *furor* (destructive madness) that they believe the Populares threaten to unleash by stoking the ambitions and resentments of the people through their foolish rhetoric and reforms. They seek to limit the power of the popular assemblies and the tribunes of the plebs, which they see as prone to supporting tyranny and valuing individuals over the common good. In general, they favor the authority of experienced *nobiles* (noble families) and oppose the ascension of *novi homines* ("new men," usually provincials, like Cicero) into Roman politics.

Indeterminates: Some senators are uncertain about which faction they should support. They are persuadable by the proper argument. They may have strong opinions about Catiline or Cicero but hesitate to join a particular faction because of their personal experience, grudges, or other motivations. They may have political goals that cannot easily fit within one of the existing factions. Note that these characters do not belong to an Indeterminate faction but instead find themselves between the other factions or drawn to more than one.

A note about factions at the time of the crisis: Although factions existed in ancient Rome and were becoming more potent at the time of the crisis of Catiline, Roman factions did not offer coherent political platforms and should not be understood through modern conceptions like "liberal" or "conservative." They are better understood as networks of associates united by a shared approach to politics and, frequently, support for similar solutions to Rome's problems. In Cicero's (biased) opinion, "There have always been two kinds of men in this state who have to engage in public affairs and to distinguish themselves therein. Of these two kinds, one aimed at being, by repute and in reality, Populares, the other Optimates. Those who wished everything that they said to be agreeable to the masses were reckoned as Populares, but those who acted so as to win by their policy the approval of the best citizens were judged as Optimates" (*In Defense of Sestius* 96).

But at the time of the crisis, a Roman politician's support for a faction might be based as much as (or more) on friendship or familial ties and expectations as on ideological support. A Roman might seem, therefore, to take conflicting positions or to switch positions in short order. But this was often because of the complex network of personal associations and moral beliefs that influenced a Roman's decision-making process. Of course, we are no different in this regard. But a Roman tended to be more aware (or honest) about the factors that shaped his decision-making process. Just because a senator supports one position associated with the Populares (for example, redistribution of land), he may not support another (for example, debt reform). This is not a sign of hypocrisy or disloyalty to his faction, since a faction, to a Roman of this period, has no claim to a Roman's loyalty.

Indeed, Romans were careful to differentiate between actions undertaken because of friendship (that is, *amicitia*; see section "Roman Virtues, or, How to Be a Good Roman") and those undertaken merely because of faction. During the time of the crisis of Catiline, Romans saw blind adherence to a faction as a twisted form of friendship, a transitory, instrumental alliance of personal interest aimed at a material goal rather than a durable connection that benefited the character of both individuals. As the historian Sallust said, "What among good men is friendship, among bad men is faction" (*The Jugurthine War* 31). Senators, therefore, are inclined to vote with their friends, but that does not always mean they vote with their factions. Some senators may disagree with their factions on specific issues. Some senators will even be convinced to switch factions as the game proceeds. Cicero, for example, began his career allied with Populares politicians and interests but saw his allegiances shift as he rose through the ranks of the *cursus honorum* (the sequence of political offices leading to the consulship).

We should also recognize that, although the senators are divided into different factions, members of the senate are all from wealthy, aristocratic families, regardless of their political beliefs. There are economic differences between senators, of course, but these do not neatly match with the divisions between factions—there are wealthy Populares (like Crassus) and more modestly heeled Optimates (like Cato). But all senators are drawn from the wealthiest stratum of Roman society. They grew up with similar family histories, values, and customs. They experienced similar careers. Even the most inconsequential senators likely had members of their extended family who served as consuls or other high-ranking officials.[1]

ROLES

Table 4.1 lists the roles in each faction *as they stand at the beginning of the game*. Once the game begins, alliances and opinions could shift dramatically. *Nonvoting roles*, for characters who are noncitizen, nonsenatorial, or outside Rome at the time of the crisis, may be assigned by the instructor. The nonvoting roles are still strongly invested in the outcome of the game and will be responsible for strategizing with senators and influencing the course of history outside of the visible debate in the senate.

Brief Outline of Each Role

Note that these biographies are listed in the order of the *Album Senatorum*. Each is annotated with the senator's faction and any official positions.

Marcus Tullius Cicero: consul and presiding magistrate; Boni; 43 years old. Cicero is a *novus homo* (new man), the first man from his family to enter the senate and rise to the consulship. As a young man, he was recognized as an unusually talented orator and poet. He studied philosophy and rhetoric in Athens, developing an innovative oratorical style that propelled his political career. Cicero won every election he entered "in his year" (his first year of eligibility), a sign of respect that he enjoys among the senate and the people of Rome. As quaestor he served in Sicily, where he compelled the farmers to supply grain needed in Rome. Yet the Sicilians considered him prudent, just, and fair. They respected him, and he prosecuted their case against Verres, who was accused by the Sicilians of grotesque abuses of power when governor. Although Verres was supported by many of the most powerful men in Rome, Cicero forced Verres to flee into exile. More success in the courts and elections followed, with Cicero often working in favor of popular reform. Recently, however, Cicero has turned toward the nobility, who supported him in his election to the consulship. Recently, he has focused all his efforts on thwarting the ambitions of Catiline.

Decimus Junius Silanus: consul designatus; Optimates; 44 years old. Silanus is from a distinguished

TABLE 4.1 Factions and their members

Optimates	Boni	Populares	Indeterminates
Decimus Junius **Silanus**	Marcus Tullius **Cicero**	Marcus Licinius **Crassus**	Manius Acilius **Glabrio**
Quintus Lutatius **Catulus**	Lucius Licinius **Murena**	Gaius Antonius **Hybrida**	Lucius Licinius **Lucullus**
Publius Servilius Vatia **Isauricus**	Lucius Aurelius **Cotta**	**Gaius** Julius **Caesar**	Quintus **Hortensius** Hortalus
Servius **Sulpicius Rufus**	**Lucius** Julius **Caesar**	Lucius Sergius **Catilina**	Lucius Calpurnius **Piso** Caesoninus
Quintus Caecilius Metellus **Celer**	Lucius **Caecilius Rufus**	Lucius Cassius **Longinus**	Publius Cornelius Lentulus **Spinther**
Quintus Caecilius Metellus **Nepos**	Publius **Vatinius**	Publius Cornelius Lentulus **Sura**	Gaius **Memmius**
Marcus Porcius **Cato**		Lucius Calpurnius **Bestia**	Gaius Helvius **Cinna**
Quintus Caecilius Metellus Pius Scipio **Nasica**		Titus Atius **Labienus**	Publius **Nigidius** Figulus
		Servius Cornelius **Sulla**	Publius Claudius **Pulcher**
		Gaius Cornelius **Cethegus**	
		Marcus Porcius **Laeca**	

Note: The most distinctive element of each name is in boldface to facilitate reference and comprehension.

family, son of Marcus Junius Silanus, who was consul in 109 BCE. He is a traditionalist and opposes reform, as he believes it will undermine the stability of the Republic. He recently won the election to the consulship for next year and, with Murena, will take office on January 1. His relationship with his wife Servilia is tense. Rumors that she is having an affair with Gaius Julius Caesar were recently confirmed when Cato demanded that Caesar read to the senate a note he received, which turned out to be a love note from Servilia.

Lucius Licinius Murena: consul designatus; Boni; 43 years old. Murena was born in Rome to a plebeian family, but is descended from aristocrats, including Lucius Licinius Murena (the elder), consul in 151 BCE. Murena served in all three wars in the East against King Mithridates and quickly climbed up the *cursus honorum*. He will assume the consulship with Silanus on January 1. After the election, he was ac-

cused of bribery by Servius Sulpicius Rufus but was acquitted, largely because Cicero gave persuasive testimony about his good character. It is widely known that he has debts and is counting on his consulship to restore his finances. He is known to be open to moderate reform.

Quintus Lutatius Catulus Capitolinus: princeps senatus; Optimates; 67 years old. Catulus's father was a close associate of war-hero and champion of the people Marius, who helped him attain a consulship. When Marius betrayed the elder Catulus and forced him to commit suicide, the younger Catulus fled Rome. Since Catulus returned to Rome with Sulla (and avenged his father, with Catiline's help), he has been a powerful voice in the senate. He is respected for his fairness, prestige, and authority. A decade ago, he led the opposition to overly hasty reform. As a result of his patient guidance, the senate achieved consensus on the restoration of tribune powers and

TABLE 4.2 Vote distribution for the *Album Senatorum* (members of the senate)

Role	Faction	Votes
Marcus Tullius **Cicero** (consul and presiding magistrate)	Boni	29
Decimus Junius **Silanus** (consul designatus)	Optimates	30
Lucius Licinius **Murena** (consul designatus)	Boni	30
Quintus Lutatius **Catulus** (princeps senatus)	Optimates	30
Marcus Licinius **Crassus**	Populares	30
Lucius Aurelius **Cotta** (censor)	Boni	30
Publius Servilius Vatia **Isauricus**	Optimates	10
Manius Acilius **Glabrio**	Indeterminate	30
Lucius Licinius **Lucullus**	Indeterminate	15–30
Quintus **Hortensius** Hortalus	Indeterminate	20
Gaius Antonius **Hybrida** (consul)	Populares	30
Lucius Julius **Caesar**	Boni	10
Gaius Julius **Caesar** (pontifex maximus, praetor designatus)	Populares	20
Lucius Sergius **Catilina**	Populares	30
Lucius Cassius **Longinus**	Populares	10
Servius **Sulpicius Rufus**	Optimates	20
Publius Cornelius Lentulus **Sura** (praetor)	Populares	20
Quintus Caecilius Metellus **Celer** (praetor)	Optimates	20
Lucius Calpurnius **Piso** Caesoninus	Indeterminate	20
Publius Cornelius Lentulus **Spinther** (curule aedile)	Indeterminate	10
Gaius **Memmius** (aedile)	Indeterminate	30
Quintus Caecilius Metellus **Nepos** (tribune designatus)	Optimates	20
Lucius Calpurnius **Bestia** (tribune designatus)	Populares	20
Marcus Porcius **Cato** (tribune designatus)	Optimates	20
Titus Atius **Labienus** (tribune)	Populares	20
Lucius **Caecilius Rufus** (tribune)	Boni	20
Servius Cornelius **Sulla**	Populares	20
Publius **Vatinius**	Boni	10
Gaius Cornelius **Cethegus**	Populares	10
Gaius Helvius **Cinna**	Indeterminate	10
Marcus Porcius **Laeca**	Populares	20
Quintus Caecilius Metellus Pius Scipio **Nasica** (pontifex)	Optimates	10
Publius **Nigidius** Figulus	Indeterminate	15
Publius Claudius **Pulcher**	Indeterminate	20

Note: The most distinctive element of each name is in boldface to facilitate reference and comprehension.

the reform of the courts. As a pontifex, he oversaw the rebuilding of the Temple of Jupiter on the Capitoline that had been destroyed during Sulla's march on Rome. For this he earned the nickname "Capitolinus." Gaius Caesar accused him of embezzling funds, but few believed the charge and the case was dismissed. He stands firmly against demagogues and unprecedented actions. Although Gaius Caesar just defeated him in the election for pontifex maximus, Catulus considers it his duty to uphold the *mos maiorum*. As princeps senatus he is responsible for preserving the decorum and traditions of the senate and will decide any procedural disputes.

Marcus Licinius Crassus Dives: ex-censor, ex-consul; Populares; 52 years old. Crassus is a savvy politician and businessman. He was a loyal supporter of Sulla and helped Sulla return to Italy in 84 BCE. Throughout his career, he has constantly been in the shadow of a younger man, Pompey, and resents that Pompey gets the credit for assisting Sulla's return and for defeating the gladiator uprisings in the 70s. Crassus is incredibly wealthy—hence his nickname, "Dives" (Rich Man)—and he uses his wealth to ensure that he and his allies continue to stay in the good graces of the Roman people. He and Cicero are often in conflict, although their disagreements have yet to come to a head and he has been known to feed Cicero evidence to use against their mutual enemies. He was elected censor with Cotta last year but has resigned, leaving Cotta the sole censor.

Lucius Aurelius Cotta: censor; Boni; 57 years old. Cotta served as praetor in 70 BCE, consul in 65, and then censor beginning last year. His family has a record of consular success: his grandfather, his father, and both of his brothers were consuls before him. Once a good friend to Sulla, he is known to be concerned with the morality of the Roman people and feels very strongly that senators must set a proper example for the people. Several years ago, he brought charges of bribery against the consuls-elect, Publius Cornelius Sulla and Publius Autronius Paetus. They were both convicted, and Cotta and his fellow prosecutor, Lucius Manlius Torquatus, were elected consuls in their place. He earned praise as an able and even outstanding consul. As a censor, it is his responsibility to monitor the moral character of his fellow senators—and he would oversee any major state-sponsored building projects. He is respected as a figure of authority in the senate.

Publius Servilius Vatia Isauricus: ex-consul; Optimates; 71 years old. Isauricus has spent his life as a champion of traditional values and the *mos maiorum*. In his lifetime he has been granted not one but two triumphs (celebratory military parades), the first for killing Saturninus and quelling the revolt that he caused and the second for defeating the pirates in Cilicia. He brought a huge amount of wealth back to Rome from Cilicia, keeping none for himself, a noble and selfless act. He recently ran for pontifex maximus but lost the election to Gaius Caesar, whom he despises.

Manius Acilius Glabrio: ex-consul; Indeterminate; 58 years old. Glabrio was tribune of the plebs in 78 BCE, praetor in 70, consul in 67, and then proconsul in the East, until his command was transferred to Pompey. Both his grandfather and great-grandfather were consuls; his father was tribune. He was a loyal supporter of the Optimates (even if he was not able to save Verres from Cicero's prosecution for corruption in 70 . . . but who could have!). But then his command in the war against Mithridates was stripped and handed to Pompey. Despite this setback, he remains a figure of authority, with friends in the senate and the respect of the people (who never disliked him; but they love Pompey more). His opinions about the current crisis are unclear, although it is known that he holds a grudge for his mistreatment and will never support any action that directly benefits Pompey.

Lucius Licinius Lucullus: ex-consul; Indeterminate; 55 years old. Praetor in 77 and consul in 74, spending most of the past two decades on a military campaign or in provincial administration. The glory of his paternal line faltered when his father was exiled after only reaching the praetorship. But, with the help of his well-connected mother, Caecilia Metella, Lucullus embarked on a successful career and has surpassed all his ancestors. An early supporter of his kinsman Sulla Felix—he was the only officer to march with the dictator on Rome in 88—Lucullus nevertheless gained a reputation for honest, efficient, and compassionate administration in his provinces, first in Asia and then Africa. Cicero and Cato recently worked together to allow Lucullus to celebrate a triumph for his campaign against Mithridates, but only after waiting for three years outside the *pomerium*, the sacred boundary of the city. This kept him from participating actively in politics and he is only now reengaging with the work of the senate, but it is not clear whether he cares more for the work of the state or the lavish gardens he is constructing. He is known to oppose Pompey, who replaced him in the East, and Pulcher, his former brother-in-law, who is rumored to have tried to lead a mutiny against him.

Quintus Hortensius Hortalus: ex-consul; Indeterminate; 51 years old. Hortensius was once unquestionably the best and most successful orator in Rome, but he has been overshadowed by Cicero, who burst into public life by besting Hortensius in Verres's corruption trial a mere seven years ago. Despite that setback, Hortensius was elected consul the following year. Like his father-in-law, Catulus, Hortensius is naturally inclined to support the Optimates, but his strong personal ties to more popular-minded politicians have seen him often side with Populares in recent years; nor can one infer from his work in court the positions Hortensius will take in the senate. He joined forces with Cicero to defend Rabirius and Murena, but the two are hardly close. First and foremost an orator, Hortensius's opinion can be persuaded by a strong oratorical display.

Gaius Antonius Hybrida: consul; Populares; 43 years old. Hybrida served in the Mithridatic Wars under Sulla and was chosen to supervise Greece after the wars concluded. During that time, he earned the nickname "Hybrida" (half-beast) because of rumored scandalous behavior. He has since embraced the name during his rise to prominence. He is currently co-consul with Cicero, although he has been spending much of his time preparing to depart to his proconsular province, Macedonia, whose riches promise to replenish his fortune. Everyone knows he cut a

deal with Cicero: in return for Macedonia, he would defer to Cicero during their consulship, allowing his colleague to remain the presiding magistrate. He ran for consul together with Catiline, and most Romans assume that he and Catiline remain friends.

Lucius Julius Caesar: ex-consul; Boni; 47 years old. Lucius Caesar was consul last year, continuing the tradition of electoral success by the Julii. He is popular with most senators, and his modest temperament leads him to support modest actions. His cautious disposition leads him to agree often with the Optimates, but just this year he joined with his cousin, Gaius Caesar, to judge Rabirius for executing a Roman citizen without trial. Known as a fair and just man, he is often called upon to moderate between opposing positions and rivals, especially as he possesses the authority to have his decisions carried out.

Gaius Julius Caesar: pontifex maximus; praetor designatus; Populares; 37 years old. Unlike his modest cousin, Gaius Caesar is the most ambitious man in a city of ambitious men. He is an up-and-coming politician with enough charisma to keep the people on his side, enough political savvy to navigate the senate with relative ease, and enough charm to be the lover of many women (including the wives of his senatorial colleagues). He proved himself a capable leader as a quaestor and aedile. Now pontifex maximus—a post to which he was elected over many older and seemingly more deserving men—he was recently elected praetor and will take office on January 1. He is an outspoken critic of the *SCU*, having led the recent prosecution of Rabirius to discredit its use. But his family has close ties to many of the Optimates, and he seems to have distanced himself from Catiline recently. He and Crassus are known to be friends.

Lucius Sergius Catilina: ex-praetor; Populares; 45 years old. Catiline stands at the center of the crisis in the senate. Brilliant and charismatic, he is descended from an ancient Roman family, but one that has not produced a consul in over 300 years. He served under Strabo in the Social War and as a young man supported Sulla and the Optimates, often through extreme measures. But he now champions the common people by pushing for debt and land reform. Throughout his life, he has been plagued by accusations of wrongdoing: in 73 BCE he was accused of committing adultery; at the same time, there were rumors that he had slept with a Vestal Virgin; in 66 BCE he was prevented from running for the consulship due to charges of corruption; in 65 BCE he was tried for abuse of power and was more recently tried for the murder of his brother-in-law Gratidianus, among others, during the Sullan proscriptions. He was acquitted of all these charges, but they have harmed his reputation. This year, he ran again for consul but lost to Cicero and Hybrida.

Lucius Cassius Longinus: ex-praetor; Populares; 45 years old. Longinus's family is well-respected and has done much for the Roman people, although Longinus himself is yet to achieve the position he craves: the consulship. He ran for consul last year but was unsuccessful and holds a grudge against Cicero for beating him in the election and for Cicero's unseemly campaign rhetoric, which often mocked Longinus's weight. He is known to be a close associate of Catiline.

Servius Sulpicius Rufus: ex-praetor; Optimates; 43 years old. Sulpicius Rufus is known as a good and just man, although he has not yet achieved significant military or political success. He is a well-known orator and rhetorician and spends most of his time in the courts. He ran for consul in the last election but was defeated by Silanus and Murena. After the election, he and Cato charged Murena with corruption and electoral bribery. Murena may have been acquitted, but Rome now knows Sulpicius is not to be taken lightly.

Publius Cornelius Lentulus Sura: praetor; ex-consul; Populares; 52 years old. Sura was a quaestor under Sulla Felix and quickly rose through the *cursus honorum*. He was elected consul for 71 BCE, but what he thought would be his great accomplishment, a command to defeat Spartacus's gladiatorial army, was handed to Crassus instead. Soon afterward, he fell out of favor and was even temporarily removed

from the senate (along with sixty-three others) on the charge of immorality. Although eventually given amnesty and allowed to return to the senate, he lost a great deal of influence. He won reelection as praetor in an effort to restart his career.

Quintus Caecilius Metellus Celer: urban praetor, augur; Optimates; 40 years old. Metellus Celer holds a great deal of military power as the urban praetor and propraetor designatus for Cisalpine Gaul, and he will use it to his advantage in the senate. He has allied himself with the Optimates and is extremely loyal to his family, the Metelli. The Metelli have recently been plagued by scandal, but unlike some of his relatives, Metellus Celer seems to be a coolheaded senator who makes reasonable and rational decisions. During the trial of Rabirius, he proved his support for the prerogatives of the senate by lowering the "red flag" (which is supposed to signal that Rome is under attack) to prevent Rabirius's condemnation by the Popular Assembly.

Lucius Calpurnius Piso Caesoninus: ex-curule aedile; Indeterminate; 35 years old. Piso is a wellknown Epicurean philosopher. Wealthy and wellconnected, he seems destined to achieve greatness. As aedile last year, he threw spectacular games that won the support of the people and the admiration (and sometimes envy) of many senators. He is known as someone who delights in bringing people with different opinions together for conversation—and for helping them find a solution that benefits both. Yet he is known to be firm in his own convictions that the Republic must be just if it is to be stable. His opinions on the current crisis are unknown.

Publius Cornelius Lentulus Spinther: curule aedile; Indeterminate; 42 years old. Spinther comes from the same family as Publius Cornelius Lentulus Sura but does not appear to share either his ambition or his talent for politics. He has close connections with the Optimates through his family, although in general it is unclear how much he supports them. He has a love for the theater and for public games and will surely be in favor of providing more entertainment for the masses. His opinions on the current crisis are unknown.

Gaius Memmius: aedile; Indeterminate; 35 years old. Memmius is one of the few supporters of Pompey who did not follow their patron to the East. Since Memmius serves as Pompey's eyes, ears, and voice in Rome, he possesses more authority than his position or achievements might suggest. Congenial and gentle by nature, he is equally passionate in his support of three things: Pompey, the prerogatives of the people, and philosophical poetry. Reconciling these interests has been difficult in recent years, as he sought to support the people while also working to thwart the ambition of their greatest champions: Caesar, Crassus, and Catiline. He recently earned the nickname "Paris" for his success at sleeping with his rivals' wives.

Quintus Caecilius Metellus Nepos: tribune designatus; Optimates; 37 years old. Nepos is a vehement defender of the Optimates. He was recently elected tribune with Bestia and Cato and will take office on January 1. There are unconfirmed rumors that his house is disordered. He has spoken out against Cicero and continues to argue that a *novus homo* should not have as much power as Cicero has accumulated.

Lucius Calpurnius Bestia: tribune designatus; Populares; 27 years old. Bestia has recently been elected to the tribunate, along with Nepos and Cato. He will take office on January 1. He is from the aristocratic Calpurnii family but is known to be in financial difficulty. He has spoken out recently in favor of land reform, amnesty, and debt cancellation.

Marcus Porcius Cato: tribune designatus; Optimates; 32 years old. Cato has quickly become a prominent senator despite his youth. He was recently elected tribune for the coming year, with Bestia and Nepos, neither of whom he seems to respect (the feeling is mutual). He makes enemies easily, as he is often unwilling to compromise on issues and has little regard for who is hurt on his quest to root out corruption and restore virtue and order to the senate and the Republic. Even so, he has earned the (grudging) respect of even those nobles he has targeted and the affection of the people, who view him as the only trustworthy man in the senate—despite the fact that he often fights against their interests. This past year, he unsuccessfully charged Murena for bribery in the most recent elections.

Titus Atius Labienus: tribune; Populares; 37 years old. Labienus is a champion of the people and has made his support of the Populares clear during his year as tribune. He showed his ambition by running for pontifex maximus last year but lost the position to Gaius Caesar. He seems to have taken the loss well, however, and instead of begrudging Caesar the position like many others, he has been working with him to support and safeguard the interests of the people of Rome. He was the lead prosecutor of Rabirius and, when Rabirius appealed his conviction to the people, presided over his chaotic, inconclusive trial.

Lucius Caecilius Rufus: tribune; Boni; 35 years old. Rufus has used his power as a tribune to fight against demagogues and to crack down on bribery. He is a staunch supporter of the Boni and, although he is bound by his office to act on behalf of the people, he fears that unwise reform will lead to mob rule.

Servius Cornelius Sulla: ex-quaestor; Populares; 45 years old. Sulla, nephew of the dictator Sulla Felix, is well-known for the grudge he has against the Optimates for their attacks on his family, especially their hypocritical actions against his cousin Publius when they prevented him from taking the consulship to which he was rightly elected due to accusations of corruption and bribery. He is known to be a staunch supporter of Catiline and has made it known that he will do whatever is necessary to restore his family's reputation.

Publius Vatinius: quaestor; Boni; 32 years old. Vatinius is a *novus homo* who has been steadily making a place for himself in a senate that does not generally respect those without family connections. Naturally sympathetic to the Populares because of his humble background, he has shown a tendency to support different factions in different debates. He has only achieved the rank of quaestor, but all assume he has ambitions for the tribunate (and higher).

Gaius Cornelius Cethegus: ex-quaestor; Populares; 42 years old. Cethegus is known as a rash man, whose recklessness has kept him from greater political success. He comes from a well-respected family, but he and his family do not get along, further casting him under suspicion by other senators. An opportunist, he has supported Marius, Sulla, and Pompey in turn. He now has allied himself with Catiline, but his true motives are unclear.

Gaius Helvius Cinna: ex-quaestor; Indeterminate; 37 years old. Cinna, a well-known poet, has participated little in the senate until now, but he appears to be compelled by a sense of civic obligation to attend debate during this crisis. He does not seem to hold any firm stances, beyond his love for the arts. Perhaps that will change as the crisis continues. His reputation recently received a blow when Cicero openly mocked his poetry.

Marcus Porcius Laeca: ex-quaestor; Populares; 37 years old. Laeca is a steadfast member of the Populares and a close friend of Catiline. He is a talented speechwriter and orator, but he has not pursued high office, choosing to bring his calls to action directly to the people rather than the senate. Cicero has accused Laeca of offering his own home in Rome as a base for those devoted to revolution.

Quintus Caecilius Metellus Pius Scipio Nasica: ex-quaestor, pontifex; Optimates; 36 years old. Nasica is just beginning his career, but he has the resources of the powerful Metelli family behind him. He recently lost the election for the tribunate to Cato, with whom he has a bitter rivalry. Thus far in his career, he has been rather conservative, favoring the Optimates, as any action that bolsters the power of the aristocracy protects the Republic, his family, and therefore his interests.

Publius Nigidius Figulus: ex-quaestor; Indeterminate; 35 years old. One of the more intriguing Romans, Nigidius is a Pythagorean philosopher, astrologer, student of Rome's distant past and the occult, and if the rumors are true, a magician! He acquired his nickname "Figulus" (little potter) from his assertion that that while the earth seems stable, it in fact "turns on its own axis at the speed of a potter's wheel." Already a renowned scholar, philosopher, and writer, he is working on a massive book on archaic language and the culture and history of Roman antiquities. Unlike most Romans, he not only has read widely in Greek philosophy but has studied Egyptian, Syrian, Etruscan, and Chaldean traditions. There are rumors that he once enchanted a boy to communicate with the souls of the dead.

Publius Claudius Pulcher: ex-quaestor; Indeterminate; 30 years old. Pulcher, still a young man, has not yet held high office, but he has close connections to some of the most powerful men in Rome. One of his sisters is married to the praetor Quintus Metellus Celer and the other was married to Lucius Licinius Lucullus, although Lucullus has since divorced her amid scandalous rumors. He is the son-in-law of Murena, who has afforded him political protection. In 65 BCE, he attempted to prosecute Catiline for his felonies in Africa but was unsuccessful. There is a rumor, possibly started by Cicero, that he was paid off by Catiline or one of his supporters to throw the case.

Public Biographies of Nonvoting Characters

Ambassador of the Allobroges: 52 years old. The ambassador is not a senator and therefore cannot vote in the senate. The ambassador represents a Celtic tribe from Transalpine Gaul (Gaul-Across-the-Alps). His people have had a brief but complex relationship with the Romans. Conquered by Rome in 121 BCE, the land of Allobroges was ravaged during the early phases of the Cimbrian War (113–101) when successive Roman armies were slaughtered by the invading Germanic tribes. Security was finally restored when Marius defeated the Cimbri, and over the past forty years Rome's attentions have shifted to other, more distant lands. In 65 BCE Roman misgovernance forced the Allobroges to revolt, which was quickly crushed and which led to the imposition of a punishing tribute. The ambassador recently arrived in Rome to seek relief from the tribute and the predatory corruption of the region's governor. The ambassador's position on the crisis is unknown.

Gnaeus Pompeius Magnus (Pompey the Great): 43 years old. Proconsul with *imperium maius* over all Roman forces in the eastern Mediterranean. Pompey should, at his age, only now be aiming for his first consulship—if he were a man who followed tradition. But for the past fifteen years he has been an unstoppable force in Roman politics. Pompey's career has been an unbroken string of successes. Besting Sertorius in Spain and the foes of Sulla in Africa and annihilating the last of Spartacus's army, he shared the consulship with Crassus when only thirty-five years old and then swept the seas free of pirates, leading to his extraordinary command in the East. Perhaps his only disappointment came when his triumphal chariot drawn by captured African war elephants proved too big for the gates of Rome (he switched to horses and finished his triumph). Word has just reached Rome that Pompey has defeated King Mithridates, who had tormented Rome in the East for a generation. There is not a Roman who doesn't respect or fear Pompey, although many envy him and some are bitter that their prestige has already been surpassed by their younger colleague.

Cornelius Nepos: 47 years old. Nepos is not a senator and therefore cannot vote in the senate. Nepos is a prominent author and biographer in Rome. Born in Cisalpine Gaul, he arrived in Rome during the end of Sulla Felix's reign. Having already published several works, he has developed a reputation as a writer who favors a straightforward record of history rather than a dramatic, embellished tale. Nepos has fostered good relationships with many prominent Romans including Titus Pomponius Atticus, a close associate of Cicero, as well as Marcus Porcius Cato, since Nepos has written a biography of Cato's great-grandfather, Cato the Elder. Nepos is known to be friends with the other writers currently gaining prominence in Rome.

Gaius Sallustius Crispus: 23 years old. Sallust is not a senator and therefore cannot vote in the senate. Sallust is an ambitious young citizen from a wealthy provincial family. As he waits to be old enough to take a seat in the senate, he has worked to establish himself as a writer and develop relationships with his future colleagues. As a young man with no established political loyalties and charisma rivaled only by Gaius Caesar, Sallust is trusted and liked by everyone.

Gaius Valerius Catullus: 21 years old. Catullus is not a senator and therefore cannot vote in the senate. Catullus is an up-and-coming *neoteros* (new poet) from Verona. His "Alexandrian" style is favored by many of the young poets of Rome, even the senator Cinna, although its witty and allusive wordplay has drawn criticism from more traditional Romans, including Cicero. Catullus has a reputation for enjoying just two things: poetry and sex, the latter of which is the subject of much gossip. Catullus has no interest in politics, but politicians are another matter. His puns and insults leveled at countless public figures become the slogans of every rival faction. Every senator knows that, should their deeds catch the attention of Catullus, they will soon be the target of jokes and the subject of vulgar graffiti.

Philodemos: 47 years old. Philodemos is not a senator and therefore cannot vote in the senate. Philodemos is a well-known poet, an authority on Epicurean philosophy, and a respected teacher of the children of Rome's elite. Originally from the province of Coele-Syria, he has lived in Rome and at the villa of Lucius Calpurnius Piso Caesoninus in Herculaneum. Due to his philosophic beliefs, Philodemos has no interest in politics, rejecting it as a waste of time and a source of no pleasure. At the same time, he seeks to teach his students the importance of virtue from which pleasure is inseparable. As a result of his strong ideals and his position as the instructor of the children of many senators, his teachings have tremendous influence on the beliefs of Rome's elite.

Publius Gabinius Capito: 32 years old. Capito is not a senator and therefore cannot vote in the senate. Capito is from a prominent equestrian family, the son of a praetor and a relative of several former tribunes. Lately he has made good use of his talent for oratory. His vigorous speeches to the people on the Aventine denounced Cicero's mistreatment of Catiline and caused many of the urban poor to rally

to Catiline's side. His family's political accomplishments, his own ambition, and his popularity among
the people lead many to believe he has his eyes set
on political office.

Sempronia: 34 years old. Sempronia is not a senator and therefore cannot vote in the senate. Sempronia may be the most famous woman in Rome, a sign
of her brilliance to some and her infamy to others.
Her husband, Decimus Junius Brutus (consul in
77 BCE), is traveling abroad, yet Sempronia continues to host parties that bring together Rome's poets,
philosophers, and politicians—at least those who
don't mind the whiff of scandal. Even those who
condemn her behavior acknowledge her talents.
She can compose Latin and Greek poetry, play
music, dance, philosophize, and orate. Rumors
swirl around her: of her communications with the
Allobroges, of her affair with Gaius Caesar, and of
her support for radical reform.

5

Core Texts

All but two of these documents were written by Romans. The other two were written by Greeks living in the Roman empire. In your speeches, feel free to mention by name those written by Cicero and Polybius. The other texts were written after the crisis of Catiline and should be attributed to "a wise/foolish Roman" (or Greek, if you quote Appian or Plutarch).

These texts will have the most value when you read them from the perspective of your character. Remember that these authors have their own perspectives, biases, and goals. Search for these as you read these texts and consider how they align or conflict with the perspectives, experiences, and beliefs of your character.

Remember too that Roman speeches were not barrages of evidence but exhortations to ideals. Wherever possible, use the texts to support specific appeals to the virtues listed in the section "Roman Virtues; or, How to Be a Good Roman" in chapter 3.

Cicero, *First Speech against Catiline*

In this speech, delivered to the senate, the consul Cicero addresses his adversary Catiline, accusing him of aiming to destroy the whole Republic and being hated by the whole city. Cicero demands that Catiline and the other traitors separate themselves from good citizens. Cicero defends both his right to act against the conspirators under his authority as consul and under the auspices of the senatus consultum ultimum *(SCU). Although Cicero hopes his words will drive Catiline from the city, proving that he is indeed an enemy of the state, his true audience is the senators who are hesitant to support his plan to suppress Catiline's coup.*

[1] When, Catiline, will you stop abusing our patience? How long will your frenzied madness mock us? Where is the limit of your unbridled arrogance? Doesn't all of this impress you? No? Not the night watch on the Palatine Hill; not the guards throughout Rome; not the panic among people; not this gather-

ing of loyal citizens; not the senate meeting here in this fortified place?[1] Look at the faces of these senators! Does none of this impress you? Don't you understand that your plans have been detected? Don't you see that our knowledge of your conspiracy has rendered it powerless? Do you think we don't know what you did last night or the night before, where you were, who attended your meeting, what you decided?

[2] Shame on this age! Shame on its character! The senate knows everything you've done. The consul sees everything.[2] Yet this man is alive. Alive? He even comes into the senate! As he takes part in public debates, he watches us and uses his eyes to mark us all for slaughter! Meanwhile we, brave men that we are, think we've done our duty for the Republic by avoiding his frenzy and his daggers. Long ago, Catiline, you should have been executed on the command of the consul. The destruction you planned for us ought to have long ago crashed on your head!

[3] Wasn't Publius Scipio, a distinguished man and pontifex maximus, a private citizen when he killed Tiberius Gracchus?[3] But the threat Gracchus posed to our traditions was minor! Shall we, the consuls, tolerate Catiline, who seeks to destroy the entire world through fire and slaughter? I won't mention an older precedent—Gaius Servilius Ahala using his own hands to kill Spurius Maelius when he plotted a revolution.[4] Once . . . once there was virtue in this Republic, when brave men would punish the traitorous citizen more ferociously than their most bitter foreign enemies.[5] We have the senatus consultum against you, Catiline.[6] This decree is powerful and authoritative. The Republic hasn't failed to make its decision. It is we—I'll say it plainly—we who are lacking.

[4] Once, the senate decreed that the consul Lucius Opimius should "see to it that the Republic suffer no harm."[7] Not a single night passed: Gaius Gracchus was executed on the mere suspicion of treason, despite the good reputation of this father, his grandfather, and his family going back generations. Marcus Fulvius, who had been consul, was executed along with his children. Another senatus consultum en-

trusted the Republic to the consuls, Gaius Marius and Lucius Valerius. Not a single day passed before the Republic exacted its punishment by executing Lucius Saturninus, a tribune of the plebs, and the praetor Gaius Servilius.[8] But for twenty days we've let the senate's authority grow dull. We have the same senatus consultum but it's tucked away in a drawer like a sword in a sheath. According to this decree, Catiline, you should have been executed immediately. Yet you live. And while you live you do not lay aside your arrogance but you strengthen it! I want, gentlemen, to be merciful. I want to not seem negligent during this crisis of the Republic. But now I condemn myself for my negligence and my failure to act.

[5] To the north in Italy an enemy base has been established against the Roman people in the mountain passes of Etruria. The number of our enemies increases every day.[9] Yet, you see the commander of that base and the leader of those enemies within the fortifications of Rome.[10] Rome? Within these very walls, plotting every day an internal strike against the senate. If now, Catiline, I order your arrest and execution, I don't fear that these good men will think I acted with too much cruelty. I will fear that they will think I acted too late. But I have a good reason for not yet doing what I ought to have done long ago: you will be executed only when no one remains who is so wicked, so perverse, so like you that he will declare your death unjust.

[6] As long as a single man dares to defend you, you will live. You will live as you live now. Besieged by my loyal guards, you won't be able to make a move against the Republic. Many eyes will watch you and many ears will stand guard against you, even if you don't know they are there.

What are you waiting for, Catiline, now that night no longer conceals your criminal meetings in its shadows and a private house no longer contains your conspiratorial voices within its walls? Everything is exposed to the light. Everything bursts into the open. Trust me: change your mind. Forget slaughter and arson. You are checked on every side. We see all your plans as clear as day. Let's review them together.

[7] Do you remember how on October 21 I told the senate that Gaius Manlius, your lackey in this brazen scheme, would begin his insurrection on October 27?[11] Wasn't I right, Catiline, not only about the act, whose savagery and brazenness I can scarcely believe, but also—and this is even more amazing—about the date? What a coincidence! I also told the senate that you had postponed the assassination of the city's leaders until October 28. Many of these men fled the city beforehand—not to save themselves but to thwart your plans. You cannot deny, can you, that on October 28 my guards and preparations hemmed you in and prevented you from moving against the Republic, even as you said that you would be satisfied by the slaughter of those leaders who hadn't fled the city.

[8] What happened? You were confident that a nighttime assault would take the stronghold at Praeneste on November 1.[12] Were you aware that I had ordered that town defended by my guards, my garrison, and my watchmen? There is nothing you do, nothing you attempt, nothing you plan that I don't hear it, see it, and know it entirely.

Review with me now the events of the night before last. Then you will understand that my efforts to safeguard the health of the Republic surpass your attempts at its destruction. I say that on the night before last you came to the Street of the Scythemakers—I'll not leave anything hidden—you came to the house of Marcus Laeca.[13] Your accomplices in this criminal insanity joined you there. You don't deny it, do you? Then why are you silent? If you deny it, I will prove that it happened. In fact, I see some of your accomplices here in the senate. [9] For gods' sake! Where in the world are we? What traditions do we have? What city are we living in? Here, gentlemen, here among us in this, the most revered and important council in the world, there are men who plot our deaths and the destruction of the city and the world! I am the consul and I see these men. I call for their opinions about state business. These men, who ought to be executed by the sword, I don't even wound with my words!

You were, Catiline, at Laeca's house that night.

It's true. You doled out the regions of Italy. You decided where each man should go. You chose men to stay at Rome. You chose men you would lead to your army. You assigned which neighborhoods in the city they should burn. You confirmed that you were about to leave the city. But you said that you delayed because I was still alive. Two knights were found to free you from this anxiety.[14] They promised to kill me in my bed just before dawn that very night.

[10] Of course, I learned everything as soon as your meeting broke up. I strengthened my guard, fortified my house. I barred my door to those whom you had sent to salute me in the morning. Yet, those very same men came at exactly the time I said they would. You see, I had revealed all of this beforehand to many of the city's leaders.

Since this is the situation, Catiline, finish what you've begun. Leave the city at last! Its gates are open. Depart! For too long has Manlius's base—*your* base—waited for its commander. Take all your men with you—or at least as many as you can. Cleanse the city. You will free me of my greatest fear once the city's walls stand between us. You cannot remain here with us any longer. I will not endure it, tolerate it, or allow it.

[11] We owe a great debt to the immortal gods and to Jupiter Who Upholds Order *[gesturing to the statue]*, the most ancient guardian of our city.[15] So many times we have already escaped this sickness, so loathsome, so foul, so deadly to the Republic. But the health of the Republic cannot be put at risk by a single man again and again. You plotted against me, Catiline, when I was consul-elect. At that time, my personal alertness defended me, not a public guard. When, as consul, I oversaw the recent election, you wanted to kill me and the other candidates in the Campus Martius. Even then I avoided public outcry and tried to thwart your wickedness by the protection and support of my own friends.[16] Wherever you attacked me, I stood in your way, although I recognized that my death would be a great disaster for the Republic.

[12] Now you openly attack the entire Republic. You summon to ruin and destruction the temples of

the immortal gods, the buildings of the city, the lives of every citizen, all of Italy. Still, I won't yet do what is best, what befits my right to command and the example of our ancestors. Instead, I shall act more leniently but with more benefit for the common good. If I order you to be killed, the rest of your gang of conspirators will remain in the Republic. But if, as I have long encouraged, you leave the city, the great and noxious sewage of your comrades will be drained from the Republic.

[13] What is it, Catiline? Surely you don't hesitate to do at my bidding what you were going to do of your own free will? The consul orders a public enemy to leave the city. You ask me, "You don't mean exile, do you?" I don't command it. But if you ask my opinion, that is my advice.

What is there, Catiline, that can now give you any pleasure in this city? Here, except among that gang of outcast conspirators, there is no one who does not fear you, no one who does not hate you. By what stain of family scandal has your life not been branded? What disgrace in your private affairs does not cling to your reputation? From what lust have your eyes ever abstained? What outrage your hands? What atrocity your body? Is there a single young man to whom, after you snared him in your net of corruption, you have not offered a sword for his recklessness or a torch for his lust?

[14] What is it? Just recently, when the scandalous death of your wife created an opening for a new bride, didn't you pile on another incredible wickedness?[17] I pass this by and willingly allow it to remain in silence so that this monstrous crime may not seem to have occurred in this city without being punished. I pass by the ruin of your fortune, which you understand looms on the next Ides.[18] I pass by your domestic difficulties and disgrace. I arrive at matters that pertain to the welfare of the Republic and the lives and health of us all.

[15] Can the daylight here please you, Catiline? Can the air here please you, when you know that every one of these men knows that on the last day of December, when Lepidus and Tullus were still consuls,[19] you stood in the Comitium armed with a weapon and readied your gang to kill the consuls and the leaders of this city?[20] Everyone knows that it wasn't fear or a change of heart that stopped this criminal insanity—it was the good luck of the Roman people. I won't mention those other crimes—they are well-known and you have committed many more since. How many times you tried to kill me after I was elected consul, how many times once I was in office! How many of your blows, which seemed destined to land, have I dodged with a slight bob or a weave? You achieve nothing. You gain nothing. Yet you don't stop trying and hoping. How often has your dagger been wrenched from your hands?

[16] How often has some chance caused it to slip and fall from your hand? This dagger—I cannot imagine what rites consecrated it since you now think that you must drive it into the body of a consul. What life is left to you now? Now I will speak with you so that you will know I am not moved by hatred— although I should be—but by a sense of pity, which you do not deserve. A few minutes ago, you entered this meeting of the senate. Did any of your friends and acquaintances greet you? No senator in memory has ever experienced this. Are you waiting for them to voice their condemnation? You have been convicted by the stern judgment of their silence. What do you think of this? At the moment you arrived, all the seats around you were abandoned. The former consuls, whom you had so often marked out for slaughter, left the seats around you bare and empty. How do you think this should make you feel?

[17] Good god! If my slaves feared me as much as your countrymen fear you, I would think that I had to depart my own home. Do you even consider that you should depart the city? If I were so deeply loathed and suspected of wrongdoing by my countrymen— even if I didn't deserve it—I would rather avoid their sight than have their hostile eyes glare at me. But you, although you acknowledge the guilt of your crimes and the justified hatred they cause, do you still hesitate to avoid the gaze and presence of those whose hearts and minds you have wounded? If your parents feared you and hated you and you were unable to reconcile with them, I think you would slink away

from their sight. Now your country, which is mother to us all, hates and fears you and long ago decided that you think of nothing but her murder. Won't you respect her authority or bow to her judgment or fear her power?

[18] She pleads with you, Catiline, and although silent, she somehow speaks: "For some years now, no crime has happened without your hand in it, no scandal without your involvement in it. You alone have slaughtered many citizens. You have tormented and plundered my allies without punishment or consequence. Not only have you ignored my laws and my courts, you have even corrupted and broken them. These earlier crimes—although they were intolerable—I tolerated as best I could. But now I am in a state of complete terror because of you and you alone. Whenever there is a thump in the night, I fear it's Catiline. There's no plot hatched against me that lacks your complicity. This I cannot tolerate. So, go! Free me from this terror. If what I fear is true, then I won't be destroyed. If it is false, at least I will no longer be afraid."

[19] If, as I said, your country said these things to you, shouldn't her request be honored, even if she couldn't force you to comply? What about the fact that you surrendered yourself into custody? To avoid suspicion, you said that you were willing to live in Lepidus's house. When Lepidus rejected you, you dared to come to me, asking that I guard you in my own home! You received the same answer from me: if I couldn't be safe when we lived together in the same city, how could we live together under the same roof! So, you approached Quintus Metellus, the praetor. When he rejected you, you went to your buddy, a most excellent man, Marcus Marcellus.[21] I suppose you thought he would keep you under the most attentive guard, under the most clear-sighted suspicion, and be the most vigorous in exacting punishment. Are you so very far from a trip to prison and chains if you deem yourself worthy of being in custody?

[20] Since this is the situation, Catiline—and if you cannot face death calmly—why do you hesitate to depart for a foreign land? Do you hesitate to entrust your very life, snatched from just punishment, to exile and solitude? "Put the matter to the senate," you say. In fact, you demand this. You say that if this group votes for your exile you will obey. I shall not put this to the senate because it is contrary to my principles. Yet I will make sure that you understand what these men think about you. Leave the city, Catiline! Liberate the Republic from its fear! If you wait for these words: go into exile! What is it? What are you waiting for? Don't you notice the silence of these men? They allow it. They are silent. Why are you waiting for their explicit request when you can see their desire expressed by their silence?

[21] Now if I had said this against this excellent young man, Publius Sestius, or that bravest man, Marcus Marcellus, the senate would have already turned violent against me—and justly too—even though I'm a consul and we are in a temple.[22] But in your case, Catiline, their inaction signals their approval, their permission their verdict, their silence their applause. I refer not only to these men, whose authority you evidently value so highly even as you deem their lives worthless. I refer also to the Roman knights, those most honorable and excellent men and all the other brave citizens that surround the senate, whose numbers you can see, whose desires you can sense, and whose voices you heard just moments ago . . . whose hands and weapons I have barely been able to keep off you. I can easily persuade these same men to escort you to the city gates, as you leave this city that you have for so long been eager to destroy.

[22] But why am I still talking? Would anything break your will? Would you ever change your ways? Would you ever consider flight or exile? If only the immortal gods had the power to plant that idea in your head. Even so, I see what a storm of unpopularity looms for me if you are frightened by my speech and decide to go into exile. The memory of your crimes may keep the storm at bay for a time, but in the future it will come. But it will be worth it, as long as this disaster falls only on me and the Republic is kept free from danger. Could you abandon your vices, fear the punishment of law, and yield to the demands

of the Republic? No, it's too much to ask. No, Catiline, you are not the kind of man whom decency could reclaim from scandal, nor fear from risk, nor reason from madness.

[23] Therefore, as I have often said, depart! If you wish to fan the flames of hatred against me, your enemy, as you have often said, go straight into exile. It would be hard for me to endure the rebukes of these men if you went. It would be hard for me to bear the burden of unpopularity if you went into exile on the order of the consul. If, however, you'd rather help my credit and reputation, leave with that savage gang of felons! Go to Manlius! Rally your outcasts! Separate yourself from virtuous men! Wage war against your country! Rejoice in your wicked banditry! Then it won't seem like I cast you out to strangers. It will seem like I invited you to join your own kind.

[24] But why am I encouraging you? I already know that you have sent armed men ahead to wait for you at Forum Aurelium.[23] I know that you have agreed with Manlius on the day. I know that you have even sent ahead that silver eagle for which you set up an evil shrine in your home.[24] I am confident it will bring death and destruction to you and all your followers. Can you bear to be parted from your precious eagle any longer? You used to worship it as you made your way to your crimes. Your hand often passed from that altar to the murder of your countrymen.

[25] At long last you will go where for a long time your unbridled lust and madness have been leading you. This outcome doesn't seem to cause you grief but some unimaginable kind of pleasure. Nature bore you for this insanity. Your will trained you for it. Your luck preserved you for it. You never wanted peace.[25] You didn't even want war unless it was despicable. You found your gang of evil men, those swept together from among the outcast souls who had lost their entire fortune and even hope.

[26] What happiness will you enjoy with them, what delights will satisfy you, with what pleasures will you debase yourself?! When you are among your friends, you will not hear or see a single decent man. Your physical training has prepared you for this kind of life. Lying on the ground? Not only to lie in wait for debauchery but even to undertake crime. Staying awake all night? Not only to ensnare husbands while they slept but even to steal the property of those you catch unawares. You have the opportunity to display your splendid endurance of hunger, cold, and total deprivation. Very soon you will realize that these talents will exhaust you.

[27] I accomplished this much when I drove you from the consulship: you could only attack the Republic as an exile rather than torment it as its consul; and the criminal acts undertaken by you would be called banditry rather than war.

Now, gentlemen, I will reject and refute a complaint by our country that may seem justified. Please listen carefully to what I say and fix it firmly in your hearts and minds. If my country, which means more to me than my life, or if all of Italy, or if the entire Republic were to say this to me:

"What are you doing, Marcus Tullius? You've discovered that this man is a public enemy. You see that he will lead an army against me. You understand that the enemy base waits for him to be its commander. He's the leader of this conspiracy, a recruiter of slaves and outcasts. Will you allow him to depart? It seems that you don't send him from the city but welcome him in! Will you not order this man to be led off in chains, taken away to his execution and to his ultimate punishment? [28] What is stopping you? The ways of our ancestors?[26] But in this Republic often even private citizens condemned dangerous citizens to death. Is it the laws that have been passed concerning the punishment of Roman citizens? But in this Republic those who rebel against the state never keep their rights as citizens. Do you fear you will be unpopular in the future? Splendid thanks indeed you give to the Roman people who have raised you so quickly through the ranks of political office, even though you made your own name for yourself and had no backing from famous ancestors.[27] Will unpopularity or fear of danger cause you to neglect the safety of your countrymen? [29] If you fear unpopularity, unpopularity caused by strictness and courage should be more fearful than unpopularity caused by inaction and negligence! Or, when Italy is being devastated by war, its cities cry in torment, its buildings aflame, will you then think that you will not be consumed by an inferno of unpopularity?"

I will respond briefly to these most holy words of the Republic and to the minds of those who share these concerns. If I thought it were the best course of action, gentlemen, to condemn Catiline to death, I would not have granted that wretched gladiator another hour of life. In fact, if our best and most illustrious citizens were not only not stained with the blood of Saturninus and the Gracchi and Flaccus and many others before them but even were glorified by it, I certainly had no reason to dread that a wave of unpopularity would crash over me because I had executed this murderer of citizens. If, however, this wave does loom over my head, I have always been of the opinion that unpopularity born from doing what is right is not unpopularity at all but glory.

[30] Nevertheless there are some in this group who either don't see what threatens us—or they pretend they cannot. These men have fed Catiline's hopes by their weak advice. They strengthened the conspiracy when it was growing because they didn't believe it existed. These men have influenced the wicked and the naive to say that I would have acted cruelly or like a tyrant if I had acted against this man. Now, if Catiline arrives at his destination—Manlius's base— I believe that no one will be so foolish or wicked as to deny that the conspiracy exists. If this man alone is executed, I believe that this disease in the Republic can be held in check for a time, but it cannot be suppressed forever. But if he banishes himself and marches away with his supporters and he gathers in one place all those castaways he's rounded up, then this disease, late-stage though it is, can be snuffed out and with it the root and source of all our misfortunes.

[31] For a long time now, gentlemen, we have lived among the dangers and plots of this conspiracy. Somehow the moment of crisis for all these crimes and this ancient, reckless madness burst forth during my consulship. If that man alone is removed from that gang of thugs, we will seem—for a short time—

to be freed from anxiety and fear. But the danger will remain, burrowed deep in the veins and vital organs of the Republic. Often men who are ill with a serious illness toss and turn with the heat of their fever. If they drink cool water, at first, they seem to have some relief. But then their affliction strikes even more seriously and acutely. Just so, if this illness in the Republic is relieved by the punishment of only one man, it will return and grow more severe as long as the others remain alive.

[32] Therefore, let these wicked men depart. Let them isolate themselves from loyal men. Let them gather in one place and, as I've often said, let the city's fortifications stand between them and us. Let them stop ambushing the consul at his home. Let them stop surrounding the tribunal of the urban praetor. Let them stop besieging the senate house with swords. Let them stop stockpiling firebrands and torches to set fire to the city. Finally, let it be written on the forehead of every man exactly what he thinks of the Republic. I promise you this, gentlemen, we consuls will show such diligence, you senators will display such authority, you Roman knights such courage, all loyal citizens such an unshakeable consensus that, when Catiline departs, you will see everything exposed, illuminated, crushed, and punished.

[33] With omens like these, Catiline, with the greatest salvation of the Republic, with disaster and ruin for yourself and destruction for all your supporters who have joined you in every crime and murder— depart to your wicked and despicable war. But you, Jupiter, whom Romulus established with the same good omens that established this city and whom we rightly call "The One Who Upholds Order" in his city and empire, keep this man and his allies from your temple and the temples of the other gods, from the buildings of the city and its walls, from the lives and fortunes of all our countrymen. And on these men, these enemies of loyal citizens, enemies of their country, plunderers of Italy, these men who joined together in an alliance of the wicked and a confederacy of crime, on them you will inflict your eternal punishment while they yet live and even after they have died. ▧

Cicero, *Second Speech against Catiline*
7–11, 17–25

In this speech, delivered to the people after Catiline has departed the city, Cicero attempts to convince the people that they should not support the Catilinarians, by describing the kinds of wicked supporters that Catiline has and why they are not looking out for the people's interests. In the game, remember that Catiline may not have fled and he may still be in the senate. Nevertheless, Cicero's characterization of Catiline and his supporters provides evidence of how those in power during the crisis viewed their opponents and the kinds of characterizations that Romans found persuasive.

In sections 1–6, Cicero rejoices that Catiline has left Rome and he invites the people to join the celebration. He also justifies his policy of allowing Catiline to depart and dismisses the threat posed by forces loyal to Catiline. He then turns to describing his opponents, who gathered around Catiline.

[7.7] . . . Throughout all of Italy, what poisoner, gladiator, outlaw, assassin, murderer, forger of wills, cheat, glutton, spendthrift, adulterer, whore, corruptor of youth, fallen and desperate man does not confess that he has lived on the most intimate terms with Catiline? What murder happened recently without him? What horrific debauchery did he not do?

[7.8] Who has shown a greater genius for seducing the youth? He shamelessly slept with some and arranged for others to do the same. To some he promised he could make their depraved dreams come true; to others, all it took was help killing their parents. In this way, he attracted a huge mob of desperate men from the city and the country. Every debtor—not only in Rome but in every cranny throughout Italy—he enrolled in this incredible confederacy of crime.

[7.9] And you can observe his diverse pursuits in different affairs: there is no one in a gladiatorial school that does not confess that he is Catiline's close associate; no foolish and disgusting actor that does

not recount that he had practically been a friend of Catiline. Yet, Catiline has trained his body to withstand cold and hunger and thirst and sleeplessness. How? By debaucheries and crimes! Those men said he was bold. Yet he consumed his wealth and resources by his depravity and recklessness. [10] But if his companions now follow him, if these disgraceful flocks of hopeless men now depart . . . how happy we will be! How lucky the Republic! How brilliantly praised my consulship!

Their depravity is no longer of the regular sort. Their recklessness is inhuman and we must not tolerate it. They think of nothing except slaughter, arson, and plunder. They have squandered their inheritances. They have mortgaged their estates. First their wealth began to fail them and recently their credit too. But the same depravity, which they had during the times of plenty, remains. If these drunken gamblers sought only their orgies and their whores, they would indeed be hopeless; but nevertheless, we could endure them. But who can endure this: these sluggish people plotting against our most courageous men, the most foolish against our most prudent, the drunkards against the sober, the lazy against the vigilant? These men—lying about at parties, embracing loose women, dulled by wine, stuffed with food, crowned with garlands, smeared with lotions, weakened by debauchery. Their conversations? They belch about the slaughter of loyal men and the torching of Rome!

[7.11] I am confident that doom hangs over these men. And punishment—long overdue—for their dishonesty, wickedness, depravity either looms or approaches. If my consulship, since it cannot cure them, removes them, it will have extended the life of the Republic by not a brief moment but by centuries. There is no foreign people that we fear; no king can make war on the Roman people. Everything abroad is peaceful, on land and sea, because of the excellence of one man.[28] But civil war remains: the threats, the danger, and the enemy are enclosed within. We must struggle with luxury, madness, and crime. I offer myself as a leader in this war, fellow citizens. I accept the hatred of desperate men. What is curable, I will cure in every way possible. What must be cut out, I will not allow to remain a danger. So let these men either depart or let them be silent or, if they remain in the city with the same mindset, let them await what they deserve.

[In sections 12–16, Cicero again defends his policy of letting Catiline depart Rome, while also criticizing those who believe that Catiline is going into peaceful exile.]

[7.17] . . . I will explain to you, citizens, the types of men that Catiline recruits as his supporters; to each group, I will offer the medicine of my advice.

[7.18] One category consists of those who are in great debt despite having even larger fortunes. They, constrained by love for their property, refuse to pay off their debts. The appearance of these men is very respectable—for they are wealthy—but their intention and motives are utterly shameless. If you possessed ample lands, buildings, silver, slaves, and every kind of possession, would you hesitate to draw from your possessions to improve your credit? What are you waiting for? War? What then? Do you think that your properties will be sacrosanct in the general devastation? Or are you waiting for the cancellation of debt?[29] They are mistaken if they expect Catiline to follow through on this. But my administration will eliminate their debt—at the auction house! There is no other way that men who have possessions can regain liquidity. If they had done this earlier and not—this is incredibly foolish—paid their interest with the income of their estates, we would still associate with them as richer and better citizens. But we need not fear these men. They can be convinced to change their opinion or, if they persist, they seem to me more likely to swear oaths than to bear arms against the Republic.

[7.19] The second category consists of those who, although they are oppressed by debt, nevertheless expect to enjoy absolute power. They want to gain possession of the government and they think that, when the Republic is in turmoil, they can attain the offices that they have no hope of reaching when the Republic is at peace. To these men—indeed to everyone—I give this advice: they have no hope of attaining this goal. First of all, I am personally on guard and watching over the Republic. Second, remember the great courage among the loyal citizens, the great harmony among the multitude, our large force of loyal soldiers, and finally the immortal gods, who will assist this unconquered people, this most distinguished empire, and this most beautiful city against so terrible and violent a crime. But if they achieved what they in their complete madness desire, can those men really hope—among the ashes of the city and the blood of her citizens—that they will be consuls or dictators or even kings? Do they not see that it is inevitable that they will lose what they desire—if they achieve it—to some runaway slave or gladiator?

[7.20] The third category consists of those who are afflicted by old age but remain strong and physically active. Manlius, whom Catiline is now replacing, is in this category. These men live in the veteran settlements established by Sulla.[30] In general, I recognize that veterans are our best and bravest, but nevertheless there are some settlers who indulged too extravagantly and recklessly in their sudden and unexpected wealth. These men built as though they were men of means and at the same time delighted in fine estates, vast numbers of slaves, and extravagant feasts. They fell into such great debt that, if they wished to be solvent, Sulla would have to be raised from the underworld. They have even enticed some weak, impoverished peasants with the hope of Sullan-style plunder. I combine both of these into a category with bandits and thieves, and I offer them this advice: let them cease their madness and thoughts of proscriptions and dictatorships. For the great anguish of Sulla's reign was so branded on our state that not even livestock—to say nothing of men—will tolerate its return.

[7.21] The fourth category is ragtag, motley, and unpredictable. These men have for a long time been in financial distress and never get their heads above water. They staggered under long-held debt, in part because of their own laziness, in part because of failed business transactions, in part because of their profligacy. Exhausted by bail summons, adverse judgments, and the forced sale of their property, many from the city and countryside are said to join Catiline's camp. These men I consider not so much eager soldiers as slow-motion defaulters. Let these men fall as soon as possible if they cannot stand on their own. But let their fall happen in such a way that not even their next-door neighbors notice it (let alone the state). For I'm at a loss. Why, if they cannot live honorably, do they wish to die in disgrace? Why do they think that they will die with less anguish in a group than if they were to die alone?

[7.22] The fifth category consists of parricides, assassins, and every other brand of criminal. These men I would not try to summon back from Catiline; for they cannot be torn away from him. Let them perish as outlaws, since they are so many that a prison cannot hold them.

The final category is last, not only in order but in character and way of life. It is Catiline's own group. He chose them, embraced them, holds them on his lap. Look at them, they have neatly combed hair, glisten (with oil), some beardless, others with a sufficient beard, with tunics down to their ankles and wrists, draped in gowns, not togas. Their entire life and their waking efforts are directed toward parties that last until dawn.

[7.23] In this throng dwell all the gamblers, adulterers, and filthy, debauched men. These boys, so delicate and soft, have learned not only to love and be loved and dance and sing but even to brandish daggers and sprinkle poisons. Unless they leave, unless they perish—even if Catiline perishes—know this: a crop of Catilines will remain in the Republic. But still, what do these wretches want for themselves? They're not about to lead their mistresses to Catiline's camp with them, are they? But how can they be away from them, especially on nights like these? How will they tolerate the frosts and snows of the Apennine Mountains . . . unless they think they will endure winter more easily because they learned to dance naked at parties?

[7.24] What an utterly terrifying war, if Catiline will have this bodyguard of whores! Now, citizens, draw up your garrisons and your armies against Catiline's glorious army. First position your consuls and commanders against that washed-up, wounded gladiator. Then, against that cast-out and weakened band of shipwrecked men, lead out the flower and strength of the whole of Italy. Yes indeed, your walled settlements and towns will be a match for Catiline's wooded hills. And I do not have to compare your other forces, equipment, and garrisons with the poverty and destitution of that pirate.

[7.25] But if we exclude all these resources which we have in abundance and which Catiline lacks— the senate, the Roman knights, Rome, the treasury, tax revenue, all of Italy, all of the provinces, foreign allies—if, omitting all these, we wished to have a contest between the causes which are opposed to each other, from just these we would understand how utterly they fail. On our side fights decency; on theirs, insolence; here, modesty; there, outrage; here, loyalty; there, treachery; here, reverence; there, crime; here, steadiness; there, insanity; here, honor; there, disgrace; here, restraint; there, lust; finally, our justice, self-control, bravery, discretion, and all the virtues struggle with their injustice, wantonness, cowardice, recklessness, and every vice. Ultimately abundance collides with poverty, good reason with corruption, sanity with insanity, sound hope with desperation in every matter. In a contest and battle of this kind—even if men's efforts falter—wouldn't the immortal gods will our illustrious virtues to be victorious over their so many and terrible vices?

[In sections 26–29, Cicero concludes by reviewing the plans that he has made for the defense of Rome and inviting Catiline's supporters to follow him out of the city.]

Sallust, *Catiline's War* 5–13

In Catiline's War, *the Roman historian Sallust (ca. 86–ca. 35 BCE) investigates the social and political factors that contributed to the crisis of 63 BCE. Drawing on personal memory, contemporary literary accounts, and a trove of documentary evidence, Sallust composed this work about twenty years after the crisis. Retelling the events of 63 BCE allowed Sallust to diagnose how the progressive degeneration of Rome's morality and politics—and the rising desperation of those Romans who failed to benefit from the globalizing economy of Rome's cosmopolitan empire—led to 100 years of escalating civil unrest and violence.*

In this excerpt, Sallust provides a vivid portrait of Catiline's virtues and vices, which in turn leads Sallust to revisit the virtues that had once made Romans great and how Roman morality degenerated into vice.

[5] Lucius Catiline was born to a noble family. He had a vigorous mind and body, but his character was wicked and depraved. In his youth, he delighted and trafficked in civil wars, slaughter, pillage, and strife. His body could tolerate incredible hunger, cold, and sleeplessness. His mind was reckless, treacherous, and fickle. He could disguise his feelings as he wished. He envied others' property; he wasted his own. His passions were ferocious. He possessed enough eloquence but too little wisdom. His insatiable mind always desired the extravagant, the incredible, the out of reach. After the tyranny of Lucius Sulla, a passion for power possessed him.[31] It made no difference how he obtained his kingdom, so long as he acquired it. Day by day his declining personal finances and the swelling awareness of his crimes stoked his mind. The character of a corrupt society also spurred him on and he was tormented by its warring evils: extravagance and greed. Since this brings to mind the character of our society, I am motivated to go back in time and recount how our ancestors behaved in politics and war, how they managed the state, how great it was when we inherited it, and how it gradually changed from the best and most glorious to the worst and most infamous.

[6] In the beginning, Trojans, as I have learned, founded and inhabited the city of Rome. These Trojans were refugees and had wandered from place to place under the leadership of Aeneas. In the same area lived the Aborigines, a wild race of people, free and uninhibited, without laws or government.[32] The Trojans and Aborigines came to live together within the same walls. Although different races, with different languages and their own customs, as though by a miracle, they easily integrated, and quickly this diverse and unsettled crowd became a harmonious body of citizens. Rome's citizens, culture, and fields all thrived. But once Rome began to appear wealthy and powerful, their prosperity produced envy, as often happens among mortals. Consequently, neighboring kings and peoples attacked the Romans. Only a few friends offered aid because most were afraid and they hoped to avoid the dangers of war. But the Romans, focused at home and abroad, prepared themselves, encouraged each other, confronted their enemies, and protected with weapons their liberty, country, and parents. After they had repelled these threats by their own excellence, they gave assistance to their friends and allies, building these friendships and alliances more by giving than by receiving support.

They had a government bound by law, and this government was called a monarchy. Select men, whose bodies were weakened by age but whose minds were strong with wisdom, gave advice about the commonwealth. These were called "fathers" (*patres*) either because of their age or the similarity of their guardianship for the state. At first, this monarchy preserved liberty and helped the commonwealth grow. But after it turned into an arrogant tyranny, they changed their custom and made for themselves two commanders with annual authority.[33] In this way, they thought that men's spirits would least be able to grow arrogant through unchecked authority.

[7] During that time, every man began to distinguish himself and display his talents. You see, kings

are more suspicious of good than bad men and they fear excellence. Once Rome had liberty, its inhabitants' desire for glory caused it to grow at an astonishing rate. The youth, as soon they were old enough for military service, trained in the fields and took greater pleasure in fine weapons and war horses than in prostitutes or parties. When they became men, they were familiar with hard work and they did not fear harsh or difficult terrain or an armed enemy. Their excellence mastered all. Their greatest concern was with the contest for glory. Every man was eager to strike down an enemy, to scale a wall—and to be seen doing so. Glory and nobility of character they considered true wealth. They were greedy for praise and generous with their money. They wanted massive glory and honest riches. I could recount many times when small bands of Romans vanquished a much larger enemy army or captured well-fortified cities by force, if this did not drag us too far from our subject.

[8] This is true: Fortune is the master of every moment. Fortune celebrates and obscures affairs according to her pleasure rather than reality. For example, the Athenians accomplished, in my estimation, great and magnificent deeds, but these are said to be more grand than they were in reality.[34] Because the Athenians produced talented authors, their deeds are celebrated throughout the entire world. Therefore, the excellence of those who undertake a deed only seems as great as the talents of the authors who praise them. But the Romans never had this advantage, since their most talented men were engaged in action rather than idle displays of intellect. The best of the Romans preferred to act rather than to speak and for his service to be praised by others rather than to describe others' service.

[9] Consequently, good character was cultivated at home and abroad.[35] They had the greatest harmony and the least greed. They were just and good by nature, not because the law compelled them. Disputes, disagreements, animosities were taken out on their enemies; citizen vied with citizen to be excellent. They were magnificent when they sacrificed to the gods, frugal at home, loyal to their friends. They pro-

tected themselves and the state by boldness in war and by justice in peace. I consider this the greatest evidence I can offer: first, in war they punished more severely those who had engaged the enemy without orders or withdrew too slowly when recalled from battle than those who dared to retreat or abandon their posts in defeat; and second, during peacetime they applied their power more through generosity than fear and, even when wronged, they preferred to forgive than to seek vengeance.

[10] But when Rome had expanded through their just and diligent labors, when it had mastered great kings by war, overcome savage tribes and mighty peoples by force, and when Carthage, Rome's rival for empire, had been annihilated, when Rome had access to every sea and land, then Fortune began to rage and sow confusion. Romans had easily endured hard labor, dangers, uncertain and harsh situations. But they found leisure and wealth, although desirable in other circumstances, to be a burden and misfortune. Consequently, they began to covet money and power, which are the sources of all evil. Greed undermined loyalty, manners, and all other good practices. In their place, greed taught arrogance, cruelty, impiety, and that everything was up for sale. The quest for power drove many men to become false, to conceal the truth in his chest while lying with his tongue, to value friendships only by advantage they offered and to have a good appearance rather than a good heart. At first these vices grew slowly and were sometimes punished; but, when this infection had spread like a plague, the community changed, and this empire, which had been the best and most just, became cruel and intolerable.

[11] First the quest for power—a vice but one close to a virtue—spurred the minds of men more than greed. You see, the virtuous and villainous both crave glory, public office, and power. But the virtuous seek these through the true path, while the villainous, who lack virtues, work by lies and deceits. Greed produces a passion for money, which no wise man craves. Greed, like something steeped with vicious poison, weakens a manly body and mind. Greed is boundless and insatiable. Neither abundance nor

poverty relieves it. But after Lucius Sulla seized control of the state and his rule became wicked after a promising beginning, everyone began to pillage, to plunder. One man coveted a house, another some property. The winners lacked all restraint and self-control. They did foul and cruel things to their fellow citizens. Also, Lucius Sulla had violated the custom of our ancestors and been overly permissive and indulgent toward the army that he led to Asia and back. Lands filled with pleasures and enjoyments softened the fierce spirits of his soldiers. It was then that a Roman army first became accustomed to sex and drink, to gawk at statues, paintings, and engraved vessels. They plundered these luxuries from private and public collections, they ransacked shrines and defiled everything. Consequently, these soldiers, when they were victorious, left nothing to the defeated. Even the wise are tormented by prosperity. But those men, with their corrupted characters, had no chance of restraining themselves in victory.

[12] Once wealth began to be respected and became a path to prestige, power, and influence, virtue lost its edge, poverty became a source of shame, and integrity was thought malicious. Consequently, Rome's wealth caused luxury and greed together with arrogance to spread into the youth. They robbed and spent. They neglected their own property but craved what belonged to others. They cared nothing for decency or modesty or any restriction, whether human or divine. Compare our houses and villas, enlarged to resemble cities, with the temples of the gods made by our reverent ancestors. Our ancestors enhanced the shrines of the gods by their piety and their own houses by their prestige. They seized from the defeated nothing except the power to do them harm. But the cowardly and wicked people of today deprive our allies of what our brave and victorious ancestors' bravest men had left them. Today, it seems that to inflict an injustice is what it means to exercise power.

[13] Should I recount things that no one will believe unless they have seen them: mountains leveled and seas paved by private property owners?[36] To these

men, wealth has become a sport. They hurried to abuse the wealth that they should have managed honorably. Then a strong passion for debauchery rushed into Roman society, alongside the gluttony of the restaurant and other indulgences. Men endured the role of the woman; women put their chastity up for sale; for the sake of their feasts, they scoured everything from the land and the sea. They slept before they needed to sleep. They did not wait for hunger or thirst or cold or fatigue but they indulged their cravings. These vices incited the youth to crime as soon as they exhausted their own resources. Their minds, steeped in wicked practices, could scarcely suppress their urges. Instead, they abandoned themselves utterly to every manner of craving and luxury.

Sallust, *Catiline's War* 37–39

In this excerpt, the historian Sallust diagnoses how moral and political corruption nurtured a desire for revolution among the poor and how elite Romans manipulated their passions and desperation in the pursuit of power.[37]

[37] Not only did this dementia hold those who had been complicit in the conspiracy, but the entire common people completely approved of Catiline's activities because of their eagerness for revolution. This they seemed to do in accordance with their custom. You see, in every community, those who have no resources envy good people and promote the bad; they hate what is old, crave the new, and are eager for everything to be overthrown because of their hatred of their own circumstances. They thrive on turmoil and civil unrest without a care, since poverty is easily preserved without loss. But the city's common people were particularly reckless for several reasons. First of all, those who were everywhere most conspicuous in their disgrace and discontent, and likewise those whose inheritance had been lost through shameful acts, and finally all those whom depravity or crime

had driven from home, these men had flowed into Rome as though into a ship's bilge. Second, many—remembering Sulla's victory, when they had seen some common soldiers become senators and others become so rich that they spent their lives in kingly feasting and entertainment—hoped for similar rewards from victory, if they took up arms.[38]

Moreover, young men, who once had endured deprivation in the fields, earning a wage with their hands, but who had grown unsettled by public and private charity, preferred urban leisure to thankless toil. Public corruption nourished these men and all others like them. It is not at all astonishing that impoverished men, with bad characters and great expectations, had the same regard for the commonwealth as they did for themselves. Moreover, those whose parents had been proscribed after Sulla's victory—their property confiscated; their rights and liberty diminished—looked forward to the end of the war with the same attitude. Additionally, those who belonged to a different faction in the senate preferred the commonwealth be thrown into disorder than for themselves to be less powerful. This, indeed, was the sickness that after many years had returned to our community.

[38] Indeed, after tribunician power had been restored during the consulship of Gnaeus Pompey and Marcus Crassus, young men, whose age and spirits were defiant, obtained the pinnacle of power and began to provoke the common people by denouncing the senate and then to inflame them more by bribery and promises: this was how they became famous and powerful.[39] Many in the nobility struggled against these men with intense effort, apparently on behalf of the senate but in fact for their own glorification. Indeed (to state the truth in a few words) after this time whoever stirred up the commonwealth on honorable pretexts—some as though defending the rights of the people, others so that the senate's authority would be preeminent—each making a pretense of "the common good," was in truth competing for power. For such men there was no moderation or limit to their struggle. Each side ruthlessly enforced its victory.

[39] But after Gnaeus Pompey had been sent to war, first at sea and then against Mithridates, the influence of the common people diminished and the power of the few increased.[40] The few held the magistracies, provinces, and everything else; they were immune to attack and lived in prosperity without fear; they intimidated others with threats of prosecution so they would control the common people when they were in office. But as soon as circumstances became uncertain and the prospect for revolution emerged, the old struggle incited their minds. ▪

Cicero, *Second Speech against Verres* 5.160–63

In 70 BCE, the people of Sicily accused their former governor, Gaius Verres, of corruption and extortion under the guise of managing a number of emergencies in his province. Exploitative behavior by Roman provincial officials was tolerated—indeed, expected; but Verres's cynical depredations of Sicily were so extreme that they shocked even the jaded sensibilities of the Romans. Cicero, at the time still a young and ambitious politician, agreed to prosecute Verres, who was defended by some of the most powerful and prestigious figures in Rome, including Hortensius, Rome's most prominent orator. Cicero's opening speech was so persuasive that Hortensius advised his client that his conviction was inevitable and that he should go into exile.

In this excerpt, Cicero denounces the illegal treatment of a Roman citizen by Verres and how the violation of the law for one has implications for all.

[5.160] Gavius of Cosa was one of a great number of Roman citizens whom Verres tossed into prison. Somehow Gavius managed to escape the Stone Quarry and make his way to Messana.[41] There he could almost see Italy and the walls of Rhegium with its population of Roman citizens. He had, he thought, emerged from the fear of death and darkness into the light of liberty and the sweet air of the law. So, he began to talk in Messana and to complain how he, a Roman citizen, had been thrown into prison. He said that he was now going straight to Rome and that he would wait there for Verres.[42]

This poor fellow did not understand that saying these things in Messana was the same as saying them in Verres's house. . . . As a result, Gavius was arrested and led before the town magistrate. . . . [5.161] Verres arrives. He thanks these men and praises their goodwill and diligence on his behalf. Then, inflamed by his criminality and madness, he enters the forum. His eyes blaze; cruelty radiates from his face. All men are waiting to see how far he would go and what he would do, when suddenly he orders Gavius to be seized, stripped naked, and bound in the middle of the forum and the rods to be readied. The miserable man cries out that he is a Roman citizen and a citizen of Cosa, too; that he served with Lucius Raecius, a reputable knight who was had a business in Panormus and who could confirm the truth of this. But Verres says that he had discovered that Gavius had been sent into Sicily as a spy by the leaders of the fugitive slaves.[43] His proof for this charge? There is no witness, no evidence, and not even the slightest hint of suspicion.

[5.162] Then Verres orders the man to be whipped violently over his entire body. In the middle of the forum of Messana a Roman citizen, dear jurors, was beaten with rods! While this was happening, no groan was heard from this miserable man, no other expression was heard, amid his agony and the crack of the whip, except these words: "I am a Roman citizen" (civis Romanus sum). He believed that the mere mention of his citizenship would ward off the blows and torture from his body. He not only failed to avert the violence of the rods by these entreaties, but as he kept repeating his pleas and invoking his citizenship, a cross—a cross, I say!—was readied for this miserable man, who had never before even seen such a cursed object.

[5.163] By the name of our sweet liberty! By the extraordinary privileges granted by our citizenship! Do the Porcian and Sempronian Laws mean nothing?[44] What of the power of the tribunes, so bitterly missed by the people and only recently restored! Do all our rights mean so little that, in a province of the Roman people—in a town of our allies!—a Roman citizen could be bound in the forum and beaten with rods by a man who owed his rods and the axes to the favor of the Roman people? What more can I say?

Cicero, *Laws* 2.7–14 and 3.2–5

The Laws *(De Legibus) is a fictional dialogue between Cicero, his brother Quintus, and their friend Titus Pomponius Atticus. Written ca. 54–51 BCE, the dialogue explores the idea that true law shapes and reveals human nature. As such, law is not a compendium of regulations but the manifestation of god's eternal wisdom. An individual law is good and durable only if it accords with this natural law. In book 3, Cicero proposes a reformed Roman constitution based on the principals articulated in books 1 and 2.*

Written around two decades after the crisis of Catiline, the work nevertheless offers insights into the philosophical approach to law and legislation during the final decades of the Roman Republic.

Book 1 establishes that the law is not merely written edicts but a fundamental part of humanity. Book 2 opens with an attempt to reconcile patriotism for one's hometown with that for one's country. When the trio arrive at an idyllic island in the Fibrenius River, their conversation turns to the difference between natural and artificial law. In the excerpts below, Cicero describes the foundations of the law and the authority of just magistrates.

[2.7] Quintus Cicero (Q): If it seems good to you, let's rest here in the shade and return to the point our conversation had reached before we started this digression.

Marcus Cicero (M): How cleverly you exact payment of my debt, Quintus! I thought I had escaped! No debt can be left unpaid to you.

Q: Then begin. We can discuss this topic for the entire day.

M: "From Jupiter the beginnings of the Muses," as my translation of Aratus begins.[45]

Q: How is that relevant?

M: Because now we must also start our conversation with Jupiter and the other immortal gods.

Q: Very true, brother! Clearly, we must do so.

[2.8] M: And so, before we approach individual laws, let's revisit the force and nature of the law itself. Then, since we must decide everything in accordance with the law, we won't repeatedly slide into error because we ignore the powerful rationale that shapes the definition of the law.

Q: Certainly, by Hercules! Your plan for the explanation is sound.

M: Therefore, I see that very wise men held this opinion: Law does not result from human intellect nor is it produced by a people. Instead, it is something eternal, which rules the entire universe through its wisdom in commanding and prohibiting. So, these wise men have said that Law is the primal and ultimate mind of god, whose reason either compels or forbids all things. Therefore, this Law, given by the gods to humanity, has been justly praised. For it is the reason and mind of a wise being applied to ordering and deterring.

[2.9] Q: You have introduced this idea several times already. But before you come to laws pertaining to the people, please explain the nature of the Law of heaven. Then, the waves of careless habit may not overwhelm us and sweep us into a common mode of conversation.

M: From the time we were children, Quintus, we have learned to call "laws" things like, "If one summons another into court. . . ."[46] But, in fact, we must understand that the true situation is like this: this and other commands and prohibitions of the people have the power to summon one to act properly or to ward one away from wrongdoing, but the real power is not only older than all nations and states but it is as ancient as the god that rules and guards heaven and earth.

[2.10] For the divine mind cannot exist without reason, nor can divine reason lack the power to establish what is holy and what is depraved. For example, there was no law that a man should stand on a bridge alone against all the enemy's troops and order the bridge destroyed behind him. Yet, this does not mean that we think it less true that the famous Cocles performed such a noble deed in accordance with the law and authority of courage.[47] The absence of a written law at Rome concerning sexual assault during the reign of Lucius Tarquinius does not mean that Sextus Tarquinius did not violate that eternal Law when he assaulted Lucretia, daughter of Tricipitinus.[48] For *reason* existed, having originated in the Nature of the Universe, impelling men toward proper conduct and diverting them away from wrong. This reason became Law not when it was written down but when it originated. And it originated at the same time as the divine mind. Therefore, the true and primal Law, applied to ordering and deterring, is the just reason of Jupiter Supreme.

[2.11] Q: I agree, brother, that what is right and true is also eternal and does not rise or fall with the documents in which this or that statute is written down.

M: Therefore, just as that divine mind is the supreme Law, so too is it supreme when it attains perfection in a wise man. When, however, things have been written down for nations in various forms and adapted to the moment, they hold the name of laws more by indulgence than in reality. Indeed, every law that truly deserves the name is worthy of praise, as wise men have proven through the following arguments. It is surely agreed that laws were invented for the safety of citizens, the security of communities, and the quiet, happy life of human beings. Those who first sanctioned statutes of this kind promised their people that they would write down and put into effect regulations that, once they were accepted and adopted, would allow the people to live honorably and happily. When such rules were drawn up and sanctioned, they called them "laws." From this perspective, we understand that those who wrote down commandments that were wicked and unjust toward the people established something other than "laws," since they did the opposite of what they promised and claimed. Thus, it is clear that designating something as a law requires the power and wisdom of selecting what is just and true.[49]

[2.12] And so, Quintus, I ask you now, just as those philosophers often do: If a state lacks something and because of this lack we would not even consider it a state, must this thing (that is, the thing lacked) be considered a good thing?

Q: One of the greatest goods, certainly!

M: And, if a state lacks Law, must for that reason it not be considered a state at all?

Q: It cannot be said to be otherwise.

M: Then Law must be considered as one of greatest goods.

Q: I agree entirely.

[2.13] M: What about the many ruinous and disastrous measures that have been ratified by various nations? These have nothing more in common with Law than statutes ratified by an assembly of brigands. If an ignorant, inexperienced man prescribes deadly poison instead of healing medicine, we can hardly call these the prescriptions of a physician, can we? Nor, if a nation accepts something that is harmful, can this thing be a law in that nation. Therefore, the Law is the distinction between the just and the unjust, conforming with that most ancient and primal of all things: Nature. And the laws of men are directed toward Nature, which inflicts punishment on the wicked, while defending and protecting the good.

Q: I understand entirely and indeed I now think that nothing else should be considered or even called a law.

[2.14] M: Then do you think that the Titian and the Apuleian laws are not really laws?[50]

Q: Not at all, nor the Livian laws!

M: This is correct, especially since the senate repealed them in an instant by a single clause. But the Law, whose power I have explained, can be neither repealed nor destroyed.

[In the rest of book 2, Cicero establishes that belief in divinity must be the foundation for the Law. At the start of book 3 the trio then agrees to discuss the nature of Roman governance, beginning with the just authority of magistrates.]

[3.2] M: You see, therefore, that the inherent power of a magistrate is that he governs and gives commands that are right and advantageous and in unison with the laws. For, as the laws govern the magistrates, so the magistrates govern the people. And it is true when it is said that a magistrate is a "speaking law," and a law a "silent magistrate."

[3.3] Moreover, nothing is so harmonious with righteousness and the conditions of Nature— when I use these terms, I wish you to understand that I mean Law—as authoritative command (*imperium*), without which it would be impossible for a household to exist, or a city, a nation, the whole of humanity, Nature, or the universe itself. You see, the universe obeys god, so too the land and sea and human life follows the commands of the supreme Law.

[3.4] But let me return to matters closer to us and better known: every nation, at one time, obeyed kings. At first, this form of authoritative command was entrusted to the wisest and most just men— this, indeed, was very much the case in our own commonwealth, for as long as it was governed by royal power. Then governance was inherited by the king's descendants. And it still remains there, among those who rule kingdoms. Now, those who were displeased with royal power did not wish that no one should rule but that they not obey only one person. But we, since we are organizing a legal system for a free people, shall at this point attune our laws to the constitution of the state that we deem best (I have spoken elsewhere, in my work containing six books, about my thoughts concerning the best form of the commonwealth).[51]

[3.5] Therefore, we need magistrates, since, without their foresight and guardianship a state cannot exist. Indeed, the whole course of a commonwealth is crafted by the nature of its magistrates. Not only must we prescribe the mode and limit of their authority but we must also set the mode and limits to which citizens are duty-bound to follow a magistrate's authority. You see, the man who rules effectively must, at some time in the past, have obeyed; the man who respectfully obeys appears worthy to rule at some point in the future. Therefore, it is right that whoever obeys have the expectation that he will rule at some point in the future. And it is right that the man who rules will soon have to obey. In fact, we must prescribe not only how citizens should act in harmony with magistrates and obey them but also, as Charondas declares in his laws, how citizens should nurture and respect their magistrates.[52] In fact, our cherished Plato decided that those who rebel against their magistrates, as the Titans did against their gods, are like the Titans.[53]

Polybius, *Histories* 6.6–9, 11–18

Polybius (ca. 208–118 BCE) was a Greek historian whose work The Histories *charted Rome's conflict with Carthage and its rise to dominate the Mediterranean in the late third to mid-second centuries BCE. Polybius had been sent to Rome when a young man as a hostage to ensure the loyalty of his father, a prominent Greek politician. In Rome, he gained the patronage of several noble families, including that of Aemilius Paullus, who entrusted Polybius with the education of his sons, one of whom would later lead the Roman army that annihilated Carthage.*

In this excerpt, Polybius summarizes the three possible modes of government, how states inevitably cycle between these modes, and how the virtues of the Roman constitution enabled it to slow its inevitable descent into tyranny.

[6.6] When, therefore, the leading and most powerful man among the people always uses his authority to advance the popular will, he seems, in the eyes of his subjects, to distribute rewards and punishments fairly. The people, then, obey not because they fear his violence but because they approve of his beneficial judgment. Even when he grows weak with age, they strive to preserve his rule with passionate unanimity and resist anyone who conspires against him. And so, step by step, the monarch becomes a king, as reason comes to triumph over raw courage and brute strength.

[6.7] This is how nature forms among men the first notions of goodness and justice—and their opposites. And this is how true kingship originates and begins. You see, the people not only preserve the authority of that man but do so for generations of his descendants. They do this because they believe that men born and raised by such men will share their character. But when they eventually grow displeased with one of these descendants, they will select their rulers and kings not according to their raw courage or brute strength but according to their judgment and reason, since they will, by then, have gained valuable experience about the difference between the former kind of qualities on the one hand and the latter on the other. In former times, therefore, men who had been selected to hold royal authority held it until they grew old. They constructed magnificent strongholds surrounded by walls to provide for the security of their subjects. They extended their territory to provide them with the abundant necessities of life. And while they pursued these works, they avoided any criticism caused by jealousy, since they hardly differentiated themselves from their subjects through their food or manner of dress. They lived very much like everyone else and shared in the typical activities of the common people.

But once royal authority became hereditary and they realized that their personal needs were provided for—and, indeed, that they had had much more than was needed—they began to indulge their appetites. They imagined that rulers ought to wear different styles of clothes than their subjects, that their meals should be different and more luxurious, and that their lust should be indulged, even if it were contrary to the law.

The first kinds of behaviors gave rise to envy and offense, while the last produced hatred and passionate resentment. And so, the kingship became a tyranny. And then the first steps toward revolution began, as his subjects began to conspire against his rule. These first conspirators were not the worst men but the noblest and most courageous, because men such as this can least tolerate the arrogant tyranny of their rulers.

[6.8] Once the people had leaders, they followed them against the dynasty for the reasons I stated above. Kingship and despotism were both completely abolished and aristocracy again emerged. For the people, who were grateful for the removal of the despotism, turned to their leaders and entrusted their interests to them. At first, these leaders took this charge seriously and looked above all to the common good, conducting all public and private business with diligence and concern.

But once again, when the sons of these leaders inherited their authority from their fathers, they had no experience in the former misfortunes and no sense of civil equality and freedom of speech, since they were raised under the protection of their fathers' power and authority. So, some abandoned themselves to greed and a passion for the corrupt acquisition of money, others indulged in drinking and the debauched partying that results, still others assaulted women and forced themselves on boys. And so the aristocracy became an oligarchy, which soon caused the people to feel as they had before. As a result, the fall of the oligarchs was very similar to what befell the tyrant.

[6.9] For as soon as there is someone who recognizes the citizens' jealousy and animosity and begins to speak out or act against the government, the whole people is ready and prepared to support him. Now, after they assassinate or exile the oligarchs, they don't attempt to put a king on the throne again, since they remain terrified of the injustice they had endured before; nor can they entrust the government to a select group, since the evidence of recent wrongs is fresh in their minds. So, since the only remaining hope is to trust in themselves, they lay hold of that as their refuge, changing their constitution from an oligarchy into a democracy, in which they themselves will take charge of the affairs of state.

As long as any person remains alive who had suffered the misfortunes of oligarchical domination, they will be very pleased with their new form of government and set a high value on equality and freedom of speech. But once new generations arise and the democracy passes into the hands of the grandchildren of the founders, their familiarity with freedom and equality leads them to no longer value these virtues and they begin to seek to become more powerful than mere ordinary citizens. It is the wealthy who are most susceptible to this temptation. And so, they begin to lust for power and public office. When they discover that they cannot attain their goals on their own or by virtue of their own merits, they ruin their estates in an effort to tempt and corrupt the common people in every way they can imagine. In this way, by their senseless craving for public reputation, they make the populace greedy and give them an appetite for bribes. The virtue of their democracy is destroyed and government becomes one based on violence and force. For the mob, which has grown used to feeding at the expense of others and looking to others' property for its livelihood, as soon as they find a leader who is ambitious enough and daring enough, yet whose poverty has excluded him from the rewards of public office, install a violent reign of terror. They hold chaotic assemblies in which they massacre, exile, and redistribute land and property. At last, having degenerated into lawless savagery, they once more find a master and despot.

This is the regular cycle of constitutional revolutions, which nature establishes for their transformation, destruction, and return to their original stage. If someone understands these principles, he may err in when a specific part of this constitutional process will occur; but unless his judgment is clouded by jealousy or animosity, he will rarely be entirely mistaken about the stage of decline in which he lives, or the form into which his government will evolve.

An inquiry into the Roman constitution will reveal to us its formation, growth, and zenith, as well as the devolutions that must necessarily follow. For this state, as I have said, more than all others, was formed and grew through natural causes, and natural causes will precipitate its decline. . . .

[6.11] I will now attempt to describe the constitution of Rome as it was when they suffered their disastrous defeat at Cannae.[54]

[Polybius justifies his knowledge of the Roman constitution, which he has observed since childhood and cautions his reader of being an overzealous critic, who would focus more on what an author leaves unsaid than what the author says in good faith.]

To return to the Roman constitution, it had all three elements of government that I described above.[55] In the construction and administration of this constitution the share of power held by each element was so attuned to equality and balance that it was impossible for even a native Roman to say with certainty whether the system was an aristocracy, a democracy, or a monarchy. This fact shouldn't cause any surprise. For, if we focus only on the power of the consuls, then the constitution seems regal and monarchical. But if we look to the senate, it will seem aristocratic. And when we turn to the power possessed by the people, it seems clear that Rome is a democracy. I will now delineate what the powers of each of these elements were and, with a few modifications, still are.

[6.12] The consuls, when they are not leading the legions, remain in Rome where they hold supreme authority over public administration. All other magistrates—with the exception of the tribunes—are under their authority and follow their orders. They introduce foreign embassies to the senate. They consult the senate when their advice is needed. They execute the senate's decrees. If some public business requires the consent of the people, the consuls see to this, summoning public assemblies, introducing proposals for their approval, and executing their decisions.

In mobilizing for war and the conduct of military operations, the power of the consuls is almost absolute. They have the authority to demand troops from the allies as they see fit, to appoint military tribunes, to draft soldiers and select those fit for service. They have absolute authority to punish active-duty soldiers under their command, they can spend as much from the public treasury as they deem necessary, and they are accompanied by a quaestor who is entirely at their command. Were someone to observe these powers alone, one would say that the Roman constitution is clearly monarchical or despotic. If there have been or will be any changes in these powers, it will not affect the underlying truth of my description, nor of what follows.

[6.13] The senate has, first of all, control of the public treasury, regulating all revenues and expenditures. For the quaestors cannot disburse any public funds for any state business without a decree from the senate—except, of course, for payments made in the service of the consuls. The senate even controls the largest and most important expenditures: those made by the censors every five years for the repair or construction of public works, which can be obtained only with the explicit consent of the senate. Likewise, all crimes committed in Italy that require a public investigation—these are treason, conspiracy, poisoning, intentional murder—fall under the jurisdiction of the senate. Moreover, if any private individual or community in Italy requires arbitration, seeks damages, or requires assistance or protection, the senate is responsible for all such matters. Looking outside of Italy, if there is need to dispatch an embassy to reconcile opposing communities, or to advise them of their responsibilities, or impose demands on them, or receive their surrender, or declare war on them, all this, too, falls to the senate. Similarly, the senate receives foreign ambassadors in Rome and decides how their petitions will be answered. The people play no part in these parts of governance. And so, if one were in Rome at a time when the consuls were absent, the constitution would appear entirely aristocratic. Indeed, this is how many Greeks and foreign kings understand the Roman constitution, since nearly all of their business with Rome is conducted through the senate.

[6.14] After this, one might naturally wonder what part of the constitution remains for the people, since the senate controls the matters I just described—especially the power over revenues and expenses—and the consuls have absolute authority over the mustering and deployment of the military. But nevertheless, a role remains for the people and it is a very important role: namely, the people have sole authority to confer honors and inflict punishment, the two things that alone hold together dynasties and constitutions and, in a word, all of human society. For, unless the distinction between honor and punishment is clearly drawn in theory and practice, then good and wicked men will be held in the same esteem. The people, therefore, are the sole arbiter in cases of capital crimes. Even when the offense is punishable by a fine, if that fine is sufficiently large, or especially if the defendant has held a higher magistracy, the people stand in judgment. Concerning capital punishment, the Romans have another practice that is particularly worthy of praise and must be mentioned. If someone is on trial for a capital crime, the accused may depart into voluntary exile, as long as the people have not yet completed their voting. Such exiles can safely reside in Naples, Praeneste, Tibur, and other allied towns.[56]

And it is the people who elect deserving men to public office, which is the most honorable reward for virtue. The people possess the absolute authority for passing and repealing laws. The people also deliberate on matters of war and peace. When the terms are established for an alliance or peace or in other kinds of treaties, the people ratify or reject them. And so, again, one might consider that the people have the greatest share of administrative power and so the constitution is democratic.

[6.15] This, then, is how power is distributed between the different elements of the Roman state. I will now explain how each of these elements can support or countermand the others, if they wished to do so.

The consul, when he departs on a military expedition with the powers I have described, indeed seems to have absolute authority to undertake his business.

Yet, in fact, he requires the support of the people and the senate, without which he can hardly bring his operations to a successful conclusion. For it is clear that his legions require continual supply, and without the support of the senate, they will have neither grain, nor clothing, nor pay. Thus, if the senate decides to shrink from danger or obstruct the consul's plans, they must fail. It is also in the senate's hands whether the consul can bring his campaign to a conclusion, since it has the authority to replace him as general, once his annual term expires, or to retain him. Finally, the senate has the power to celebrate and glorify the successes of a general or, on the other hand, to obscure and diminish them, since they can decree "triumphs," parades in which the generals bring the spectacle of their achievements before the eyes of the citizens. These cannot be held or even organized before the senate consents and authorizes the requisite funds.

Turning to the people, the consuls must certainly court their favor, even if they are distant from Rome on campaign. For, it is the people (as I said above) that ratify or reject the treaties and peace terms made by the consul. And, even more important, when the consuls step down from office, they are obliged to provide the people an account of their administration. Therefore, the consuls cannot with impunity neglect the goodwill of the senate or the people.

[6.16] As for the senate, it possesses great power, as I have already described. But first, it must take into account the common men and respect the will of the people in public affairs. It cannot exact penalties for the most serious offenses against the state, those that are punishable by death, unless their decrees are ratified by the people. And even in matters that concern only the senators themselves—for example a law that removes some of the senate's traditional authority, or that abolishes a privilege enjoyed by senators, or limits their property in some way—it is the people and the people alone that can ratify or reject the measure. But this is the most important check: if a single tribune of the plebs interposes his veto, the senate cannot pass a decree about any matter; indeed, it cannot even meet in formal session.

Since the tribunes are always obliged to carry out the decrees of the people in accordance with the people's will, the senate, for this reason, stands in awe of the populace and is obliged to consider the will of the people.

[6.17] Similarly, the people are not independent of the senate and must respect its members, both as a group and individually. The censors distribute a vast number of contracts (too many to list) on matters throughout the entirety of Italy for the construction and repair of public works. There is also the collection of revenue generated from rivers, ports, gardens, mines, and land—that is everything under the control of the Roman dominion. And the people are deeply engaged in these matters. As a result, there is hardly a single individual who is not engaged either as a contractor or an employee. For certain people purchase the contracts from the censors, others partner with the contractors, others pledge collateral or loan them money. The senate has absolute control over matters like these. It can grant extensions. If an accident occurs, it can relieve the contractor of some of their obligations. If the work proves impossible, it can cancel the contractor's obligation outright. And there are many minor ways in which the senate can benefit or harm those who contract with the public, since they hold the right to appeal in these cases. Most important, in most civil trials with high stakes, whether public or private, the judges are appointed from the ranks of the senators.[57] As a result all citizens might find themselves at the mercy of the senate, and since they worry that they may, at some point, require its assistance, they are cautious about obstructing or opposing the senate's will. For a similar reason, men avoid rash resistance to the consuls, since they may soon find themselves subject to their absolute authority on campaign.

[6.18] The final result of this situation, in which each element of the state has the power to assist or obstruct the others, is that their constitutional union is prepared for any emergency and it is impossible to find a better constitution than the one that they possess. For whenever an external threat emerges to the general welfare that compels them to work in unison and support each other, the power of the state becomes so great that it can accomplish everything that is required through the zealous rivalry of the three elements in meeting the needs of the hour. Nor does any determination, once reached, fail for want to prompt execution, since everyone cooperates in public and private to accomplish the business at hand.

Consequently, the Romans' peculiar form of constitution makes the power of their state irresistible and able to obtain any objective that it decides to attempt. And when they are freed from the external threats—and they again enjoy their good fortune and the wealth that flows from their victories and their prosperity begins to corrupt them through flattery and idleness, leading them to grow arrogant and violent—in these circumstances, which happen frequently enough, we see that the constitution possesses the power to correct any abuses. For when one element has grown too powerful and strives for supremacy by encroaching on the others, the fact that the aims of one element might be checked and thwarted by the others (as explained above) means that no element can dominate the others and treat them with contempt. So, the proper balance is maintained, as any aggressiveness by one element is checked by its fear of the others. ▨

Livy, *From the Founding of the City*
2.23–24, 32–33

Livy (64 or 59 BCE–12 or 17 CE) was a Roman historian who composed a massive 142-book history of Rome from the origins of the Roman people down to his own time. Only about a quarter of his work survives, most recounting early Roman history as well as Rome's victories over Carthage and Greece in the late third and second centuries BCE.

In this excerpt, Livy recounts an episode from the first years of the Roman Republic: the First Plebeian Succession (ca. 494 BCE), a labor strike by plebeians to force the patricians to treat them more fairly.[58]

[2.23] Not only did a war with the Volscians loom, but the community was enflamed by internal hostilities between the patricians and plebeians, especially over the matter of debt-slavery.[59] The indebted complained that, while they were abroad fighting for Rome's liberty and empire, they were enslaved and oppressed at home by their fellow-citizens and that the liberty of the plebeians was more secure in times of war than peace and more secure among the enemy than among their fellow-citizens.

These ill feelings, which were growing on their own, burst into flame because of the miseries of one man. Old and bearing the marks of all his misfortunes, he rushed into the Forum. His clothes were smeared with grime, the condition of his body was even filthier, and he was pale and emaciated. Besides this, his unkempt beard and hair gave his face a savage look. Even in this shocking state, he was recognized and some people began to recall how he had commanded ranks of soldiers, while others, pitying the man, boasted that he had won various military honors. The man himself displayed the scars on his chest, witnesses to his honorable service in many far-flung battles. When a crowd gathered around him and inquired how he came to be in such a filthy condition, he spoke out, as though before an assembly:

"While I served in the Sabine War, I lost my crops because of the depredations of the enemy. They burned my house. They plundered all my belongings. They stole my livestock. When I was in this desperate situation, the war-tax was imposed and I contracted debt. First, my debt swelled through usurious interest and they confiscated my farm, which had been my father's and my grandfather's before him. Then, they took the rest of my property. Finally, like a disease that reached every part of a body, my creditor led me not into slavery but into jail and the torture-chamber."

At this point, the man displayed his back, disfigured by the marks of recent blows. When the crowd saw and heard these things, there was a great uproar. At this point, the commotion was no longer confined to the Forum but had spread throughout the entire city. The debt-slaves, whether they were enchained or not, broke into the public spaces on every side and begged for help (*fides*) from the citizenry. No part of the city lacked volunteers for the uprising. Large columns of men rushed chaotically through the streets toward the Forum. The senators who were, by chance, in the Forum found themselves in great danger when they encountered this crowd, which would not have hesitated to resort to violence had not the consuls, Publius Servilius and Appius Claudius, intervened and beat back the mob.

But the mob turned on the consuls and displayed their chains and other marks of mistreatment. These, they said, were their rewards, and they reproached the consuls with details of when and where they had served in the army. They called out—in a manner more threatening than beseeching—for the consuls to convene the senate and they surrounded the Curia, thinking that they should monitor and control the public debate. But the consuls collected only a few senators, whom chance had led to the vicinity. Fear excluded the other senators not only from the Curia but even from the Forum. Thus, the senate could not do anything because it lacked a quorum.

At this point the mob believed that they were being toyed with and put off, thinking that the senators were absent not because of chance or fear but to prevent any action and that the consuls themselves were equivocating. Nor did they have any doubt that their miseries were being mocked. Just as it seemed that not even the majesty of the consuls could control the wrath of these men, the senators, who were uncertain whether they risked more by delaying or coming forward, came at last into the senate. But even when the Curia was full, there was disagreement among the senators and even between the consuls themselves. Appius, a violent and impetuous man, advised that the matter should be settled through consular authority; when one or two men had been arrested, he said, the others would quiet down. Servilius, who was more inclined to gentler remedies, thought it would be easier—and safer—to redirect their agitation rather than break it.

[2.24] Even as this was happening, a greater threat arose: Latin cavalrymen arrived at a gallop with the disturbing news that the Volscians and their cursed army were coming to attack the city. This report affected the senators and the plebs very differently, so completely had their dissension split the community in two. The plebs were overjoyed; the gods, they said, had come as the avengers of patrician arrogance. They encouraged each other not to give their names (for the levy), since it was preferable to perish together than alone. Let the senators serve in the army, they said, let them take up arms, so that those who reaped the rewards of war should be closest to its dangers. In the Curia, however, the mood was gloomy and nervous. In their twofold fear—of their fellow-citizens and the enemy—the senators begged Servilius, who was more popular than his colleague, to extricate the community beset by such threats. At once, the consul dismissed the senate and went into the assembly. There, he revealed that the senators had intended to consult the plebs but that during their deliberations over this part of the community—a very important part but nevertheless only a part—fear for the entire commonwealth had intervened. It was impossible, he said, when the enemy was almost at the city's gates, to consider anything before the war. Nor, if there was some relief from that threat, would the plebs have behaved honorably if they had only taken up arms in defense of their own country if they first received some compensation. Nor would it

be suitable for the senators to have been forced to pass legislation dealing with the misfortunes of their fellow-citizens when they would have done so later of their own free will. He then added credence (*fides*) to his speech through an edict that said that no one should hold a Roman citizen in chains or confinement and prevent him from giving his name to the consuls, nor should anyone seize or sell the property of any soldier, for as long as he is in service, nor harass his children or grandchildren. After this edict had been published, the debt-slaves who were present submitted their names at once and from everywhere in the entire city, they rushed from private houses, where their creditors no longer had the right to detain them, into the Forum to take the military oath. It was a massive crowd, and their courage and usefulness was very distinguished in the war against the Volscians.

The consuls led their troops against the enemy and pitched their camp just a short distance from them.

[The Romans successfully repulsed the Volscian attack at dawn and then advanced, forcing the Volscians to sue for peace (2.25). They then repulsed further attacks by the Sabines and Auruncans (2.26). Victorious, the plebs expected the consuls to fulfill their promises, but Appius began to issue harsh sentences against the debtors and hand them over to their creditors (2.27), forcing the plebs to begin organizing resistance. In the new year, the plebs refused to answer another muster until their liberty was restored (2.28), but as the senate first debated what to do and then decided in favor of the hard line advocated by Appius Claudius (2.29), a combined force of Volsci, Aequi, and Sabines invaded. After the dictator Marcus Valerius promised them fair treatment, the plebs answered the muster and the Romans crushed their foes (2.30) but senatorial opposition at the behest of the moneylenders led the triumphant Valerius to resign in disgust (2.31).]

[2.32] At this point the senators grew worried that, once the army disbanded, the plebs would again take up their secret meetings and conspiracies. Although the dictator had conducted the levy, the soldiers had sworn their oaths to the consuls. The senate, therefore, decided that the plebs were still bound by oath *[despite Valerius's resignation]* and ordered them to march out of Rome, using as a pretext the renewed hostilities with the Aequi.

This was the act that caused the revolution. It is said that at first the plebs agitated to slaughter the consuls, since by their deaths they would be discharged from their oaths. But when they learned that a sacred obligation could not be undone by a crime, they decided, at the prompting of a certain Sicinius, to ignore the consuls' command and withdraw to the Sacred Mount on the other side of the Anio River, three miles from the city.[60] They set out carrying only the bare necessities, and on the mount, although they had no commander, they established a regular, fortified encampment and held out for several days in peace, making no further provocations.

A great panic seized the city, as affairs hung in suspense in an atmosphere of mutual distrust. The plebeians who had been left behind in the city feared violence from the patricians; the patricians feared the plebeians who remained, and they were unsure whether they would rather have them go or stay. They wondered how long the multitude that had seceded would remain peaceful and what would happen if a foreign war broke out. They felt that any hope they had rested on harmony among the citizens and that this must be restored at any cost.

Therefore, they decided to send Menenius Agrippa to plead their case to the plebs. He was an eloquent man and, since he was himself of plebeian origin, liked by the plebs. Agrippa was received into the camp and it is said that he told them this simple story in an old-fashioned and gruff style:

"There was a time when the parts of the human body did not, as they do now, work together, but each member kept its own council and had its own language. The extremities grew indignant when they saw that everything acquired by their laborious exertions went to the belly, which, undisturbed at the body's center, did nothing but enjoy the pleasures they provided. So, they formed a conspiracy: the hands would not bring food to the mouth, the mouth would not accept food if it were offered, the teeth would not

chew it if it were received. So, although they, in their animosity, intended to use starvation to conquer the belly, the extremities themselves wasted away and the entire body reached a point of extreme weakness. By this it became clear that the belly provided a vital service and the nourishment it received was returned to all parts of the body through the blood that allows us to live and be strong, equally distributed through our veins after it was fortified by the digestion of food."

Through this comparison, which showed how the internal strife among the parts of the body was like the animosity the plebeians held against the patricians, Agrippa succeeded in persuading the plebeians to change their minds.

[2.33] Discussions about reconciliation then began. An agreement was reached on the following conditions: the plebs should have their own inviolable magistrates to protect them against the consuls, and no patrician would ever be allowed to hold this office. Two tribunes of the plebs were elected: Gaius Licinius and Lucius Albinus. These selected three colleagues, among whom was Sicinius, the initiator of the secession . . . and it was there, on the Sacred Mount, that the "holy law" was passed.[61]

Valerius Maximus, *Memorable Doings and Sayings* (Selections)

In the early first century CE, Valerius Maximus composed a compendium of exempla, or anecdotes, mostly drawn from Roman history but with non-Roman examples as well. His work was intended for use by Roman orators, who used the exempla as evidence to support their arguments. It also served as a handbook for moral instruction by illustrating examples of good behavior to emulate and bad behavior to avoid.

The excerpts below feature exempla on reconciliation, mercy, and severity. They provide examples of when Romans compromised—and when they did not.

Book 4.2: On Those Who from Enmity Were Reconciled into Friendship

Let us pass to the honorable deflection of the human mind from hate to kindness and let us pursue this course with a cheerful pen. You see, whenever the sea turns from rough to calm or the sky from cloudy to clear, we observe it with smiling faces. If war changes to peace, this brings us extraordinary happiness. Likewise, putting aside bitter wrongs ought to be celebrated outright.

Marcus Aemilius Lepidus, who was pontifex maximus and had twice been consul, enjoyed a seriousness in his life that equaled the splendor of his official positions.[62] He had waged a long and violent enmity with Fulvius Flaccus, a man who had attained the same lofty status.[63] Yet, when it was announced that the pair had been elected censors, Lepidus publicly repudiated their enmity, judging it improper for persons who were joined publicly in the highest authority to be in a state of antagonism because of private hostilities. Lepidus's contemporaries approved of his judgment, and the old writers of the annals have related it to us for commendation.

In the same way, the annalists refused to allow posterity to forget Livius Salinator's famed decision to end his feud.[64] Salinator had gone into exile burning with hatred for Nero, whose testimony had grievously damaged him.[65] But after Salinator was recalled from exile and his fellow-citizens elected him to the consulship with Nero as his colleague, he forced himself to forget his previous mindset, which was the harshest imaginable, and the injury he had received, which was the gravest. For he feared that, if he showed that he was steadfast in his hostility, he would reveal that he was acting like a bad consul if he shared authority with a colleague with whom he was antagonistic. Shifting his mind to greater tranquility greatly contributed to the salvation of Rome and Italy in a dangerous and difficult time. For the two men, challenging and matching each other with their passion for virtue, beat down the awesome power of Carthage.[66]

Famous, too, is the example of hostilities laid aside by Scipio Africanus the Elder and Tiberius Gracchus.[67] These men came to the rites of a shared table as enemies who hated one another. But they left that table joined in friendship and affinity. For Scipio was not content with merely reaching an understanding with Gracchus at the banquet of Jupiter on the Capitol (as he had been advised to do by the senate) but straightaway betrothed his daughter Cornelia to him.

Book 5.1: On Humanity and Mercy

[Preface] What more suitable partners could I give to generosity than humanity and mercy, since they strive for the same kind of praise?[68] Generosity should be granted in times of poverty, humanity in struggle, mercy in perilous misfortune. While you may not know which of these you should approve of most, praise seems to flow first to the virtue whose name was drawn from our very spirit *[that is, humanity]*.[69]

[5.1.1] First of all, I shall recount the senate's most humane and merciful actions. When Carthaginian delegates came to Rome to ransom their prisoners, the senate immediately returned 2,743 young men without accepting any ransom.[70] What a perfect act! How large an army of enemies released! How much money despised! How many Punic injuries forgiven! I think the delegates themselves were stunned and said to one another: "The munificence of the Romans is equaled only by the magnanimity of the gods! Our mission has succeeded beyond our prayers! In truth, we have received a gift we never would have given!"

The following is also no small indication of the senate's humanity: it decreed that Syphax—who had once been the exceptionally wealthy king of Numidia but had been captured and died in prison at Tibur—should be buried with a public funeral, adding the honor of a proper tomb to the gift of life.[71] It displayed the same mercy in the case of Perseus.[72] When he died at Alba, where he had been imprisoned, the senate sent a quaestor to bury him with a public funeral, lest it allow his royal remains to lie disrespected.

These were the duties the senate paid to enemies, to miserable men, to the dead. Now let's recount what it bestowed upon friends, the prosperous, and the living.

After the conclusion of the Macedonian War, the victorious Roman general Paullus dispatched Musochanes, the son of Masinissa, back to his father along with the cavalry that he had brought to assist the Romans.[73] But Musochanes's fleet was scattered by a storm, and Musochanes was carried into the port of Brundisium as a sick man. When the senate learned of this, it immediately ordered a quaestor to go to Brundisium and prepare lodgings, medical treatment, and everything that Musochanes's health required, sparing no expense in the care of the young man and his entire force. The quaestor secured transports that could carry him and his men to Africa in safety and comfort. Each cavalryman was given a pound of silver and five hundred sesterces. After such humane behavior had been shown by the senate on behalf of the conscript fathers (so timely and diligent!), even if the young man had died, his father might have borne his loss with more equanimity.

The same senate heard that Prusias, king of Bithynia, was traveling to Rome to offer them his congratulations on their defeat of Perseus.[74] They sent the quaestor Publius Cornelius Scipio to Capua and decreed that the best possible house be rented for the king in Rome and that he and his retinue be supported at public expense. When the city received

him, it wore the expression of a humane friend. And so, a king, who was already very affectionate toward us when he arrived, returned to his kingdom with his goodwill doubled.

Not even Egypt lacked humane treatment from the Romans. When its king, Ptolemy, had been robbed of his kingdom by his younger brother, he traveled to Rome to request assistance.[75] Only a few slaves attended him, he was covered in grime, and he was forced to take up lodgings with a painter from Alexandria. When this was reported to the senate, they immediately summoned the young king and apologized that they had not sent a quaestor to greet him, in accordance with their ancestral custom and had not received him with public hospitality. They said that this was due not to any negligence on their part but to the king's sudden and secret arrival. Straightaway, they led him from the Curia to public lodgings and encouraged him, once he had put aside the grime of his travels, to request a day when he could visit the senate. The senate even took care to send a questor to him every day bearing presents. By these repeated gifts, the senate raised him from abjectness to the pinnacle of royalty and brought it to pass that he possessed more hope in the assistance of the Roman people than fear in his own situation.

[5.1.2] Let me move from the collective actions of the senate's conscript fathers to individuals. Lucius Cornelius was consul during the First Punic War when he captured the town of Olbia, for which Hanno, the Carthaginian general, had died, fighting with extraordinary courage.[76] The consul gave Hanno a lavish funeral, carrying the Carthaginian's body out from his own tent and not hesitating to celebrate an enemy's funeral in person. For he believed that the victory that excited the least ill will among gods and men was precisely that which displayed the greatest humanity.

[5.1.3] What should I say about Quinctius Crispinus, whose gentleness could not be shaken, even by those most powerful emotions: anger and the desire for glory?[77] He had once welcomed Badius the Campanian into his home with the most generous hospitality. When that man had fallen ill, Crispinus had seen to his recovery with the most attentive care. After the infamous treason of the Campanians, Badius challenged Crispinus to solo combat. Crispinus, however, although he was far stronger in body and more courageous in spirit, preferred to admonish that ungrateful man rather than defeat him. You see, he said, "What are you doing, madman? Where has this perverse desire carried you, so far from your true course? It's bad enough that you rage with public betrayal. Are you also to fall into private betrayal? It seems that, disgracefully, it would please you to use your weapons on Quinctius, alone of all the Romans, despite the fact that you owe his household gods both the reciprocity of a service and your very life! As for me, the bonds of friendship and the gods of hospitality—pledges as sacred to the Roman people as they are cheap to your hearts—forbid me from joining you in a hostile struggle. Indeed, even if by chance, in the clash of our armies, I had recognized you lying on the ground, laid low by the impact of my shield, I would have recalled my blade even as it met your neck. Therefore, may your criminal desire to kill your host be on your head; I will not bear the crime of a slain guest. And so, seek another hand by which you might die, since mine has learned to save you." The celestial spirits gave to each man the outcome he deserved during that same battle: Badius was decapitated; Quinctius fought nobly and survived the battle as a hero.

[5.1.4] Come, how memorable and famous should we consider the example of the mercy shown by Marcus Marcellus![78] After he had captured Syracuse, he mounted its citadel to observe from on high the situation of the city, which had been so exceedingly wealthy but was then in such dire straits. Gazing on the city's sad fate, he could not check his tears. If someone who did not know Marcellus had seen him then, he would have thought that his victory belonged to another. And so, citizens of Syracuse, into your greatest disaster you enjoyed a dash of thanksgiving, since, although it was not fated that you should withstand our assault, you fell under so gentle a conqueror.

[5.1.5] Quintus Metellus, when he was fighting the Celtiberians in Spain, besieged the city of Centobriga.[79] When he advanced his siege engines and was about to destroy the only part of the fortifications that were able to be battered down, he placed humanity before a victory that was in his grasp. You see, the Centobrigians placed the sons of Rhoetogenes, who had deserted to the Romans, in the path of the engines. Although Rhoetogenes himself refused that there be any delay in the completion of the assault, even if it meant the annihilation of his own flesh and blood, Metellus broke off the assault, lest those boys suffer a cruel mode of death before their father's own eyes. Indeed, by this act of extraordinary mercy, he captured not just the walls of a single community but the hearts of every Celtiberian city, with the result that he removed the need for many sieges to bring the Celtiberians under the sway of the Roman people.

[5.1.6] Africanus the Younger also displayed his exquisite humanity far and wide.[80] For, after Carthage was sacked, he circulated a letter to the communities of Sicily saying that they could recover the temple treasures that the Carthaginians had stolen and restore them to their original positions. This gift was welcomed equally by the gods and men!

[5.1.7] The same man undertook another equal act of humanity. When the quaestor was auctioning off war-prisoners, an exceptionally handsome boy with a gentlemanly disposition was put up. Scipio learned from the boy that he was Numidian and had been raised by his uncle Masinissa after he was orphaned. A precocious youth, he had taken up arms against the Romans without Masinissa's knowledge. Scipio judged it appropriate to pardon the boy's mistake and respect the friendship owed to the king who was the most loyal to the Roman people. So, he gave the boy a ring, a gold brooch, a broad-striped tunic, a Spanish cloak, and a well-equipped horse and sent him to Masinissa with a cavalry detachment as an escort. Scipio reckoned that the greatest fruits of victory lay in restoring treasures to the gods and relatives to their kin.

[5.1.8] In praising humanity, we must also hold tight the memory of Lucius Paullus.[81] When Paullus learned that Perseus—a captive who only a moment before had been a king—was being led before him, Paullus met him adorned with the tokens of Roman authority. When Perseus attempted to fall to his knees, Paullus raised him up with his right hand and, addressing him in Greek, encouraged him not to despair. Paullus even led him into his private tent, sat him at his side during deliberations, and did not despise honoring him at his table. Let's compare the battle that had laid Perseus low and the sequence I just described. Men will doubt which spectacle delights them more: for if it is a glorious thing to lay an enemy low, it is no less praiseworthy to know how to pity him in his misfortune.

Book 6.3: On Severity

[Preface] It is necessary to steel one's heart with hardness when acts of terrible, sorrowful severity are recounted. Putting aside all gentler thoughts, make space for affairs that are harsh to hear. Severe affairs and inexorable retributions and diverse modes of punishment will rush into view and the useful defenses offered by the law too, but these will hardly amount to a few peaceful and quiet pages.

[6.3.1] Marcus Manlius was hurled headfirst from the same place from which he had driven off the Gauls because he had tried, infamously, to oppress the liberty he had so bravely defended.[82] Surely this would have been the preface to that just vengeance: "You were my Manlius when you routed the Senones; but after you began to imitate them, you become one of the Senones."[83] His execution made a mark known to eternal memory: for because of him a law was established that no patrician could reside on the citadel of the Capitoline, because he had a house where now we see the Temple of Juno Moneta.

Equal disdain broke out among the citizenry against Spurius Cassius, for whom the suspicion that he desired to become a tyrant did more harm than his three magnificent consulships and two incredible triumphs did him credit.[84] For the senate and people of Rome, not content with inflicting capital punishment on the man, threw the ruins of his own house upon his corpse, so that he be additionally punished

by the destruction of his household. On the grounds of his house, they build the Temple of Tellus. In this way, what before had been the dwelling of an ambitious man is now a monument to reverent severity.

The fatherland punished Spurius Maelius, who made a similar attempt at tyranny, with the same outcome.[85] In fact, the site of his house acquired the name "Aequimelium" so that the justice of his execution continues to be well-known to posterity.[86] Thus, through the ruins of the walls and roofs of where these men lived, the men of old bore witness to the great hatred they held in their hearts against the enemies of liberty. This is why, when the bodies of Marcus Flaccus and Lucius Saturninus, those most seditious of Roman citizens, had been slaughtered, their households were razed to their lowest foundations.[87] The site of Flaccus's house, after it had remained more or less empty for a long time, was decorated with the spoils won from the Cimbri by Quintus Catulus.[88]

The lofty nobility and bountiful promise of Tiberius and Gaius Gracchus once flourished in our community.[89] But because they attempted to overthrow our community's constitution, their bodies lay unburied and the final honors paid to the human condition were denied to the sons of Gracchus and the grandsons of Africanus.[90] Indeed, even their acquaintances were thrown headfirst from the Tarpeian Rock, lest anyone wish to be a friend to the enemies of the commonwealth.

[6.3.2] Publius Mucius, the tribune of the plebs, believed he had the same power as the senate and people of Rome when he burned alive all his colleagues who had, under the leadership of the consul Spurius Cassius, called the community's liberty into doubt by not holding elections for new magistrates.[91] In truth, nothing is more courageous than this act of severity: for a single tribune dared to inflict on his nine colleagues a punishment which nine tribunes would have shuddered to exact from a single colleague.

[6.3.3] Up to this point, severity has been the guardian and avenger of liberty. But she is also equally serious in respect to dignity and discipline. For the senate surrendered Marcus Claudius to the Corsi because he had made a shameful truce with them.[92] When the Corsi would not accept him, the senate ordered that he be jailed and executed. The majesty of our empire was wounded once; but in how many ways was the senate an unyielding avenger of its wrath! It annulled his actions, deprived him of liberty, extinguished his life, and befouled his corpse by the shameful indignities of jail and the Gemonian Steps.[93]

Claudius had earned the senate's hostility. Gnaeus Cornelius Scipio, however, the son of Hispalus, experienced it before he could earn it.[94] You see, when the province of Spain was allotted to him, the senate decreed that he should not go, with this justification: he did not know how to do the right thing. And so, Cornelius, although he never went to his province, was in effect found guilty under the law against provincial corruption because of the dishonor of his lifestyle.

Nor did the severity of the senate hesitate in the case of Gaius Vettienus, who had amputated the fingers of his left hand to avoid service in the Italian War.[95] The senate decreed that his property be confiscated and that he be thrown in chains for the rest of his life. Thus, in chains and disgrace he wasted the life he did not wish to shed with honor in battle.

[6.3.4] Manlius Curius imitated this severity.[96] When he was consul, he was suddenly compelled to order a fresh levy of soldiers. When none of the young men responded to the summons, he made a lottery of all the tribes. The token of Pollia came first, but when he ordered a name from this tribe to be drawn from the urn and summoned there was no response. So he ordered the property of this young man to be auctioned off.

[6.3.5] Lucius Domitius was equally steadfast in his purpose.[97] You see, when he was the praetor who governed Sicily, a boar of extraordinary size was brought before him. He ordered the shepherd who had killed it to be led before him. He asked the shepherd how he had killed the beast. When Domitius learned that the shepherd had used a hunting spear, he crucified him, because, in an attempt to suppress the banditry that was devastating the province, he had decreed that no one should possess a weapon. Some have said that this act is balanced between severity and cruelty (it is possible to argue either side). But a proper reckoning of public authority does not allow us to deem the praetor's actions as overly harsh.

Seneca the Younger, *On Mercy* 2.3–5, 7

Seneca the Younger (ca. 4 BCE–65 CE) was an author, dramatist, Stoic philosopher, and politician. He became the tutor and adviser of the emperor Nero during the early years of his reign but was eventually implicated in a plot to assassinate Nero and forced to commit suicide.

This treatise about the importance of mercy in the application of justice was written in an attempt to educate the young emperor Nero on how to be a benevolent ruler. Although it was composed circa 56 CE, more than a century after the crisis of Catiline, it provides insight into how an ethical Roman could justify showing mercy to one who has committed a wrong.

[2.3] We should not let the attractiveness of the word "mercy" (*clementia*), deceive us and lead us into its opposite. So, let us consider what mercy truly is, what qualities it possesses and what are the limits of this virtue.[98] Mercy is when we restrain our mind from vengeance when it has the capacity to avenge itself, that is to say, it is the leniency shown by the more powerful when assigning punishment to the weaker. To avoid losing my case, so to speak, it is safer to give multiple definitions, since just one might not contain all the possibilities for mercy. Mercy might be defined as "an inclination toward leniency when inflicting punishment." Some might object to this definition, even if it is closer to the truth than other possible definitions, since, if we say that mercy requires "moderation that excuses some of a punishment that is deserved," they might object that a virtue can never give someone less than what they deserve. True, but everyone understands that mercy consists in stopping short of a punishment that justice might inflict.

[2.4] The ignorant think that the opposite of mercy is strictness (*severitas*). But no virtue has as its opposite another virtue! What, then, is the opposite of mercy? Cruelty (*crudelitas*), which is simply savageness in the mind when exacting punishment. "But," you say, "there are men who do not exact punishment yet are still cruel. For example, a man who murders a stranger he just met, not to rob him but for the sake of killing. And there are men, unsatisfied with merely killing, who torture the stranger, like Busiris and Procrustes and those pirates who whip their captives and burn them alive."[99] This indeed appears to be cruelty. But because it does not result from vengeance (since there had been no injury) and is not caused by any offense (for no crime preceded it), it falls outside our definition, which is limited to immoderation in the mind when exacting *punishment*. If a man takes pleasure in such actions, we can say that this is not cruelty but savagery (*ferocitas*)—we might even call it madness (*insania*). You see, there are many kinds of madness and none is clearer than that which reaches the point of indulging in murder and mutilation. I shall, therefore, call those persons "cruel" who have a reason for exacting punishment but who do so without moderation. For example, Phalaris was said to have tortured criminals and did so with inhuman and unbelievable savagery.[100] Let's avoid empty sophistry and define cruelty like this: cruelty is "the inclination of the mind toward harshness." Mercy repels cruelty and demands that it stand far away from her. But mercy is agreeable with strictness (*severitas*).

At this point, it is relevant to ask what pity (*misericordia*) is. Indeed, many praise pity as a virtue and call good the man who engages in pity. But to do so is a mental vice. Just as we should avoid cruelty, we should avoid pity, although both are near to strictness and mercy. For, in the guise of strictness we fall into cruelty; in the guise of mercy into pity. The danger is less when we are misled into pity, but both are mistaken, since they both lead us away from the truth.

[2.5] Consequently, just as religion honors the gods and superstition harms them, good men will display mercy and kindness and avoid pity, which is the vice of weak minds succumbing to the sight of another's suffering. Pity, therefore, most often appears in the worst sort of people, like old women and little girls who, moved by the tears of the vilest criminals, would break open the prisons if they could. Pity looks to the misfortune but not its cause; mercy is allied with reason.

I know that Stoicism has a bad reputation among the inexperienced who deem it a philosophy that is excessively harsh and not at all likely to provide good advice to kings and princes. Stoicism is criticized because it rejects the possibility that a wise man might show pity or grant pardon. These doctrines, if taken in isolation, are indeed odious, since they would seem to leave no hope for human error and to require that every mistake be punished. And if this is true, what kind of wisdom orders us to unlearn our basic humanity and to shut off what would offer the most secure port for our misfortunes: mutual aid and support?

But no philosophy is kinder or gentler, none more full of love for men, none more attuned to the common good, since its maxims are designed to be useful and helpful and not make decisions for the self alone but for the interests of all. Pity is a disease of the mind contracted by the sight of others in sorrow or sadness that had been caused by misfortunes that seem undeserved. But disease does not befall the wise man. His mind is calm and nothing can befall it that would cause it turmoil. Nothing so befits a person as a superior mind. But superiority of mind cannot coexist with sorrow. Grief dulls the mind, casts it down, constrains it. Even the greatest personal calamities cannot inflict this on a wise man. He will beat back the rage of misfortune in its entirety and shatter it. He will always maintain the same composure, calm and unshaken. He could not do this if sorrow affected him. . . .

[2.7] "But," you ask, "why not grant pardon?" Come now, let us clarify what indulgence is. Then you will know why a wise man must not grant it. Indulgence is "leniency toward deserved punishment." The doctrine of why a wise man must not grant leniency has been explained by others at greater length. But I will summarize their position, as one conveying the opinions of other men, as follows: "One pardons someone whom he ought to punish. But the wise man does nothing that he ought not do and omits nothing that he ought to do. Therefore, he does not excuse a punishment that he ought to exact. But in a more honorable way he will bestow upon you that which you wish to obtain by pardon. For the wise man will spare you, he will consider your true interest, he will correct you. He will do the same thing as if he pardoned you but he will not pardon you, since the one who pardons admits that he has failed to do something that he should have done. Some men he will punish by reprimanding them, inflicting no other punishment if he thinks that they are of an age that allows reformation. Some, who were undeniably implicated in a heinous crime, he will nevertheless release, because the wrongdoer had been deceived or had faltered because of wine. The wise man will even release his enemies—and perhaps even praise them—if they were spurred to fight by honorable motives, like preserving loyalty, an oath, or their liberty. These are acts not of pardon but mercy. Mercy is free in its judgments. Its decisions do not follow the letter of the law but what is good and equitable. Mercy may acquit or assess damages as it wishes. It does nothing that seems anything less than just, but whatever it decides seems most just of all. But to pardon is to not punish someone whom you deem worthy of punishment. To pardon is to excuse a punishment that ought to be exacted. Mercy excels most of all in this: to those whom it releases it announces that they should have suffered nothing other than they did. It is more complete than pardon—and more honorable."

In my opinion, this is a semantic difference but we are agreed about the matter itself. The wise man will excuse many punishments and we will preserve men who, although their characters are not sound, may become sound. He will be like the good farmer, who not only tends to his trees that are already straight and tall but will apply props to those that for some reason have grown crooked so that they might grow straight. Other trees he will prune so that their branches not restrict their growth. He will fertilize those that have been weakened because they have been planted in poor soil. He will expose to sunlight those that have been cast into shade by other trees. Thus, the wise man will see which method of treatment will improve a given character and how the crooked might be straightened. . . . ■

Cicero, *On the Agrarian Law* 2 (Selections)

Cicero delivered this speech before the Popular Assembly in January of 63 BCE. In speaking directly to the people, Cicero attempts to diminish popular support for the land reform bill introduced by the tribune P. Servilius Rullus (but, in reality, the work of Crassus and Caesar). The law would establish a Board of Ten (the decemvirs) to oversee the execution of the law. Cicero had previously spoken against the law to the senate on January 1, his first official speech as consul.

Cicero begins by thanking the people for electing him, a novus homo, *to the consulship (2.1–6). In the excerpt below he describes his plan for his consulship to be brave, cautious, and "popular" (which he further defines). He then reminds the people how Rullus's agrarian law was introduced and summarizes its general features. Technical or repetitive sections are summarized using bullet points.*

[2.7] I know that I was elected consul by the judgment of the entire Roman people, not by the partisan support of the powerful nor by the extraordinary influence of the few. And I know, too, that a large majority preferred me to other men of the very highest rank. How, then, could I, first while I am consul and then for the rest of my entire life, not devote myself to being a populist (*popularis*)?

But I have urgent need of your wisdom in describing the proper meaning and interpretation of "populist." For, many men are spreading a great error under insidious pretenses. These men not only attack and hinder the interests of the people but even the safety of the people. Yet these same men, through their speeches, want to achieve recognition by being "populist."

[2.8] I recognize, my fellow-citizens, the condition of the commonwealth when it was handed into my care on January 1: it was full of anxiety, full of fear. At that moment, there was no evil, no calamity that good citizens did not dread—and that the wicked did not anticipate! Every manner of sedition against the constitution of our commonwealth and against your tranquility was being discussed. Some, indeed, had already been put in motion, others were designated to begin as soon as we became consuls.[101] All confidence was banished from the Forum, not by the blow of any new calamity but by the suspicions directed toward the courts and their disruption and by the overturning of matters you thought already decided. New forms of despotism were being considered, extraordinary powers befitting not the military commander but a king!

[2.9] Now, since I not only suspected these things but understood them clearly (although they were hardly being organized in secret!), I declared in the senate that, for as long as I held this office, I would be a "populist" consul. After all, what is more advantageous to the people than peace? Isn't it true that all whom nature granted sense enjoy peace? And also our homes and farms? What is more advantageous to the people than liberty? Is this not yearned for and preferred above all, by man and beast alike? What is more advantageous to the people than tranquility? Did your ancestors and the bravest men deem tranquility so pleasant that immense effort should be expended so that someday tranquility—accompanied by authority and dignity—might be enjoyed? Surely, therefore, we owe exceptional praise to our ancestors because we owe to their efforts that we can enjoy tranquility without the threat of danger. How, therefore, could I not be a "populist," my fellow-citizens, when I see all of this—peace abroad, liberty as the property of your name and nation, domestic tranquility—everything, in short, that is near and dear to you, placed in my trust and, in a manner of speaking, into the protective patronage of my consulship?

[2.10] Indeed, my fellow-citizens, no proposed act of welfare should please you or seem to be "populist" if it can only be promised with words and there is no way for it to become reality without exhausting the public treasury.

Nor should the following be considered "populist": the disruption of the courts, the overturning of matters you thought already decided, the restoration of the condemned.[102] These are often the final acts of destruction in cities already on the verge of ruin. Nor does one act as a "populist" when he promises land to the people—or if he displays false pretenses while secretly aiming at different objectives.

For, if I were to speak truthfully, my fellow-citizens, I cannot disparage agrarian laws in general, since I remember that two of our most illustrious men, two of our most clever men and most devoted to the Roman plebs—I speak of Tiberius and Gaius Gracchus—settled plebeians on public land that had formerly been occupied by private citizens.[103] I am not one of those consuls who thinks it a crime (as most do) to praise the Gracchi. I recognize that many aspects of our commonwealth were strengthened by their counsel, wisdom, and laws.

[2.11] And so, when I was consul-elect and I was informed that the tribunes-elect were drawing up an agrarian law, I was eager to learn about their plans. In fact, I thought that, since we would all be magistrates in the same year, it would be appropriate if there was some unanimity between us concerning the proper administration of the commonwealth.

[2.12] But when I attempted to offer myself as a confidant in their conversations, I was shut out and excluded. And when I made it clear that, if I thought that the law was helpful to the Roman plebs, I would support and promote it, they scorned my generosity and declared that I could never be encouraged to support any act of public welfare. I halted my offers of assistance, lest my persistence have the appearance of treachery or impudence. In the meantime, they continued to meet in secret, to invite only certain private citizens to join them, and to choose night and seclusion for their secret gatherings. You can easily imagine my concerns at this time from the anxieties that also gripped you.

[2.13] At last the tribunes entered office. The speech of Publius Rullus was greatly anticipated, since he was the chief proponent of the agrarian law and he was more belligerent than his colleagues. As soon as he had been elected, he practiced a different expression, a different tone of voice, a different gait, wearing more traditional clothing, his body was unkept and wild, his hair longer and beard untrimmed, so that his eyes and entire look seemed to threaten everyone with the power of the tribunate—indeed, he seemed to menace the commonwealth.[104]

I was waiting for his man's speech and his law. At first no law was proposed. He schedules a speech for the Ides of December.[105] Men gather with immense anticipation. He unrolls an extraordinarily long speech full of the finest words. There was just one thing, one fault that I could detect. . . . In that massive crowd there was not a single person who could understand a single thing he said. Did he do this through some nefarious design or because he delights in this kind of oratory? I don't know. The sharper men who attended his speech suspected that he wished to say something about the agrarian law. But at last, after I had been elected consul, the law was proposed publicly. The copyists, on my orders, immediately rushed to bring me an exact transcript of the law.

[2.14] I can assure you, my fellow-citizens, that I applied myself to reading and understanding this law with a mindset that I would support and promote it if I understood it to be appropriate and advantageous for you. For the consulship has not, either by natural disagreement or deep-seated animosity, undertaken some sort of war against the tribunate, although good and brave consuls have had to oppose wicked, seditious tribunes from time

to time and the power of the tribunate has sometimes had to resist the passions of the consuls. It is not the incompatibility of their powers but different intentions that create dissension between them.

[2.15] And so, I took this law into my hands with the sincere hope that it would be suitable and advantageous to you and that a consul, one who not only spoke but acted out of devotion to being "populist," could defend it freely and with honor. And I discovered, from the law's first clause to its last, my fellow-citizens, that its only thought, its only intention, its only aim is to appoint ten kings of the public treasury—all the tax revenue of every province, of the entire commonwealth and all the allied kingdoms and free peoples. Indeed, they aim to establish ten masters of the entire world under the pretense and false name of an agrarian law.

Thus, I assure you, my fellow-citizens, this "beautiful agrarian law that only has the people's interest at heart" gives you nothing but it bestows everything on a few individuals. This law dangles land before the eyes of the Roman people while it steals their liberty. It increases the wealth of private individuals and drains the wealth of the state. Finally—and this is the most shameful thing of all—thanks to a tribune of the plebs, which our ancestors established as the protector and guardian of your liberty, kings are to be established in our community! After I have revealed these facts to you, my fellow-citizens, if they appear to you to be untrue, I will yield to your authority and change my opinion. But if you understand the plots being laid against your liberty, then do not hesitate—and you will have a consul to assist you—to defend that liberty which your ancestors won with such blood and sweat and handed down to you without any effort on your part.

In the first clause of this agrarian law, they make a light attempt, or so it seems to them, to see how you will bear a diminution of your liberty. For it orders "the tribune of the plebs who has passed this law to create ten decemvirs by the votes of seventeen tribes, so that whosoever a majority consisting of nine tribes elects shall be a decemvir."[106]

[In the bulk of the speech, Cicero provides a detailed criticism of the law, revealing the ways it violates the mos maiorum *and diminishes the authority of the people whom it claims to help. He emphasizes:]*

- *The election method of the decemvirs is unprecedented (16–32).*
- *The decemvirs will be elected by a simple majority of seventeen of the thirty-five tribes that are first selected by lot; therefore, the decemvirs might be elected by the votes of only nine tribes (16–19).*
- *Rullus, suspiciously, is to preside over the selection of the tribes and the election (20–22).*
- *Because candidates must appear in person, this is, in effect, an ad hominem exclusion of Pompey's candidacy from the decemvirs; who benefits from this? The powerful forces behind the law, namely Crassus and Caesar (23–25).*
- *The law was proposed in such a way that it avoided the possibility of a tribunician veto; why do this if it is beneficial to the people? (26–32)*

Cicero then cautions against the powers invested in the decemvirs and the high probability of their corruption.]

[2.33] Just observe the immense authority they are invested with and you will see that this law follows not the madness of private individuals but the intolerable arrogance of kings. First, they are granted boundless authority to acquire vast sums of money out of your revenues, not by tax-farming them but by confiscating them. Second, they claim the authority to examine the conduct of every country and of every nation, without judicial oversight; to punish, without any right of appeal; and to condemn, without fear of a tribune intervening.

[2.34] For five years these men will be able to sit in judgment on the consuls, or even on the tribunes of the people themselves. But during that time no one will be able to sit in judgment on them. They can run for magisterial offices, but they cannot be brought to trial. They will have power to purchase whatever lands they wish, from whomsoever they choose, at whatever price they decide. They are allowed to establish new colonies, to restore old ones, to fill all Italy with their colonies. They have absolute authority to visit every province, to deprive free peoples of their lands, to buy and sell kingdoms. They may stay in Rome when it is convenient to them. But they also have the right to wander about wherever they wish with absolute military and judicial authority over everyone and everything. They dissolve our courts. They can remove from the bench any judge they wish. They can individually decide the most important matters. They can delegate their power to a quaestor. They can send out surveyors, and then the same decemvir who sent the surveyor can ratify whatever the surveyor reports!

[2.35] I fail to find the right word, my fellow-citizens, when I call this power "royal." In fact, it is something much greater. For there has never been a royal power that was not restrained to some extent—if not by some law, at least within certain bounds. But this power is infinite: all the kingdoms, all of your empire at its widest extent, all nations that are free from your rule and even those that are unknown to you, fall under the purview of this law.

In the first place, they are granted the ability to sell everything that was authorized to be sold by the resolutions of the senate during the consulship of Marcus Tullius and Gnaeus Cornelius or afterward *[that is, beginning in 81 BCE]*.

[2.36] Why is this fact so obscure and so hidden? What could it mean? Could not all those places about which the senate passed resolutions *[in 81 BCE]* be mentioned in the law by name? There are two reasons for their obscurity, my fellow-citizens. The first reason is shame, if such outrageous impudence can have any shame. The second reason is criminal intent. The law does not dare to name individually those places that the senate resolved to sell because they are public places in the city and its shrines, which since the restoration of the tribunician power no one has touched and which our ancestors intended as refuges in the city during times of danger. But all these things the decemvirs will sell by this tribunician law. Besides these, there is Mount Gaurus.[107] There are willow-beds at Minturnae.[108] There is the road to Herculaneum, valuable because of the delightful and fertile fields that abut it. There are many other places that the senate advised should be sold because of the poverty of the public treasury, but which the consuls did not sell because of the unpopularity of such measures.

[The law orders the sale of what became the property of the Roman people outside Italy after the year 88 BCE (38–46), which includes "Pergamum and Smyrna and Tralles and Ephesus and Miletus and Cyzicus and, in short, all Asia, which has been recovered since the consulship of Lucius Sulla and Quintus Pompeius" (39–44); this punitive measure will lead to serious conflict with the allies (45–46).

- *The law permits the sale both inside and outside Italy of certain rent-producing lands (*vectigalia*) with special reference to new* vectigalia *acquired by Pompey (47–55).*
- *The law authorizes the decemvirs to make sales whenever they see fit (55–56).*
- *The law authorizes the decemvirs to conduct (both inside and outside Italy) an investigation of all public and private land and imposes a tax (with some exceptions in Sicily and Africa) (57–59).*
- *The law confiscates for the decemvirs all treasure acquired by generals, unless it has been spent upon the erection of a monument or paid into the treasury; treasure already captured by Pompey is excepted, but revenue from lands captured by Pompey will go to the decemvirs instead of the public treasury (59–62).*

In the next section, Cicero focuses on the excessive power of the decemvirs—who would be elected to five-year terms, could not be removed, and were not subject to tribunician veto—and the irregularity of how they will purchase land (63–72).]

[2.63] Now learn about the rest of their enormous, intolerable business. Then you will understand that this agrarian law that they designate as "populist" is only an attempted scheme to satisfy the insatiable greed of certain men. Rullus orders lands to be bought with this money. You will be led there as colonists. I am not accustomed, my fellow-citizens, to call men unnecessarily harsh names—unless I am provoked. I wish I could, without insulting them, name those men that hope they themselves will be appointed decemvirs. Then you would immediately see the kind of men to whom you would entrust the power of selling and buying everything.

[2.64] Nevertheless, the names that I have decided I ought not say . . . yet, you can imagine. This one thing, however, I think that I can say in plain truth: once upon a time this commonwealth had men like the Luscini, the Calatini, the Acidini, men distinguished not only by the honors the people conferred on them and by their own great accomplishments but also by their patient endurance of poverty.[109] And later we had Catos and Phili and Laelii, men whose wisdom and moderation you recognized in public, private, forensic, and domestic affairs.[110] Even then, was such power as this ever entrusted to them? Did we allow the same man to be both assessor and seller and to act thus for five years over the whole world and also to have power to confiscate the lands that generate revenues for the Roman people and after he had amassed a vast fortune, without witnesses and according to his whim, to purchase whatever seemed pleasing from whomever he pleased?

[2.65] Do you now, my fellow-citizens, entrust such powers to the men whom you suspect of sniffing after the Decemvirate? You will discover that some of them think they never possess enough and some think they never have enough to squander.

Here, I will not debate another obvious point, my fellow-citizens, namely that our ancestors did not give to us the custom of buying lands from private individuals on which the plebs might be settled. In all their laws it was on *public* lands that *private* citizens were settled. I confess that that I expected something like this from this aggressive, brutish tribune of the plebs. Nevertheless, I always thought that this most profitable yet most shameful business of buying and selling was utterly inconsistent with the duties of a tribune—and utterly inconsistent with the dignity of the Roman people.

[The law is too vague about which lands will be sold; why would the law be vague and why would it say "which can be plowed or cultivated" instead of "which has been plowed or cultivated"? (66–67)]

[2.68] But now consider the force of this agrarian law. Even those men who occupy public lands will not yield their title unless they are tempted by advantageous terms—and a large sum of money. The law reverses the previous situation. Before, when a tribune mentioned an agrarian law, immediately everyone who occupied any public lands, or who had possessions that made them unpopular, began to be alarmed.[111] But this law makes them rich and relieves them of any unpopularity. How many men, my fellow-citizens, do you suppose there are who cannot defend the boundaries of their possessions or who cannot bear the unpopularity of lands given them by Sulla? How many of these wish to sell these lands but cannot find a purchaser? How many who, in fact, would be overjoyed to get rid of those lands by any means possible? Such men who, just a little while ago, quaked day and night at but the name of the tribunate, who feared your might, who were terrified at the mere mention of an agrarian law, will now be asked and begged to surrender to the decemvirs (at whatever price they like) these same lands, some of which are public property and others that are teeming with unpopularity and risk. This tribune sings this song not for you but for his own ear.

[The decemvirs will purchase lands that (1) the wealthy have appropriated and to which they have no right and (2) are worthless for farming (69–71).

The law forbids reimbursement of unspent funds back to the state treasury; therefore, the funds will remain a slush fund for the decemvirs, and the people will receive no land (71–72).

The law does not define, as is typical, the location of the colonies that will be founded; this is a threat to liberty and the commonwealth (73).]

[2.74] "And into whatever other places seem appropriate." What reason, therefore, would prevent them from placing a colony on the Janiculum Hill and so placing their garrison on our heads and necks?[112] Will you not define how many colonies you wish to lead forth, into what places, and with how many colonists?[113] Will you occupy any place you consider suitable for your violence? Will you fill these places with as many colonists as you wish? Will you strengthen it by whatever garrisons you wish? Will you use the revenues and all the resources of the Roman people to coerce, to oppress the Roman people itself, and to bring it under the power and command of your decemvirs?

[2.75] But I beg you now, my fellow-citizens, to consider how this tribune plans to besiege and occupy all of Italy with his garrisons. He authorizes the decemvirs to lead whomever they wish into every municipality and into every colony throughout all of Italy. He orders lands to be assigned to those colonists. Can there be any doubt that seeks greater powers than your liberty can tolerate? And stronger defenses? Can there be any doubt about how this royal power is being established? Can there be any doubt about how your liberty is being destroyed? For when the same group of men have all the money, when they command a great mob, when they lay siege to all of Italy through these resources, when they will have surrounded your liberty with their garrisons and colonies—what hope, what capacity for recovering your liberty, is left to you?

[Cicero denounces at great length the plan to place a colony in Capua, with the decemvirs selecting the colonists, who he says will be "fit instruments for violence and atrocity and slaughter, from which they (the decemvirs) may be able to make war and which may be able to equip them properly for war" (76–79).

The state will be weaker because of this colony, as it will lose valuable revenue and productive people will be driven from their homes; the land will be divided to the point of unproductivity (80–84).]

[2.85] Indeed, I think that, if the Campus Martius were divided and each of you were allotted two square feet of ground on which to stand, you would instead prefer to enjoy the whole in common than for each of you to possess a small portion for it as his own private property.[114] Therefore, even if a portion of these lands came to each of you—as is now dangled before your eyes, but is, in reality, being readied for others—still it would be more honorable to possess the whole, than for each of you to possess a portion separately. But since in fact nothing at all will be shared by you, and instead everything is being prepared for others and stolen from you, will you not resist this law with your utmost efforts, just as you would resist an armed enemy in defense of your lands?

[The Roman ancestors treated Corinth, Carthage, and Capua very differently when they defeated them. The first two they annihilated; but Capua they left to be an economic engine in Campania and a source of revenue for the commonwealth (87–97).]

[2.98] You, Publius Rullus, have preferred to follow in the criminal footsteps of Marcus Brutus, rather than the wise memorials of our ancestors.[115] You and those supporters of yours have plotted to plunder our established revenues, discover new ones (for your own benefit), and oppress Rome with a new city that will rival her dignity. You and those supporters of yours have plotted to bring beneath your law, command, and power cities, nations, provinces, free peoples, kings, in short, the entire world. You and those supporters of yours have plotted to drain all the money from the public treasury, extract anything that might be owed in taxes, extort as much as you can from kings, nations, and even our own generals. Yet everyone may still have to pay you money at the nod of your head. Then, after buying lands—some the hate-inducing lands of the Sullan occupiers; some desolate and diseased—from your supporters and even yourself, you might inflict them on the Roman people at whatever price you wish. Then you might occupy every municipality and colony in Italy with new settlers. Then you might establish new colonies wherever and with whomever you wish. [2.99] Then you might surround our entire commonwealth and oppress it with your soldiers, cities, and garrisons. Then you might rob Gnaeus Pompey, on whose protection and assistance our commonwealth has repeatedly relied against our fiercest enemies—and our most nefarious citizens—and you might deprive him of the sight of these men.[116] Then you will steal and hold in your power everything that can be tampered with through gold and silver, corrupted through the mob or voting fraud, shattered by force and violence. Meanwhile, you might fly through every nation and every kingdom with your absolute military authority, unchecked jurisdiction, and limitless funds. Then you might, if it were to your advantage, enter Pompey's camp and sell it out from under him! And meanwhile you might stand for magistracies, unhindered by any laws, without any fear of the courts, without any risk. Then no one will be able to lead you before the Roman people, or summon you before any court, or compel you to attend the senate, and no consul will be able to control you, nor a tribune of the plebs restrain you.

[2.100] I am not surprised that you, given your folly and immoderation, desired these powers. But I am amazed that you hoped to obtain them while I am consul. For every consul must protect the commonwealth with his utmost care and diligence. And this is especially important for those who have been elected consul not in the cradle but in the campus.[117] None of my ancestors cosigned on my behalf to the Roman people. Credit has been given to me. You ought to seek from me what I owe. When I was a candidate for the consulship no ancestor from my family recommended me to you. Just so, now, if I have committed a mistake, there are now ancestral images which will beseech you on my behalf. Therefore, for as long as my life remains, I will attempt to defend our commonwealth from the crimes and plots of those wicked men. And I promise this to you, my fellow-citizens, in good faith: you have entrusted your commonwealth to a vigilant man, not a timid one, to an active man, not a lazy one. Am I a consul who fears a public assembly . . . ?

[Cicero concludes by saying that, as consul, he has nothing to fear from the people and he will do everything in his power to protect them from unscrupulous men who will disturb the peace in order to acquire wealth for themselves. He reminds them that "there is nothing so 'popular' as that which I, the consul of the people, am this year bringing to you, namely, peace, quiet, and tranquility" (101–3).]

Appian of Alexandria, *Civil Wars* 1.7–13, 54

Appian of Alexandria (b. late first century CE) moved to Rome, where he composed a twenty-four-book Roman history, of which just less than half survives. For an ancient historian, Appian was unusually interested in economic matters; as a result, his history provides a unique window into the necessity and challenge of land and debt reform in Republican Rome.

In the first excerpt, Appian recounts the first attempt at land reform by Tiberius Gracchus in 133–132 BCE. Although Gracchus passed his legislation, it led to his assassination. Tiberius had been motivated primarily by how the collapse in the number of small farmers was reducing Roman military manpower. This problem was solved by the Marian reforms a generation later; but the account of Tiberius's efforts remains valuable for the light it sheds on the connection between farming and citizenship, as well as the risks of reform from the Roman perspective.

[1.7] The Romans, as they conquered Italy region by region, used to confiscate a part of the conquered territory on which they either built towns or enrolled Roman colonists to settle in preexisting towns. These settlements served in place of garrisons. The Romans immediately distributed to these colonists, by sale or lease, the cultivated part of the land acquired in each war. But, since they did not have time to assign land that had become unworked because of the war (this was generally the greater part of the region), they declared that, in the meantime, those who were willing to work it might do so in return for a tax on their annual harvest: 10 percent of the grain and 5 percent of the fruit. A tax was also imposed on livestock, both cattle and smaller animals. They did this to encourage the proliferation of the population in Italy, which the Romans considered the most hardworking race in the world, with the intention that they might enjoy many allies at home.

But the very opposite happened: for the rich gained possession of the greater part of the undistributed lands and, being emboldened by the passage of time, they came to believe that they would never lose title to this property. Then they absorbed adjacent plots and their poor neighbors' allotments, partly by persuading them to sell and partly by force. Thus, the wealthy came to cultivate vast tracts of land instead of single estates, using slaves as laborers and herdsmen, since free laborers might be drafted away from their farms into the army. At the same time, owning slaves brought the landowners immense profit, because the slaves had so many offspring, who continued to increase because they were exempt from military service. Thus, certain powerful men became extraordinarily rich and the number of slaves multiplied throughout Italy, all while the Italian people dwindled in numbers and strength, worn down by poverty, taxes, and military service. Even if they enjoyed any rest from these evils, the Italians could only pass their time in idleness, since the land was owned by the rich, who employed slaves instead of freemen as their farmhands.

[1.8] Because of this the Roman people grew concerned that their Italian allies might no longer be able to supply sufficient quantities of soldiers and that Roman authority itself might be challenged by the immense number of slaves. Nevertheless, they failed to formulate any plausible reform, for the situation was not simple nor did it seem just to deprive men of property that they had held for such a long duration of time, including trees they had planted, buildings they had erected, and other improvements they had made. But at last and with reluctance, the tribunes carried a law that no one should hold more than 500 acres of this public land or pasture on it more than 100 cattle or 500 smaller livestock.[118] The law also required a certain number of freemen be employed on the farms, who would observe and report what happened there. After passing this law, the Romans took an oath that they would obey the law and fixed penalties for breaking it.

The Romans had assumed that the remaining land would immediately be divided into small parcels and distributed to the poor. But no one showed any respect to the law or their oaths. Even those few who pretended to respect the law and the oath fraudulently transferred their lands to their relatives. [1.9] The majority, however, disregarded the law and their oaths entirely. At last, the tribune Tiberius Sempronius Gracchus, a nobleman known to all for his love of public glory and a most persuasive speaker, delivered an eloquent oration concerning the state of the Italians. He lamented that a people so distinguished in war and related by blood to the Romans were dwindling little by little into abject poverty and depopulation without any hope of salvation. He denounced the mass of slaves, who could not fight in the army and were never faithful to their masters. He pointed to the recent disaster that slaves had inflicted on their masters in Sicily, where the demands of increased agricultural productivity had led to a great increase in the number of slaves. Tiberius recalled the war the Romans had waged against them, which was neither easy nor short, but drawn-out and full of the reversals and dangers of fortune.[119] After he finished his speech, he again proposed the law that would forbid anyone from holding more than the 500 acres of the public land. But he added this provision to the former law: each son of the landowners might also hold one-half of that amount and the remaining land should then be distributed among the poor by three elected commissioners, who would be elected annually.

[1.10] This proposal greatly upset the wealthy because the land commissioners could prevent them from disregarding the law as they had done before, nor could they just buy back the land that was allotted to the poor, since Gracchus had foreseen this maneuver and banned the resale of the distributed property. So the wealthy huddled together and took turns complaining to the poor that their estates, vineyards, and buildings had been held by them for a very long time. Some asked whether, in addition to the land, they would lose the money that they had paid when they purchased it from their neighbors. Others said that the graves of their ancestors were on these lands, which had been allotted to them in the division of their fathers' estates. Others said that they had spent their wives' dowries on these estates,

or that the land had been given to their own daughters as a dowry. Moneylenders could show loans made with these lands as collateral. In short, the proposal caused great commotion and indignation.

From the other side arose the complaints of the poor. They were being reduced from prosperity to extreme poverty and then to childlessness because they were unable to afford to raise children. They listed the military campaigns in which they served— often campaigns that had acquired that very land. They were angry that they were being robbed of their fair share of the common property. At the same time, they criticized the wealthy for making use of slaves— who were always faithless and hostile and for those reasons not subject to military service—instead of freemen, citizens, and soldiers.

While these factions were thus complaining and accusing each other, large groups of colonists, inhabitants from free towns and those who, because they had some other interest in the lands, were apprehensive about the reform, surged into Rome and took sides with one faction or the other. Emboldened by their swelling numbers and exasperated against each other, they touched off many civil disturbances while waiting to vote on the new law. Some intended to prevent its enactment by any means necessary; others prepared to enact it whatever the cost. In addition to individual interest, a spirit of rivalry spurred both sides in their preparations against each other as the day of the vote approached.

[1.11] For Gracchus, the intent of this law was not welfare but manpower. Inspired by the great utility of his proposed program and believing that nothing more advantageous or beneficial could happen for Italy, he dismissed the difficulties that were piling up around it. When the day of the vote arrived, he advanced many persuasive and detailed arguments in support of his law. Was it not just to distribute common property in common? Was a citizen not always worth more consideration than a slave? Wasn't a man who served in the army more useful than one who did not? Wasn't a man who participated in public affairs more devoted to the public interest?

Tiberius did not dwell long on these comparisons,

which he considered degrading, but quickly proceeded to review his hopes and fears for the country. He said that the Romans acquired most of their territory by military conquest and that they had hopes of conquering the rest of the habitable world. But now the entire issue was at stake: Would they gain the rest through a sufficient supply of manpower, or, because of their weaknesses and jealousies, would their enemies strip away what they now possessed? He exaggerated the glory and riches of the former outcome and the dangers and fears of the latter. Then he called on the wealthy to consider giving their lands as a gift so that the poor might rear children. They should not, he said, overlook more important matters while bickering about trivial ones, especially since they would be amply compensated for any effort they had expended and they would receive undisputed, perpetual title to 500 acres of highly productive land at no expense and another 250 acres for each son, for those who had sons. After delivering a long speech in this manner, stirring the poor, as well as all who were moved by reason rather than by the desire for gain, he ordered the clerk to read the proposed law.

When a tribune, Marcus Octavius, vetoed the legislation, Gracchus reintroduced it and barred Octavius from attending. On the verge of a riot, Gracchus brought his proposal to the senate but was denounced. When Gracchus again introduced the bill to the people, he first had them take the unprecedent step of voting to remove Octavius from the tribunate.

[1.12] When the first tribe voted to remove Octavius from the tribunate, Gracchus turned to him and begged him to put aside his veto. As Octavius would not yield, he took the votes of the other tribes. There were thirty-five tribes at that time. The seventeen that voted first vehemently supported the motion. If the eighteenth should do the same it would make a majority. Again Gracchus, before the people, urgently begged Octavius, who found himself in extreme danger, not to block a work that was divinely sanctioned and extremely beneficial for all Italy and not to frustrate the express will of the people. As tribune, Octavius should yield when the people expressed their strong desire and not risk losing his office by public

condemnation. After saying this, Tiberius called on the gods to witness that he did not willingly strip his colleague of his rights. As Octavius still refused to yield, Tiberius resumed the vote. Octavius was reduced to a private citizen and slipped away unnoticed. Quintus Mummius was elected tribune in his place and the agrarian law was passed.

[1.13] The first land commissioners appointed to distribute the land were Gracchus himself, as proposer of the law, his brother of the same name, and his father-in-law, Appius Claudius. The people were afraid that the law would not be enacted unless Gracchus and his family led the way. Gracchus assumed a swagger after the passage of the law and was escorted home by the crowd as though he were the founder not of a single city or people but of all the peoples of Italy. After this, the victors returned to the fields from which they had come to attend to their business. But the defeated took their loss badly and remained in the city, spreading word that, as soon as Gracchus was a private citizen, he would regret that he had used force against the sacred and inviolable office of tribune and had sown in Italy the seeds of so much future strife.

[This second excerpt recounts Asellio's attempted debt reform and his assassination in 89 BCE.]

[1.54] During the same period, unrest broke out in the city between debtors and lenders. The lenders were attempting to extract the money due to them with interest, although an ancient law explicitly forbade lending on interest and imposed a fine upon any one who did so. It seems that the ancient Romans, like the Greeks, shunned the taking of interest on loans as something that was mercenary and hard on the poor and led to disputes and hostility. The Persians forbade all borrowing as contributing to deceit and lying for the same reason. But, since long-established custom authorized the practice of charging interest, the lenders demanded it, according to custom. The debtors, on the other hand, put off their payments, as was typical during wars and civil unrest. Some of the debtors even threatened to sue and exact a fine from the interest-takers.

The praetor Asellio, in whose jurisdiction these matters fell, tried but failed to reconcile these groups by persuasion and so allowed them to take each other to court, thus bringing before the juries the impasse caused by a conflict in the law. But the lenders, outraged that an obsolete law was being revived, murdered the praetor. It happened like this. Asellio was sacrificing to the Dioscuri in the Forum. A crowd stood around him, as was typical for such a ceremony. At first, when a single stone was thrown at him, he dropped the libation-bowl and ran toward the Temple of Vesta. But the crowd outran him and prevented him from reaching the temple. Asellio fled into a tavern. When they found him, they cut his throat. Many of his pursuers, thinking that he had taken refuge with the Vestal Virgins, ran in there, although the law forbade men to enter. So it was that Asellio, while serving as praetor and pouring a libation and wearing the gilded vestments for sacred sacrifice, was murdered at eight in the morning among the shrines of the Forum. The senate offered rewards to anyone who could give testimony leading to the conviction of the murders of Asellio—money to any free citizen, freedom to any slave, immunity to any accomplice—but nobody provided any information. The moneylenders covered up everything.

Livy, *From the Founding of the City* 6.14, 6.31–32, 42.5

Livy composed a massive 142-book history of Rome from its founding up to his own day under the first emperor, Augustus. Only a portion survives, but this contains many references to Roman attempts to manage repeated debt crises.

The first excerpt describes a confrontation in 385 BCE between the dictator Aulus Cornelius Cossus and Marcus Manlius Capitolinus, a wealthy war hero who took up the cause of the indebted. According to Livy, Manlius was the first Roman aristocrat to act like a "populist" (popularis).

[6.14] The dictator held his army in camp, since he had no doubt that the senators would declare war against these peoples.[120] But a greater trouble emerged in Rome, compelling the senators to recall him, since sedition was growing day by day and its leader made the situation even more serious. For at this point not only the speeches made by Marcus Manlius but also his actions, which seemed designed to curry the favor of the people on their face, aimed in fact at revolution.

A centurion, well-respected for his military service, had been condemned for debt. When Manlius saw this man being led away, he burst into the Forum with a band of followers and grabbed hold of the centurion. Manlius denounced the arrogance of the senators, the cruelty of the moneylenders, and the miseries suffered by the common people, as well as the virtues and misfortune of the centurion. "Then in truth," Manlius said, "I protected the citadel and the Capitoline with my own right hand in vain, if I now see my fellow citizen and brother-in-arms led away in chains to slavery as though he had been captured by the victorious Gauls." Then, before the assembled people, Manlius paid off the centurion's debt to his creditor and through the ceremony of "the scales and bronze" he freed the debtor, who called upon the gods and men to thank Manlius as his liberator and the true father of the Roman plebs.[121] The centurion was at once welcomed by the agitated crowd and he added to their agitation when he showed them the scars he had received against the Veians and Gauls and in Rome's other battles, saying, "While I was serving as a soldier and restoring my ruined home, I paid many times more than my principal in interest, but because the interest overwhelmed the principal, I found myself buried by debt. That I now see the light of day and the faces of my fellow citizens is the work of Marcus Manlius. His support for me has been like that of a parent for a child. To him I pledge whatever power remains in my body, my life, and my blood. Whatever justice bound me to my country and the gods of my household and the state, now binds me to this man alone." The plebs, excited by the centurion's speech, were already aligned with Manlius. Then something else happened that seemed even more calculated to throw the state into revolution: Manlius declared he would auction off an estate in the region of Veii that was the main part of his fortune, saying, "May I not allow any of you, Roman citizens, to be indicted and condemned to slavery as long as a piece of my property remains." Indeed, this so inflamed their spirits that they appeared they would follow their champion of liberty in any action, right or wrong.

In addition, Manlius delivered speeches in his house, as though in a public assembly, that were full of recriminations against the senators. He hurled accusations with little consideration for their truth or falsehood, saying that the senators were hiding the treasure of the Gallic gold and that they were no longer content to lay claim to public land unless they could also embezzle public funds, funds that, if they were distributed openly, would be able to settle the debts of the plebs. Once this hope was held out to them, they thought it a shameful crime that the gold to ransom their city from the Gauls had been raised through general taxation, but when it was captured from their enemies it became the plunder of the few. They insisted, therefore, in discovering where the stolen treasury had been concealed; but Manlius kept putting them off, declaring that he would reveal it at a time of his choosing. Meanwhile this question

consumed everyone's attention to the exclusion of all other matters. It was evident that there would be boundless loyalty (*fides*) if the accusation proved true—and limitless anger if it proved false.[122]

[In this excerpt, military necessity forces a modification of debt payments in 378 BCE.]

[6.31] The start of the new year blazed with violent political disturbances. . . . Debt was the source and cause of the trouble. Spurius Servilius Priscus and Quintus Cloelius Siculus had been appointed censors to investigate the situation, but they were prevented from doing so by the outbreak of war. At first frightened messengers and the folks fleeing from their fields reported that the army of the Volscians had entered Roman territory and was devastating the countryside. Despite this panic, the external threat hardly suppressed the civil strife. On the contrary the tribunes pressed even more vehemently to obstruct the levy of new troops until the senate agreed to their terms, namely that until the completion of the war, no one should have to pay a war-tax or be sued for debt.

[The Romans rout the Volscians and ravage Volscian territory.]

[6.32] The debtors had received a short space to catch their breath, but as soon as hostilities were settled, the courts were as crowded as ever, and not only did they have little hope of paying off their old debts, but new debt had been incurred because a war-tax had been imposed to repair the city wall with hewn-stone, as contracted by the censors. The plebs were compelled to submit to this new burden, since there was no levy that their tribunes could obstruct.

[In this excerpt Romans mediate a debt crisis in Asia.]

[42.5] It was not only the Aetolians who were in a state of civil unrest because of the crushing burden of debt. The Thessalians, too, were in the same state and the trouble had spread, as though by contact with the plague, to Perrhaebia.[123] When the news arrived that the Thessalians had taken up arms, the senate at once sent Appius Claudius to investigate and manage the situation. Claudius chastened the leaders on both sides. Since the debt had grown more serious because of illegal interest, he reduced the amount with the consent of most of the creditors who had created the burden in the first place. He then arranged that the sum of the legal debt should be paid off by ten annual installments. He settled the situation in Perrhaebia in the same way.

Cicero, *On Duties* 2.80–84

In the final years of his life, Cicero was isolated from political power and turned his energies to philosophy, composing a stunning array of philosophical treatises. His final work, On Duties *(43 BCE), is among the most important and influential works on ethics in the western tradition. It was the second book printed on the Gutenberg press, after the Bible. It is written in the form of a letter to his son who was studying in Athens.*

In this excerpt, he explains why the virtuous man must avoid falling into debt.

[2.80] What can we say about our own Gracchi, sons of the illustrious Tiberius Gracchus and grandsons of Africanus? Were they not destroyed by political disputes over their agrarian laws?

[2.81] Aratus of Sicyon, on the other hand, is justly praised.[124] For fifty years his community had been controlled by tyrants. Arriving from Argos, he entered Sicyon in secret and seized control of it by quickly attacking the tyrant Nicocles. He recalled 600 exiles, who had been the wealthiest men in the city, and so by his arrival he liberated his country. But he discovered great difficulties in the matter of property and its occupancy. He considered it most unjust that those whom he himself had restored to the city should be impoverished because others now occupied their property; conversely, he thought it completely unfair to displace those who had occupied that same property for fifty years, since during that long period of time, much of that property was acquired through innocent means, many by inheritance, many by purchase, and many by dowry. He therefore judged that it would not be appropriate to deprive those who

held the property or to let them keep it without making sufficient restitution to its former owners. And so, when he had decided that he needed funds to remedy the situation, he announced that he wished to travel to Alexandria and ordered that the matters should stay as they were until his return. He quickly arrived at the halls of Ptolemy, his friend, who was then ruling as the second king of that dynasty.[125]

Aratus explained to Ptolemy that he wished to liberate his country and presented his case to him, and since he was such a prominent man, he easily secured the assistance of a great sum of money from the wealthy king. When Aratus brought these funds to Sicyon, he summoned fifteen leaders of the city to deliberate with him. With these men he investigated the cases of those who were holding property that belonged to another and those who had lost their property. By assessing the value of the properties, he brought it to pass that some of those who held the property preferred to surrender the property for cash, while others, who had lost property, reckoned that it was more convenient to take a fair payment than to try to recover what had once been theirs. Thus, it was brought to pass that public concord was restored and all withdrew without complaint.

[2.83] What a great man Aratus was! He would have been worthy of being born in our own commonwealth! Indeed, this is the just way to act with one's fellow citizens, not, as we have already twice seen, by setting up that cruel spear in the Forum and subjecting the property of the citizenry to be summoned to the auctioneer.[126] But that Greek, because he was a man of extraordinary wisdom, thought that he should consider all the citizens. For this is the highest consideration and wisdom in a good citizen: not to tear asunder the common interests of the citizenry but to unite them all through impartial fairness. "Let them live in another's house rent-free!" Why is that? So that, after I have bought, built, maintained, and spent my resources on a house, you might enjoy what is mine without my consent? [2.84] How is this any different than to rob one man of his own possessions and give what doesn't belong to him to another man? What is the logic of debt cancellation (*tabulae novae*) except that you buy a farm with my money and then you have the farm and I don't have my money?

We must, therefore, see to it that there should be no debt of the sort that risks harm to the commonwealth. There are many ways by which this situation can be avoided. But if such debt has been incurred, the debtors should not profit while the wealthy lose their property. For there is no matter more important to maintaining the commonwealth than credit (*fides*), and no credit is possible unless the repayment of debt is mandatory. Never was the repayment of debt questioned more vehemently than during my consulship. Men of every sort and rank attempted to force this program through arms and armies. But I resisted all their efforts so effectively that this evil was utterly expelled from the commonwealth. Indebtedness was never greater and yet was never repaid more easily or fully. For, after I removed any hope of defrauding the creditor, repayment followed of necessity. ▨

Plutarch, *Why We Ought Not Borrow*

Plutarch (46–ca. 119 CE) is best known for his Parallel Lives, *which compared the biographies of forty-eight notable Greeks and Romans. But he also composed nearly eighty essays, collectively known as the* Moralia, *on a range of serious philosophical and lighthearted topics such as "Can Virtue Be Taught?," "How to Praise Oneself," "How Hearing Works," "How to Profit from Your Enemies," "What Is the Face in the Moon?," and "Are Land or Sea Animals More Clever?". Among the* Moralia *is this essay warning of the dangers of debt and why it should be avoided.*

[1] Plato, in his *Laws*, forbids people from taking water from a neighbor's land unless they have first dug a well on their own land down to the "potter's clay," as it is called, and determined that their land will not produce flowing water.[127] For this "potter's clay," which is oily and firm, retains groundwater beneath it. But, Plato says, those who cannot procure water on their own land can have a share of that on their neighbor's land, for the law gives relief to those in need. Shouldn't there also, then, be a similar law about money, namely that people should not borrow from others—or resort to other people's wells—unless they have first examined their domestic resources and gathered together what would be useful and necessary, like a large amount of water from little drips? But now, luxury, weakness, and overindulgence cause people to make no use of their own possessions but to take from others at a high rate of interest, though they have no need of doing so. I can give you clear evidence that this is so: loans are not made to people in need but to those who wish to acquire some luxury for themselves. A man produces witnesses and collateral to pledge that he deserves credit since he has property. But, since he has property, he ought not borrow!

[2] Why do you wait on a banker or broker? "Borrow from your own table!" You already have drinking-cups, silver plates, and small bowls.[128] You can pawn these to satisfy your needs. Beautiful Aulis or Tenedos can still decorate your table with pottery that is cleaner than silverware. And this pottery lacks the potent, pungent smell of interest, which day by day, like rust, tarnishes the surface of your indulgence. Your pot won't remind you of the first of the month, that holiest day coinciding with the new moon, which the moneylenders have made shunned and reviled.[129] Not even the god of property can save those who pledge their belongings as collateral instead of selling them. Men like this are ashamed to sell but not ashamed to pay interest on their belongings. The ornaments of the goddess Athena weighed forty talents of pure gold and the famed Pericles ordered that they should be removable, "so that," he said, "we can use it for wartime expenses and then pay back an equal amount."[130] Let us do likewise, since we are besieged by our needs and reject the garrison of our enemy, the moneylender, or allow our property to be sold into slavery. Instead, let us preserve our liberty by removing everything that is useless—from our table, our bed, our carriage, our

entire mode of life—with the intention of paying it back when and if we again find ourselves in good fortune.

[3] The Roman women fashioned their jewelry into a golden bowl that they sent as an offering to the Pythian Apollo in Delphi.[131] The women of Carthage shaved their heads and gave their hair to make ropes for the catapults and other military engines that would defend their native city.[132] But we are ashamed to be independent and enslave ourselves by mortgages and other debts. Instead, we should restrict ourselves to the bare essentials. From the proceeds we earn from the sale of useless luxuries we can build a sanctuary of Liberty for ourselves, our children, and our spouses.

The goddess Artemis at Ephesus protects debtors when they seek refuge in her sanctuary, and within her shrine debtors are safe from their debts. But another refuge is open everywhere to responsible men: the sheltering, inviolable sanctuary of frugality, which offers the pleasant, honorable span of bountiful leisure. Just as when, during the Persian Wars, the Pythian oracle told the Athenians that the god offered them a wooden wall and the Athenians therefore abandoned their lands, their city, their belongings, and their houses and retreated onto their ships for the sake of freedom, so god offers all of us a wooden table, a ceramic dish, and a coarse cloak, whenever we wish to live as free men.[133]

Don't wait for fancy horses or chariots decorated with horn or inlaid with silver. Speedy interest will outstrip and outpace these. Instead hop onto whatever donkey or nag happens by. Just flee from your tyrannical enemy, the moneylender! Unlike the Persian, the moneylender won't demand earth and water but attacks your freedom and brings suit against your dignity.[134] If you fail to pay him, he harasses you. If you have money, he defers payment. If you sell, he lowers the price. If you won't sell, he forces you to do so. If you sue, he takes you to court. If you swear your oath, he makes you fulfill it. If you go to his house, he shuts the door in your face. If you stay home, he stands there and keeps knocking at your door.

[4] Did Solon really help the Athenians when he forbade them from giving themselves as collateral for debt?[135] Indeed, all debtors are enslaved to the men who ruin their lives—or rather not to men (would that be so bad?) but to arrogant, barbarous, savage slaves, like those who Plato says stand in hell, the fiery tormentors and executioners of those who have transgressed.[136]

These moneylenders make the public square a place of the damned for miserable debtors, devouring them like vultures or flaying them, "diving into their entrails." Or they loom above them and inflict the tortures of Tantalus by preventing them from tasting the produce that they themselves have harvested.[137] Just as Darius sent Datis and Artaphernes against Athens bearing chains and fetters for their captives, these moneylenders bring their fetters—jars full of signatures and promissory notes—as they march against and through the cities of Greece.[138] They don't come like Triptolemus, sowing grain for our advantage.[139] Instead they plant the roots of debt, which require much toil and much interest and are difficult to escape and which, as they sprout and grow, oppress and strangle the cities. Rabbits are said simultaneously to give birth to one litter, suckle another, and conceive a third. But loans made by these barbarous rogues birth interest before conception.[140] For, when they give a loan, they at once demand payment. They pick up their money as they lay down on the table. They lend again what they receive with interest.

[5] There is a saying among the Messenians: "Before that famous Pylos, there was Pylos and another Pylos too."[141]

But concerning moneylenders we might say: "Before the interest, there was interest and yet more interest."

Moneylenders mock the natural philosophers that say that "nothing arises out of nothing." For their interest arises out of something that lacks being or existence. Now moneylenders consider it disgraceful to be a tax-collector, which the law allows. Yet the moneylenders lend money contrary to law and then collect taxes from their debtors—or rather, truth be told, their lending cheats their debtors, since anyone who receives less than face value for his note has been cheated. This is why the Persians regard lying as the second worst form of wrongdoing but consider being in debt as the first.[142] For, while debtors often lie, moneylenders lie more than debtors! They cook their books, jotting down that they lent so much to whoever, while in reality they loaned less. It is greed, not want or need, that causes the moneylenders to lie, insatiable greed, which brings them neither pleasure nor profit but brings ruin to those whom they wrong. For when they seize a farm from a debtor, they do not cultivate its fields; they don't live in the houses from which they evict the owner, nor do they eat at their tables or wear their clothes. They ruin someone and then hunt another, using the first as bait.

For their savagery spreads like fire, growing by the destruction and consumption of whoever falls into it, devouring one after another. But the moneylender who fans and feeds this conflagration that ruins so many men gains nothing, except that, from time to time, he can read his ledgers to learn how many men he has ruined, how many he has driven from their homes, and where his silver, rolling in and piling up, has made a profit.

[6] But know this: I don't say these things because I have declared war against the moneylenders: "They never have harassed my cattle, never made off with my horses."[143]

But I wish to show those who are eager to become borrowers just how much shame and subservience borrowing causes and that it is an act of boundless folly and weakness. Do you have money? Then don't borrow, since you are not in need. Do you not have money? Then don't borrow, since you will not be able to repay your loan. Let's examine each of these alternatives individually. Cato, when some old man was misbehaving, once said, "Man, when old age already has so many evils, why do you add the shame of wickedness?"

Therefore, if you are in poverty, which already has so many evils, don't pile on complications from borrowing and debt; don't strip poverty of the only ad-vantage it possesses over wealth: freedom from care. Don't make mockery of the proverb, "I can't carry the goat; let me try the ox."

If you cannot carry the burden of poverty, will you put the moneylender on your back? This is a heavy load for even the wealthy to bear. "How, then, will I live?" Are you really asking this, when you have hands, when you have feet, when you have a voice, when you are a man who can love and be loved, who can do favors and receive them with grace?

Teach the ABCs. Escort children to school. Be a doorkeeper. Work as a sailor or a boatman. Are any of these honest professions more disgraceful or un-pleasant than hearing "pay up"?

[7] Rutilius, a well-known Roman, once approached the philosopher Musonius and said, "O Musonius, Zeus the Savior, whom you imitate and emulate, doesn't borrow." But Musonius smiled and replied, "Nor does he lend." For Rutilius, who was a money-lender, was criticizing Musonius for borrowing. This is an example of the madness of the Stoics. Why dredge up Zeus the Savior when you can refer to things that appear before you? Swallows don't borrow; ants don't borrow. And nature has bestowed on these neither hands, nor reason, nor art. But man-kind uses its exceptional intellect and ingenuity to support horses, hounds, partridges, rabbits, and jackdaws. Why, then, despise yourself, thinking that you are less persuasive than a jackdaw, less articulate than a partridge, less noble than a hound? Do you think that you can't obtain help from someone by waiting on him, entertaining him, protecting him, or fighting for him? Don't you see how many oppor-tunities exist on land and on the sea? As Crates says, "Indeed, I have observed Miccylus carding wool and his wife carding wool at his side, fleeing famine through their 'terrible rivalry.'"[144]

King Antigonus once met Cleanthes in Athens, after not seeing him for a long time and asked, "Still grinding, Cleanthes?"[145] "Oh yes, my king," he an-swered, "I do this so that I don't abandon the lessons of Zeno's philosophy."[146] How great was the spirit of that man, who came from the mill and the kneading-trough and, using the same hand that had ground flour and baked bread, wrote about the gods, the moon, the stars, and the sun! But we consider such labor slavish. And so, in order to be "free," we borrow and fawn over men who wear away households. We act as their bodyguards, dine them, give them presents and taxes, not because of poverty (for no one lends to poor men!) but because of our need for luxury. If we were just satisfied with life's necessities, there would be no race of moneylenders any more than there are centaurs or gorgons! But luxury produced moneylenders just as it did goldsmiths, silversmiths, perfumers, and dyers of bright colors. We don't go into debt for bread or wine but for estates, slaves, mules, dining-rooms, and tables and because we stage shows in cities with abandon, vying with one another in fruitless, thankless rivalries. But once a man is ensnared, he remains in debt all his life, exchanging, like a bridled horse, one rider for the next. There can be no escape to their former pastures and meadows. Instead, they wander about, like the spirits described by Empedocles, who have been expelled by the gods and driven from heaven:

> "The might of the ether drove them into the
>   ocean's waves.
> Then the sea vomits them forth onto the earth's
>   hard ground.
> But earth ejects them into the ray of the tireless
>   sun,
> who throws them back into the swirling ether."[147]

And so "one after another takes over" the one who's in debt: first a Corinthian usurer or broker, then one from Patrae, then an Athenian, until, beset on all sides by all of his creditors, he is dissolved and chopped up to pay off the interest. For just as a man who has fallen into the muck must either get up or stay where he is, but whoever rolls over only covers his water-logged person with yet more dirt; so, by transferring and exchanging loans, by plastering themselves all over with additional interest, they burden themselves more and more. These men are like a patient stricken with cholera who refuses treatment and vomits up his prescriptions and so collects more and more disease. Just so borrowers who don't wish to be purged and always, through every time of the year, toss up the interest, despite their pain and convulsions, while immediately another interest payment piles up and oppresses them, leading to another attack of nausea and migraines. They ought to do this: pay off their debts and so become healthy and free.

[8] At this point I address only those who are better off and more comfortable, men who say, "Should I, then, lack slaves, a hearth, a home?" Imagine if a sick man, bloated with dropsy, said to his physician, "Should I, then, become thin and empty?" Why, yes! If you can make yourself healthy! And so, yes, you should do without slaves, so that you may not become a slave. You should do without property, so that you may not become another's property.

Remember the tale of the vultures. One vulture had an acute attack of nausea and said he was vomiting out his bowels, but another vulture said, "Why's that so terrible? You're not vomiting out your own bowels but those from the corpse we tore apart a little while ago." In the same way, a debtor sells not his own land nor his own house but those belonging to his creditor, whom by law he has made their owner.

"No! By Zeus," he says, "my father left me this field." True. Your father also left you your freedom and your dignity, which you ought to value more. Your parent also gave you your foot and your hand, but when it begins to rot, you pay to cut it off. Calypso clothed Odysseus in one of her own garments, "putting fragrant clothing upon him," a gift and a token of her love that smelled of her divinity.[148] But when Odysseus capsized and was drowning in the waves and could hardly stay afloat, since the garment had become waterlogged and heavy, he stripped it off and tossed it away and with a simple cloth bound over his naked breast, "he swam along the shore, looking toward land."[149]

And when he reached shore safely, he didn't lack clothing or food. Well, then, doesn't a storm break over debtors when the lender approaches over and over again to say "pay up"?

"Having spoken thus, he gathered the clouds and

stirred up great waves. The East and South and West Winds raged furiously."[150]

Just so, interest piles on interest and the debtor, drowning, continues to grip them as they drag him down. He cannot swim away or escape. He sinks down into the depths, vanishing along with any friends who vouched for him.

Crates the Theban abandoned an estate valued at eight talents.[151] He wasn't even being harassed for payment. He didn't even owe anything! But he detested managing his property, with its attendant cares and distractions. So, he grabbed a cloak and a leather sack and fled into philosophy and poverty. Anaxagoras also allowed his land to become a pasture for sheep.[152] But why mention these men when there's Philoxenus the musician?[153] He had been allotted lands in a colony in Sicily that guaranteed him a livelihood and a wealthy household. But when he saw how common were luxury, indulgence in pleasure, and lack of culture in the colony, he said, "By the gods! These good things shall not make me lose myself. Instead, I shall lose them." And so, he abandoned his allotment to others and he sailed away. But people in debt are content to be harassed, to pay tribute, to be enslaved and cheated. They are like Phineus—they endure, only to feed the winged Harpies that steal their food and devour it. They buy their grain, not in the proper season, but before it is harvested. They purchase the oil before the olives have been harvested.[154] The borrower will say, "I have wine at a predetermined price," and he gives a promissory note for the wine's value—but the grape cluster still clings to the vine and awaits the rising of Arcturus.[155] ▩

Juvenal, *Satire* 3 (Selections)

In most literary genres, Romans consciously built on brilliant prior works by Greek authors. But the Romans claimed that verse satire was, according to the rhetorician Quintilian, "entirely ours." Key to the genre was a moralizing narrator who observed the foibles and errors of his society and exposed them to scrutiny and mockery. Juvenal was a prolific satirist and composed sixteen satires in the late first to early second centuries CE.

In this excerpt from Satire *3 (beginning on the next page), the satirist complains about the terrible living conditions that afflict the nonelite inhabitants of the city of Rome. Although Juvenal wrote more than 100 years after the crisis of Catiline, when the population of the city had grown considerably, his vivid (if exaggerated) portrait of the city offers a glimpse of life in the ancient metropolis. The poem begins by revealing that one of the poet's friends, Umbricius, plans to flee the city for more peaceful living down south.*

At this point Umbricius spoke: "There's no room in Rome
for honest skills and no reward for hard work.
My wealth is less today than yesterday and tomorrow
will erode still more. That's why I've decided
to move to where Daedalus took off his tired wings. . . .[156]   25
I'll say goodbye to my homeland. Let rich Arturius   30
and Catulus live in Rome. Let men who turn black white remain,[157]
men who find it easy to win contracts for temples, rivers,
harbors, waterworks, and transporting corpses to the pyre,
who offer themselves for sale at auction,
and those men who once tooted horns—they once played during rural
gladiatorial games, known through all the towns   35
for their puffed-out cheeks; but now they stage games themselves,
killing to please when the mob's downward thumb demands it . . .
then they return to their public restroom contracts![158]
Fortune raises these men up to the heights
from the lowest sewer, whenever she needs a laugh.   40
What can I do in Rome? I don't know how to lie or praise
a bad book or beg a copy. Astrology?
I'm ignorant. Prophesy the death of someone's father
I can't and won't. I've never inspected
the entrails of frogs. To smuggle to a cheating wife what her   45
lover sends . . . others know how to do that. No thief will ever
have me as their partner. And so, I'm never in the in-crowd. . . .
. . . May the sands of wealthy Tagus mean   55
less to you, despite all its gold washed down to the sea,[159]
than lost sleep and taking (and losing) bribes with a sad face,
and thus, always fearing your powerful "friends."
[Umbricius complains at length about the success of foreigners
    in the city, especially Greeks.]
Besides, not to flatter ourselves, but what office or service is left
for a poor man here? Even if he risks donning his toga, running
around before dawn, he finds the praetor rushing his lictor
to make the morning greeting of wealthy, childless widows,
like Albina or Modia, before his colleague gets there first.   130
In Rome a freeborn son escorts a rich man's slave:
that slave can pay out as much as a military tribune's
salary to Roman Calvina or Catiena, just to flop
around on top of her once or twice. Meanwhile you,
liking the look of some whore's dress, stutter
about helping "Snow White" descend from her high seat.[160]
Produce a witness in Rome as holy as the man
who escorted the goddess from Mount Ida;[161]
let Numa come forward, or Caecilius Metellus,

who rescued nervous Minerva's statue from the temple.[162]
His character would be the very last thing questioned! The first? His net-worth.   140
"How many slaves does he support? How many acres of farmland does he have?
How many and lavish are his banquets, how many courses served?"
The number of coins a man keeps in his treasure chest—that's
the only credit he has. Though you swear by the altars of Roman   145
or Samothracian gods, it'll be thought that, since you're poor,
you'll just despise the divine lightning bolt, with the gods approving.[163]
And what about this? The same poor man provides the rich
with matter and cause for amusement: if his cloak's dirty and torn,
if his toga's weathered and stained, if one shoe gapes open where   150
the leather has cracked, or when more than one patch shows
where a tear has been stitched up with coarse new thread.
The hardest thing to bear about poverty's misfortune
is that it leaves you open to ridicule. . . .
What prospective son-in-law can pass the test, if his net-worth   160
is less, or can't carry the girl's luggage?[164] What pauper becomes an heir?
When do aediles vote them onto the board of assessors? Impoverished citizens
should all have assembled long ago and emigrated from Rome.
It's never easy to climb the ladder when meager means
block your talents, but at Rome the attempt is harder still: 165
lodgings are expensive and wretched; expensive, too, the bellies
of slaves; even a meagre supper is expensive. . . .
[The poor suffer under the expense of trying to keep up with wealthy
*   fashions in dining, at the theater, in clothing, etc.]*
It's a universal vice; in Rome we all live in pretentious poverty.
Why do I keep talking? Everything in Rome comes at a price.
What do you pay so you can say good morning to Cossus,
or that Veientus will give you a tight-lipped glance?   185
When this slave's beard is trimmed, or another's lock of hair is dedicated,[165]
the house is full of celebratory cakes—(that you'll have to pay for! "Take my money
and keep your yeast!" We clients must fork over
such taxes to supplement the savings of well-groomed slaves.
Who fears now, or ever did, that their house might collapse   190
in cool Praeneste, or among Volsinii's wooded hills,
or at simple Gabii or the sloping hills of Tibur?
We inhabit a Rome held up, mostly, by rickety
props—that's how the superintendents prevent buildings
from falling down. Once he's covered the chasm of some   200
ancient crack, he tells us to sleep tight—on the brink of ruin.
The place to live is far away, where there are no fires, no
nocturnal panics. Ucalegon is already calling for water,
shifting his things, and your third floor's already smoking.
But you don't know, since if the alarm was raised downstairs,   205

the last to burn will be the one a bare tile protects from
the rain, where gentle doves nest on their eggs.[166]
Cordus had a bed, too small for Procula, and six tiny
jugs to adorn his sideboard, and, underneath it,
a little Chiron, a centaur made of that very same "marble,"   210
and a box, ancient now, that holds his Greek books,
even as barbarous mice gnawed away at immortal poems.
Cordus had nothing, who'd disagree? Yet, that poor man
lost all the "nothing" he had! And the pinnacle
of his misery is this: naked and begging for scraps, no one   215
will give him food, or help, or a place to rest.
But if Assaracus's great mansion burns down. . . .
[Since the wealthy more than restore the fortunes of a fellow elite
     who suffers a loss, some will even burn down their own houses
     in hopes of improving their possessions.]
In Rome, many invalids die from insomnia, though their
fevered stomachs are sick because of undigested food. Where can you
lodge to have a good night's sleep? You have to be filthy rich to sleep   235
in Rome. That's the source of our sickness. The endless cart traffic
in narrow twisting streets, the driver swearing at his halted cattle
would deprive a Drusus of sleep, or the seals in the ocean.[167]
When duty calls, the crowd gives way as the rich man's litter
rushes by, right in their faces, in his huge Liburnian galley.[168]   240
On his way he reads, writes, sleeps inside.
(You know how a coach with windows shut makes you drowsy!)
Yet, he arrives first. As I hurry, the tide ahead blocks my way,
while huge massed ranks behind crush my kidneys:
this guy pokes me with his elbow; that one spins twirling a hard pole;   245
this guy smacks my head with a plank; that one with a cask.
My legs are caked in mud. Soon, I'm trampled by powerful feet
on every side. A soldier's hobnailed boot impales my toe. . . .
[Umbricius gives an extended description of an unstable portable
     kitchen perched on a wagon that threatens to crush passersby.]
And now ponder all the various other dangers at night.
It's a long way down for a tile from the highest roof when it falls   270
on your head! How often cracked and leaky pots plunge down
from a windowsill! What a crash when they strike the pavement, chipping
and cracking the pavement! You're considered careless and oblivious
to the sudden dangers that may strike you if you head out
without first making out your will! At night, there are as many opportunities
to die as there are open windows watching you pass.   276
So, as you set out, make a wish and a pathetic prayer that they'll
be content with emptying their chamber pots on you.
The drunken thug's annoyed if, by chance, there's no one for him

to fight. He spends the whole night grieving, like Achilles for   280
Patroclus, lying on his face and then turning onto his back again.[169]
He needs a brawl to get sleepy. But, however fired up he is with youth
and unmixed wine, he steps aside when a man's scarlet cloak
orders him to steer clear—and his long line of attendants,
with plenty of torches and bronze lamps. Yet he confronts me,   285
as I pass by, by the light of the moon or flickering candlelight,
whose wick I anxiously care for and protect.
Observe the preliminaries of this pathetic brawl, if you can call it a brawl,
when one beats and the other (me) takes the beating.
He stands in my way and he tells me to stop. I have to obey.   290
What can you do, when a madman has the upper hand and is stronger
than you as well? "Where've you been?" he shouts. "Whose sour wine
and beans swell your gut? Which shoemaker has been dining with you,
stuffing your face with boiled sheep's head, gorging on fresh spring onions?
Nothing to say? You'd better speak up fast, or I'll stomp you!   295
Tell me where you're staying: In what bawdy prayer house can I find you?"
If you try to say something, or try to retreat in silence, it's all the same:
he'll beat you regardless. Then, still enraged, he'll indict you
for assault! This is the poor man's liberty:
when he's beaten, smacked down by fists, he can beg and plead   300
to be allowed to make his way home while he still has a few teeth left.
And that's not all we need to fear! There's someone who'll rob you,
after the houses have been locked up, when the shops' shutters
have been chained shut and everywhere's silent.
Sometimes there's the homeless robber, ready to ply his blade: 305
whenever the Pontine Marsh, or the Gallinarian forest,
are temporarily rendered safe by an armed patrol, they all rush
here, heading for Rome as if to a game preserve.[170]
Is there a furnace or anvil somewhere not busy fashioning chains?
Most of our iron is hammered into chains. You should worry about   310
an imminent shortage of ploughshares, a lack of mattocks and hoes.
You might call our distant ancestors fortunate, fortunate those generations
long, long ago, when they lived under kings and tribunes,
that witnessed a Rome content with a single prison. . . .

Acknowledgments

The Crisis of Catiline was first developed for the elementary Latin class at Haverford College and has since been deployed in several other courses at Haverford. I owe deep thanks to Hannah Weissmann and Lena Breitenfeld, who played earlier versions of the game in Haverford's introduction to Roman culture, Roman Revolutions, and then helped improve the game mechanic, role sheets, and overall experience for instructors and students alike. Additional thanks go to Mara Miller, Aileen Keogh, Jacob Horn, Florencia Foxley, and Emma Mongoven, who assisted in the initial assembly of materials for the game; Jeremy Steinberg, who helped with the revision of the role sheets; and Liam Mears, Anna Fiscarelli-Mintz, Celine Pak, and Felix Townley Bakewell, who helped with final revisions. The game was improved immeasurably from comments by play testers, reviewers, and instructors experienced with Reacting to the Past, including Nick Proctor, Martha Payne, John Moser, Charles Umiker, Marina Giovanna Maccari-Clayton, Rebecca Kennedy, Ted Gellar-Goad, Paul Wright, Peter Andersen, and many more. Special thanks go to Saundra Schwartz, who pioneered the *pedarii* point mechanic. Ray Kimball provided services as a development editor on behalf of the Reacting Editorial Board.

The game design and mechanic for *The Crisis of Catiline* are indebted to other Reacting to the Past games, in particular *Beware the Ides of March: Rome in 44 BCE* by Carl A. Anderson and T. Keith Dix. Procedures for the operation of the Roman senate are based on references to senate meetings in the speeches and letters of Cicero and on the handbook of senate procedure written by Marcus Terentius Varro in 70 BCE at the request of Pompey the Great, which was quoted by the antiquarian scholar Aulus Gellius (14.7). These instructions have been adapted from those found on the Nova Roma website (novaroma.org/nr/Senate_procedures). The evaluation rubrics that accompany this game are based on originals by Ted Gellar-Goad. B. McManus's "Roman Nomenclature" www.vroma.org/~bmcmanus /roman_names.html) provided the inspiration for (and a few of the examples in) "A Guide to Roman Names" (used with permission).

Appendix
A Guide to Roman Names

Roman names can be confusing because the Romans involved in politics generally came from only a few families, and Romans tended to use only a limited number of given names.

During the time of the crisis of Catiline, the names of most elite Roman men had three parts:

praenomen: the given name, bestowed by a father on his infant child;

nomen: the hereditary name that indicated the child's extended clan (*gens*); and

cognomen: the hereditary nickname, indicating the child's family or branch within the clan. It was originally a nickname (or agnomen, see below) of an important ancestor; often humorous or derogatory—for example, Calvus, "baldy"; Crassus, "fatty"; or Cicero, "chickpea"—it became inherited to mark the descendants of this famed ancestor. Less noble Romans (like the famous general Gaius Marius) may not possess an inherited cognomen.

Each of these elements, known collectively as the "three names," or *tria nomina*, had different significance and could be used in different combinations depending on the social status of the speakers and the social context in which the name was used.

Roman women would receive a nomen (for example, Sempronia), sometimes modified with a nickname like "older" (Agrippina Maior) or "second" (born) (Claudia Secunda) or a diminutive (Tulliola or "little Tullia").

Romans could acquire other names, such as a nickname, known as an *agnomen* because it was added to an official name (*ad-nomen → agnomen*); it could be bestowed on a Roman by popular acclamation after a great achievement or because of widespread recognition of a personal characteristic. So Catulus acquired the agnomen Capitolinus because of his role in restoring Jupiter's temple on the Capitoline Hill. Crassus acquired the agnomen Dives ("rich man") because of his vast wealth. An agnomen could be a cherished sign of honor (or a mark of shame), and might be passed on to descendants.

USING THE *TRIA NOMINA* LIKE A ROMAN

Close friends and family would use the praenomen or cognomen in addressing one another: "Marcus" or "Cicero."

Friends would use the nomen and cognomen in addressing one another: "Tullius Cicero."

Colleagues and clients would show polite respect to fellow senators by using their praenomen and nomen: "Marcus Tullius." This was the customary form of address in the senate. When in doubt about the nature of one's relationship, this mode of address was favored, with additional elements like cognomens and agnomens added if there was a need to distinguish the addressee from a relative.

Formal contexts could call for the use of all three names: "Marcus Tullius Cicero." Using a familiar form of address in a formal setting ("Marcus")—or even in private if such familiarity has not been earned—would be considered a great insult.

Notes

CHAPTER 1

1. Romans identified a year by the names of the consuls of that year or the time since the city was founded. For example, a Roman might call 63 BCE the year "when Marcus Tullius Cicero and Gaius Antonius Hybrida were consuls" or "690 AUC" (*ab urbe condita*, "from the founding of the city"). To ease comprehension, this book uses the more familiar BCE ("before the Common Era") whenever possible.

2. The names of most elite Roman men during this period consisted of three elements: the *praenomen* (e.g., Lucius), *nomen* (Licinius), and *cognomen* (Lucullus). Enslaved people would typically have a single name (e.g., Eros, Thais), while nonaristocratic citizens would have only a *praenomen* and *nomen*—for example, Quintus Sextilius; see the appendix, "A Guide to Roman Names" for additional information about Roman names and their significance.

3. Roman relationships outside of the family were defined in part by the system of patronage, or *clientela*, which established a complex set of mutual obligations between a patron and his many clients. The number of clients a patron had was one manifestation of the social authority, or *dignitas*, wielded by powerful Romans.

4. Lucullus was known for his botanical experiments, including the creation of the vegetable known today as Swiss chard.

5. The Roman senate during this period consisted of approximately 300 elite Romans who had served as quaestors and met a (high) minimum property qualification. Senators voted on legislation, controlled expenditures, oversaw foreign policy, and proposed candidates for higher-level magistracies.

6. After Lucius Cornelius Sulla Felix ("Lucky Sulla") had occupied Rome in 82 BCE and forced the senate and people to appoint him dictator, he enacted proscriptions, in which Roman citizens were arbitrarily declared public enemies (*hostes*) and executed; their murderers were allowed to keep a portion of the estates confiscated from the proscribed.

7. The Subura was one of the roughest neighborhoods of ancient Rome, near the Forum but full of narrow streets and crowded high-rise apartments known as "islands" (*insulae*).

8. Tribunes were elected by the people and empowered to protect the life and property of all non-aristocrats (the plebeians) against arbitrary abuses by nobles (the patricians). Because the bodies of tribunes were declared sacrosanct, it was a religious offense to harm a tribune when they exercised their power of *intercessio*, or interposition, on behalf of a plebeian.

9. Cicero delivered four "Speeches on the Agrarian Law" (*De Lege Agraria*), three of which survive; selections from his second speech, delivered to the people, are included in the core texts in this book.

10. Two consuls were elected annually. The consulship was the most prestigious regular political office. They were responsible for the legal, political, and diplomatic apparatus of the Roman state. They frequently led Roman armies. Although by 63 BCE any adult, male citizen could enlist in the Roman army, until the late second century BCE, only those who owned land could enlist.

11. In January 63 BCE Cicero blocked a bill that would have restored civic rights to the supporters of Marius who had been condemned by Sulla, and another that would have granted amnesty to all convicted politicians and debtors.

12. For a more detailed account of the *senatus consultum ultimum*, or "final decree of the senate," see the section "History of the *Senatus Consultum Ultimum*" in chapter 2.

13. Pompey and Crassus had been elected consuls for 70 BCE after their suppression of the slave revolt led by Spartacus (73–71 BCE). Pompey and Crassus had overturned a number of political reforms enacted by Sulla. They restored the powers of the tribunate, expanded the pool of jurors, and added large numbers of Italians to the voting rolls.

14. During Sulla's proscriptions, Catiline lured his brother-in-law, Marcus Marius Gratidianus, to his death. Quintus Lutatius Catulus Capitolinus (the current princeps senatus), who blamed Gratidianus for the death of his father, killed Gratidianus on the tomb of the elder Catulus. Catiline, however, was said to have committed

sacrilege by mutilating and decapitating the corpse of his brother-in-law and then parading Gratidianus's head through the streets of Rome before depositing it at the feet of Sulla as proof that he should receive the bounty for Gratidianus's death.

15. Knights (equites) were the second class of the Roman elite, below senators. Because knights were involved in business and trade, some were as, if not more, wealthy than many members of the senate, but they lacked the full range of political powers enjoyed by the members of the senatorial class.

16. Hannibal was the leader of what had been Rome's most tenacious foe, Carthage in North Africa, and he masterminded a devastating invasion of Italy during the Second Punic War (218–201 BCE). The Cimbri were a Germanic tribe that had invaded Roman territory and slaughtered as many as 120,000 Romans and allies at the Battle of Arausio in 105 BCE.

17. The Aventine was one of Rome's seven hills and the site of a temple to the patrons of the plebeians. It was routinely the site of plebeian resistance to patrician tyranny during the early Republic.

18. Praetors were magistrates who oversaw the foreign and citizen law courts and assumed the administrative or the military duties of consuls when the consuls were absent. Celer, as the urban praetor for 63 BCE, was one of the most powerful politicians in Rome.

19. GAIUS QUINTO FRATRE S.D.P.: Roman letters often opened and closed with formulary abbreviations. SDP stood for *salutem dicit plurimum* (warmly greets); a typical closing might be STVBEEV, or *si tu vales bene ego etiam valeo* (if you are well, I too am well).

20. In one of Aesop's fables (373), the diligent ants worked all summer planting and harvesting for the winter, while the carefree grasshopper played music. When winter came, the ants refused the starving grasshopper's pleas. A Latin version of the fable survives by Avianus (*Fables* 34).

21. Cincinnatus occupied a constitutional office. In times of severe crisis, the consuls could nominate a dictator (ratified by the senate) to take control of the entire apparatus of the Roman state. Other officials, including consuls, remained in office but became subordinate to the dictator during his six-month term.

22. More information on the Gracchi can be found in the section "The Reforms of the Gracchi and the Collapse of Civil Peace" in chapter 2.

23. Tarpeia was the daughter of the commander of the garrison on the Capitoline Hill when early Rome was besieged by the nearby Sabines. Entranced by the Sabines's gold armlets, she offered to betray the city if the Sabines promised to give her what they had on their left arms. After the Sabines entered the city, they fulfilled their pledge by crushing the hapless Tarpeia under their shields, which they also carried on their left arms. Tarpeia's lifeless body was then tossed from a rock on the Capitoline that later bore her name; see Livy 1.11 and Plutarch, *Life of Romulus* 17. The Gauls sacked Rome around 390 BCE; it was said that their attempt to capture the last spot of resistance on the Capitoline was thwarted when the sacred geese who lived in Juno's temple began honking, alerting the garrison to the Gaul's attack (Livy 5.47–49).

24. Gaius Mucius Scaevola volunteered to assassinate Lars Porsena, an Etruscan king who had laid siege to Rome in the first years of the Republic. Captured and threatened with torture, Scaevola ("Lefty") thrust his right hand into the fire and held it there until it burned off, declaring that he was only the first of 300 Roman youths who had sworn to kill the king. A stunned Porsena sued for peace; see core text Livy, *From the Founding of the City* 2.12–13.

25. Catullus, poem 49 (one of 113 poems by the author that survive).

CHAPTER 2

1. See core text Livy, *From the Founding of the City* 2.23–24, 2.32–33.

2. See core text Appian of Alexandria, *Civil Wars*.

3. For a more detailed account of the *SCU*, see the section "History of the *Senatus Consultum Ultimum*" in chapter 2.

4. See core text Cicero, *On the Agrarian Law*.

5. Sallust, *Catiline's War* 19: *consules darent operam ne quid detrimenti res publica caperet.*

CHAPTER 3

1. *Patres conscripti, quod bonum faustum felix fortunatumque sit populo Romano Quiritium, referimus ad vos. . . . De ea re quid fieri placet?*

2. *Dic, Marce Tulli (quid censes).*

3. *Murenae adsentior.*

4. *Qui hoc censetis, illuc transite; qui alia omnia, in hanc partem.*

5. *Haec pars videtur maior.*

6. The *Rhetoric for Herennius* (3.2–9) includes a wealth of more detailed advice for crafting speeches that make recommendations and offer advice; see "The *Rhetorica ad Herennium*" on Lacus Curtius, penelope.uchicago .edu/Thayer/E/Roman/Texts/Rhetorica_ad_Herennium /home.html.

7. Cicero recounts the (macabre) origin of this system in *On the Orator* 2.351–54. See also *Rhetoric for Herennius* 3.28–40 and Quintilian's *Institutes of Oratory* 11.2. For a summary of these, see L. A. Post, "Ancient Memory Systems," *Classical Weekly* 25, no. 14 (1932): 105–10, www.jstor .org/stable/4389681.

8. This list of the "ten greatest and most excellent things" in life is drawn from the eulogy of Lucius Caecilius Metellus (twice consul and pontifex maximus), delivered by his son in 221 BCE.

CHAPTER 4

1. For more on factions at the time of the crisis, see E. D. Eagle, "Catiline and the *Concordia Ordinum*," *Phoenix* 3, no. 1 (1949): 15–30, www.jstor.org/stable/1086989.

CHAPTER 5

1. "This fortified place" is the Temple of Jupiter Stator. Roman temples, with their massive stone walls and restricted entryways, made for ideal strongholds. The Roman senate consisted of approximately 300 elite Romans who had served as magistrates. They voted on legislation, controlled expenditures, oversaw foreign policy, and proposed candidates for higher-level magistracies.

2. Cicero refers to himself.

3. The pontifex maximus, as the chief priest of the state religion, managed the public calendar and sacrifices. This was a political position and the only elected magistracy in the Republic that served a lifetime term. Tiberius Sempronius Gracchus was tribune in 133 BCE; when his attempts at land reform languished, he attempted to run (anomalously) for reelection and was assassinated by a mob of senators led by Publius Scipio Nasica, an ex-consul but at the time no longer a magistrate.

4. Gaius Servilius Ahala was the assistant (*magister equitum*) of the dictator Cincinnatus; he assassinated Spurius Maelius with a dagger concealed in his armpit (*ahala*) when Maelius disobeyed the dictator and seemed to be currying favor among the people as a prelude to overthrowing the state.

5. Cicero often uses virtue, or *virtus*, to refer to the act of doing something in the service of the well-being of the state. It is a characteristic that is often used to describe Romans of the past who lived more justly. Learn more about these virtues in the section "Roman Virtues, or How to Be a Good Roman" in chapter 3.

6. The *senatus consultum ultimum*, or "final decree of the senate," authorized the consuls to safeguard the Republic during civil unrest; see the section "History of the *Senatus Consultum Ultimum*" in chapter 2.

7. Lucius Opimius was consul in 121 BCE; he was entrusted by the senate through the *SCU* to thwart the actions of Gaius Sempronius Gracchus; in the ensuing violence, Gaius and 3,000 of his supporters were killed. Among these was Marcus Fulvius, consul in 125 BCE, who had allowed himself to be elected tribune to support Gracchus.

8. Lucius Appuleius Saturninus, his associate the praetor Gaius Servilius Glaucia, and many of his supporters, were killed in 100 BCE after the senate promulgated an *SCU* to check their increasing violence. Their ally, the consul Gaius Marius, was unable to save them. Tribunes of the people were elected to protect the rights and well-being of the plebeians, or nonaristocratic and generally poorer Romans. Praetors were high-ranking magistrates who oversaw lawcourts and assumed the duties of the consuls when the consuls were absent from Rome.

9. Throughout the speech, Cicero uses "enemy," or *hostis*, to refer to both foreign enemies and the legal designation for Romans who are publicly expelled from Roman citizenship and its legal protections, typically for treasonous or tyrannical actions.

10. Walls and the pomerium (5, 6, 10, 32, 33): Cicero makes several statements in which he makes a distinction between being inside and outside of the walls of the city. In addition to portraying Catiline as an invader through this contrast, Cicero is also referencing the religiously significant pomerium, the sacred boundary that separated the city of Rome from the rest of the world.

11. Gaius Manlius was a skilled veteran of Sulla's army; he had raised an army in Etruria (to the north of Rome) in support of Catiline.

12. Praeneste was a strategically important town in Latium, approximately thirty-five kilometers east of Rome.

13. Marcus Porcius Laeca was one of Catiline's supporters, who often met at Laeca's house.

14. Knights, or equites, were the second highest socioeconomic class in Rome, after senators.

15. The cult of Jupiter Stator, or "Jupiter Who Upholds Order," was established by Romulus, the founder of Rome, after Jupiter prevented the rout of the first Roman army and saved the nascent state.

16. The senate had declined Cicero's request to postpone the elections and grant him a personal bodyguard.

17. Catiline was rumored to have murdered his son.

18. "Fortune" can denote both an individual's luck and his economic standing. Cicero charges that, because of his debts, which come due on the Ides (or the middle of the month, when the moon is full), Catiline will soon not have enough wealth to qualify to sit in the senate, ending his political career.

19. Manius Aemilius Lepidus and Lucius Volcacius Tullus were consuls in 66 BCE.

20. The Comitium was the area in the Roman Forum where citizens gathered to hear speeches and vote.

21. Nothing more is known about this Marcus Marcellus.

22. Publius Sestius was quaestor in 63 BCE. Marcus Claudius Marcellus is different from the Marcellus mentioned above. Both Sestius and this Marcellus were supporters of Cicero.

23. Forum Aurelium was a small town in Etruria on the Aurelian Way, about eighty kilometers north of Rome.

24. Catiline was said to possess an eagle from the standard of one of the legions that Marius led in defense of Rome in 101 BCE.

25. Peace: Cicero is speaking more about a period of rest (*otium*) from work for the state (*negotium*) rather than the absence of war (*pax*). He castigates Catiline for the turmoil he has caused Rome.

26. In the absence of a written constitution, the guiding principles for the running of the state were determined by precedent, or the "custom of our ancestors" (*mos maiorum*).

27. The ranks of political office, or *cursus honorum*, was the standardized sequence of high-profile political offices, beginning with the quaestorship and culminating in the consulship. Cicero was a so-called *novus homo*, a "new man," or a politician with no ancestors who had attained high office.

28. Cicero refers to Gnaeus Pompeius Magnus, who cleared the sea of pirates in 67 BCE and had recently defeated King Mithridates, the last ruler in the Mediterranean to oppose Rome.

29. Debt forgiveness, or *tabulae novae* (new ledgers), was a common promise made by radical reformers.

30. On Sulla Felix, see "Sulla heads east" in the section "The Storm before the Storm" in chapter 2.

31. On Sulla Felix, see "Sulla heads east" in the section "The Storm before the Storm" in chapter 2.

32. The Aborigines are the Sabines, an Italic tribe, who lived in the vicinity of Rome.

33. In time these would become the annually elected consuls.

34. Sallust refers to the Athenians' accomplishments in the fifth century BCE, when they forged an empire, built the Parthenon, invented Greek comedy and tragedy, and attracted the greatest thinkers and artists of the age.

35. Romans conceptualized the world as organized into two spheres: home (*domi*), or domestic matters in Rome, and war (*militiae*), or foreign affairs.

36. The manipulation of nature, especially in the construction of lavish villas, was a common complaint in moralizing literature of Sallust's age.

37. See core text Sallust, *Catiline's War* 5–13, for a general introduction to Sallust's work.

38. On Sulla Felix, see "Sulla heads east" in the section "Storm before the Storm" in chapter 2.

39. Pompey (the Great) and Crassus were co-consuls in 70 BCE. They restored the powers that Sulla had stripped from the tribunes but otherwise agreed on and accomplished little.

40. The disruptions of the 80s and 70s BCE in Rome had left a power vacuum around the Mediterranean that led to the rise of large-scale piracy. After Rome's own port of Ostia was attacked in 68 BCE, Pompey was given an extraordinary command of Roman land and sea forces around the Mediterranean and tasked with suppressing the pirate menace, which he did with stunning speed and success. This led to popular support to give him command of the stalled efforts against Mithridates in the East, whom he defeated and drove to suicide in 63 BCE.

41. A king of Syracuse had long ago converted an old quarry into a prison to hold large groups of prisoners. Verres would arrest the crews and passengers from ships bound from Spain under the pretense that they were

rebels. Those who could pay a lavish bribe were released; the others were executed.

42. Gavius planned to wait for Verres to return to Rome after the end of his governorship and prosecute him for administrative corruption.

43. The fugitive slave army led by Spartacus had moved toward southern Italy with the intention of crossing into Sicily using pirate ships. There he planned to spread the rebellion among the island's vast number of enslaved peoples. Although the pirates betrayed Spartacus, Verres, as governor, would have been guarding the island against Spartacus's forces.

44. The Porcian Laws (or more properly, the Valerian-Porcian Laws) were a series of laws that exempted Roman citizens from corporal punishment and guaranteed the right of a condemned citizen to appeal to the people (*provocatio*). The nature of the Sempronian Law is unknown but likely restated that provincial governors were bound by the Valerian-Porcian Laws.

45. Cicero composed a verse translation of the *Phaenomena*, a popular Greek poem by Aratus of Soli (ca. 315–240 BCE) on the constellations and other astronomical phenomena. Cicero quotes the opening of his own translation.

46. Cicero quotes from Rome's earliest written law code, the Twelve Tables (449 BCE).

47. In 509 BCE, the Etruscan king Lars Porsena invaded Rome and was on the verge of taking the city when Horatius Cocles staged a ferocious defense on the Sublician Bridge over the Tiber River, which allowed the panic-stricken Romans time to withdraw and destroy the bridge. Horatius was heavily wounded, losing an eye and earning the agnomen Cocles, or "one-eyed."

48. Lucius Tarquinius Superbus was the last king of Rome (535–509 BCE); Sextus was one of his sons. Lucretia's suicide galvanized the Romans to overthrow the monarchy and establish the Republic.

49. Cicero bases this argument on his etymology that "law" (*lex*) derives from "to choose" (*legere*).

50. Cicero mentions the agrarian and grain laws proposed by the tribune Sextus Titius in 99 BCE and the tribune Lucius Appuleius Saturninus in 100 BCE; Quintus then mentions similar laws by the tribune Marcus Livius Drusus in 91 BCE.

51. Cicero references his work on the ideal state, *The Republic*.

52. Charondas, perhaps a pupil of Pythagoras, was a celebrated lawgiver of the Greek city of Catania in Sicily. His verse laws were adopted by many neighboring Greek communities in the late sixth and early fifth centuries BCE. He was said to have committed suicide after he accidentally entered an assembly wearing a sword, a violation of his own law.

53. In *Laws* 701c, the Greek philosopher Plato (ca. 428/423–348/347 BCE) describes how lawful authority declines in a state, which he says passes from excessive freedom to a loss of respect for rules, elders, and parents and finally to the rejection of all oaths, pledges, and gods, leading the inhabitants to revert to a primal state of brutal suffering.

54. In 216 BCE, outside of the strategic town of Cannae in southern Italy, the Carthaginian general Hannibal annihilated both consular armies: as many as 70,000 Romans and allies were butchered in a single afternoon—among the worst defeats ever suffered by Rome or, indeed, by any army. Polybius, therefore, sets his description of the Roman constitution not in his own present (ca. mid-second century BCE) but at the moment when the Republic experienced its most profound challenge.

55. In the first section of book 6, Polybius had described the attributes of monarchy, aristocracy, and democracy.

56. By the first century BCE, Romans were required to leave Italy when they went into exile.

57. The composition of juries for major political crimes like bribery and extortion became a source of significant tension in the first century BCE, with various reformers seeking to seat the mercantile class (the knights or equites) in these juries, while conservatives attempted to preserve this as a senatorial prerogative.

58. Livy's most likely source for this section of his history, the annalist Licinius Macer, committed suicide in 66 BCE after being convicted by Cicero for corruption while he was praetor in 68.

59. At the time, the poor, since they lacked property to put up as collateral for loans, had to pledge their own bodies as collateral. If they failed to repay the loan, they became "bound" (*nexus*) to the creditor, essentially falling into slavery.

60. On August 15, 1805 (2,300 years later), Simón Bolívar swore on the same Sacred Mount that he would not rest until he had "broken the chains" of Spain's colonial occupation of South America.

61. Under the holy law (*lex sacrata*), anyone who injured a tribune was condemned to death and damned to the infernal gods, along with their wives, children, and property.

62. Marcus Aemilius Lepidus (ca. 230–152 BCE) was known as the handsomest and bravest man in Rome.

63. Valerius confuses his Fulvii here. Marcus Fulvius Nobilior (ca. 230–? BCE)—not Fulvius Flaccus—had thwarted Lepidus's attempts to be elected consul in 189 and 188. Nobilior and Lepidus were elected censors in 179. Fulvius Flaccus was censor in 174.

64. Gaius Livius Salinator (254–ca. 191 BCE) led a successful campaign against the Illyrians in 219 but went into exile after he was found guilty of misappropriating the spoils of that campaign. During the Second Punic War, he was recalled and elected consul in 207.

65. Gaius Claudius Nero (ca. 247–ca. 189 BCE) had testified against Salinator during his corruption trial in 218.

66. Salinator and Nero led the Roman army that smashed the Carthaginian forces under the command of Hasdrubal at the Battle of Mataurus, ending Carthage's last hope for victory in the Second Punic War.

67. Publius Cornelius Scipio Africanus (236/5–183 BCE) spearheaded the Roman conquest of Carthaginian Spain and then defeated Hannibal at the Battle of Zama in 202, effectively ending the Second Punic War. His popularity led to animosity among the other aristocrats, who repeatedly attempted to bring him to trial for corruption. In 185, he was defended by Tiberius Gracchus, who would later wed Cornelia, one of that century's most illustrious Roman women (and the mother of Tiberius and Gaius Gracchus).

68. Valerius aligns three core Roman virtues, generosity (*liberalitas*), grace (*humanitas*), and mercy (*clementia*); see the section "Roman Virtues, or How to Be a Good Roman" in chapter 3.

69. Valerius refers to *humanitas* (compare "humanity").

70. Valerius refers to the Carthaginian delegation that brokered the end of the Second Punic War (218–201 BCE).

71. Syphax ruled Numidia in North Africa during the Second Punic War. He was captured after his defeat in the Battle of Great Plains and died in Roman custody in 201 BCE.

72. Perseus, or Perses (ca. 213/2–165 BCE), was the last king of Macedonia. His defeat at Pydna in 168 ended the Third Macedonian War (171–168 BCE). He was captured in Samothrace later that year.

73. Rome's victory in the Third Macedonian War ended the political independence of the Kingdom of Macedonia. Masinissa (ca. 238–148 BCE) originally fought against the Romans in the Second Punic War, but his defection to the Roman side helped Scipio defeat Hannibal and the Carthaginians at Zama in 201. Thereafter, he was a loyal ally to Rome, and Numidia flourished under his rule.

74. Prusias II (ca. 220–149 BCE) ruled Bithynia, a kingdom on the shores of the Black Sea, until his abdication.

75. In 164 BCE, Ptolemy VI Philometor (186–145 BCE) was briefly deposed by his younger brother, Ptolemy VII Euergetes II.

76. Lucius Cornelius Scipio was consul in 259 BCE and led an expedition against Carthaginian territory in Corsica and Sardinia during the First Punic War (264–241 BCE). Olbia is a town in northeast Sardinia.

77. Titus Quinctius Crispinus shared the consulship with Marcus Claudius Marcellus in 208 BCE during the Second Punic War (218–201 BCE).

78. Marcus Claudius Marcellus (270–208 BCE), known as the "Sword of Rome," captured Syracuse in Sicily after a lengthy siege in 212.

79. Metellus besieged Centobriga at the start of the Third Celtiberian, or Numantine, War (143–133 BCE).

80. Publius Cornelius Scipio Africanus the Younger (185/184–129 BCE) sacked Carthage at the end of the Third Punic War (149–146 BCE).

81. Lucius Aemilius Paullus Macedonius (ca. 229–160 BCE) defeated Perseus, king of Macedonia, in the Third Macedonian War (171–168 BCE).

82. Marcus Manlius Capitolinus had been consul in 392 BCE and led the final resistance to the Gallic sack of Rome in 390, becoming the first man of equestrian rank to win the mural crown for exceptional bravery when defending fortifications. The plebeians suffered terribly during the sack and its aftermath, with many falling deep into debt. In 384, when Manlius saw a centurion being led to prison for his debt, he bought his freedom with his own money and then sold his property to relieve the debt of other impoverished plebeians. The aristocrats suspected him of aiming to become a tyrant and condemned and executed him. The Manlii never again named a child Marcus, consigning his name to eternal obscurity; see core text Livy, *From the Founding of the City* 6.14.

83. The Senones were a people of Gaul.

84. Spurius Cassius Viscellinus was one of the most illustrious figures in the first decades of the Republic, but when he proposed Rome's first agrarian law, which sought to distribute conquered lands to the urban plebs and their Latin allies, he was condemned for aiming to become a tyrant and executed in 485 BCE; see Livy 2.41.

85. During a severe famine, Spurius Maelius bought a large amount of wheat with his own money and resold it at a reduced price to the people of Rome. Lucius Minucius Augurinus, the praetor in charge of the grain supply, accused him of plotting a coup. When Maelius refused a summons by the dictator Cincinnatus, he was assassinated by Gaius Servilius Ahala in 439 BCE.

86. The name Aequimelium contains a pun, as it can mean both "Maelius's square" and "Maelius's justice."

87. On the praetor Marcus Flaccus and the tribune Lucius Saturninus, see "Reforms of Marius" in the section "The Storm before the Storm" in chapter 2.

88. Quintus Catulus and Gaius Marius had defeated the invading Cimbri at the Battle of Vercellae in 101 BCE.

89. On Tiberius and Gaius Gracchus, see the section "The Reforms of the Gracchi and the Collapse of Civil Peace" in chapter 2.

90. Tiberius Sempronius Gracchus (ca. 217–154 BCE) was twice consul and twice celebrated a triumph; Publius Cornelius Scipio Africanus (236/5–183 BCE) spearheaded the Roman conquest of Spain and led the invasion of Carthaginian Africa during the Second Punic War (218–201).

91. Publius Mucius Scaevola was tribune in 486 BCE; the action Valerius describes is of dubious historical authenticity.

92. Marcus Claudius Glicia was a freedman who had accompanied his former master, Publius Claudius Pulcher, when the latter was given command of a Roman fleet in Sicily in 249 BCE during the First Punic War (264–241 BCE). After Pulcher's disastrous defeat at Drepana (in which he arrogantly drowned the sacred chickens), he was recalled by the senate, which asked him to appoint a dictator to continue the war in Sicily. He mocked the senate by appointing his former slave. Although the senate refused to ratify Glicia's dictatorship, he nevertheless attended public games in the regalia of a former dictator, which the senators took as a sign of impertinence and which they used to insult members of the Claudii forever

after. As legate to the consul Varius in 236, Glicia made an unauthorized treaty with the Corsi on Corsica.

93. The Gemonian Steps were a flight of stairs on the Capitoline Hill. The bodies of executed criminals were thrown down the stairs and left to rot before being thrown into the Tiber River.

94. Gnaeus Cornelius Scipio was consul in 139 BCE; the historical accuracy of Valerius's account is questionable.

95. On the Italian, or Social, War, see "The Social War" in the section "The Storm before the Storm" in chapter 2; nothing else is known of this Vettienus.

96. Manlius Curius Dentatus (d. 270 BCE) was thrice consul and a hero of the Samnite War. In 275, when he was consul for the second time, he thwarted King Pyrrhus's invasion of Italy. Curius was said to be incorruptible: when the Samnites attempted to bribe him, their delegates found him humbly roasting turnips over a fire; Curius said he preferred to rule those who possessed gold than to possess it himself (see Valerius Maximus 4.3.5).

97. Lucius Domitius Ahenobarbus governed Sicily around 96 BCE, when the island was still in turmoil following the Second Servile War (104–100 BCE).

98. For Seneca, the opposite of mercy is pity (*misercordia*), discussed below.

99. Busiris was a mythological king of Egypt who murdered travelers until he was killed by Hercules. Procrustes was a brigand who murdered travelers in Attica by stretching them or cutting off their legs to make them fit his bed until he was killed by Theseus.

100. Phalaris (d. ca. 554 BCE) was the tyrant of Acragas in Sicily. He was said to have roasted criminals alive inside a bronze bull—and eventually met the same fate.

101. Cicero refers to the supposed assassination attempt by Catiline and his followers on January 1, 63 BCE.

102. Cicero refers to the children of those who had been condemned by Sulla.

103. On the reforms of the Gracchi and their assassinations by the aristocrats, see the section "The Reforms of the Gracchi and the Collapse of Civil Peace" in chapter 2.

104. It had been fashionable for Romans to shave since the third century BCE, when Licinius Moenas introduced Greek barbers to Rome.

105. That is, December 12, 64 BCE.

106. Elections of this sort were typically held using thirty-five voting tribes. The effect of Rullus's law would be that seventeen tribes would be chosen by lot (of thirty-

five, so less than a majority, which was safely controlled by members of the senatorial and equestrian classes) and the decemvirs would be elected by a majority of those seventeen tribes.

107. Mount Gaurus in Campania possessed valuable vineyards.

108. The marshland of Minturnae sat at the border of Latium and Campania. It was a fertile and thriving region, and Romans often planned to create more cropland by draining the marshlands, which were frequently the haunt of outlaws. Marius hid himself in the marshes during his flight from Sulla.

109. Cicero refers to notable figures from the third and second centuries BCE. Gaius Fabricus Luscinus (consul 282 and 278) fought Pyrrhus of Epirus and was famous for his frugality. Aulus Atilius Calatinus (consul 258 and 254) was a general in the First Punic War; once, when summoned by the senate, he was discovered humbly sowing his own land. Lucius Manilius Acidinus (consul 179) was a general in the Second Punic War; presumably he was also known for his embodiment of some traditional virtue, but this is lost to us.

110. Cicero now refers to important families from the second century BCE, a few generations in the past, all of whom were known for their virtue, wisdom, and patriotism.

111. Property that had been procured during the Sullan proscriptions would be unpopular; see "Sulla's second march on Rome and the Sullan terror" in the section "The Storm before the Storm" in chapter 2.

112. The Janiculan Hill, or Janiculum, was the tallest hill in Rome, on the west bank of the Tiber and so outside the sacred boundaries of the city. Because of its tactical importance, it was early incorporated into Rome's defenses, although this did not prevent Lars Porsena from occupying the hill in 508 BCE and using it as a base to threaten Rome.

113. Cicero addresses Rullus directly.

114. The Campus Martius ("Field of Mars") was the plain in northern Rome, the site of military musters and public meetings. In the time of Sulla, wealthy landowners had begun building large houses in the area.

115. Marcus Junius Brutus had been tribune in 83 BCE and founded a colony in Capua. His actions were discredited when he joined Lepidus's unsuccessful revolt in 78. He was captured and executed by Pompey.

116. Cicero is probably addressing the Roman citizens,

but he clearly wishes to call to mind Pompey's soldiers, who would likely revolt if their victorious general were threatened.

117. Cicero distinguishes "new men" like him, who won their place through open elections in the Campus Martius, from those who attained prominence because of their noble birth.

118. A Roman acre (*iugerum*) was equivalent to approximately two-thirds of a modern acre.

119. The First Servile War (135–132 BCE) was an uprising of enslaved persons in Sicily.

120. When Cossus had defeated the Volsci, he discovered among the captured soldiers leading youths from many Latin towns that were supposedly allies to Rome.

121. This ceremony symbolically sold the debtor from his creditor to the goddess Liberty.

122. Manlius was eventually condemned and hurled from the Tarpeian Rock.

123. The Greek historian Diodorus makes it clear that it was the violent reaction of the creditors to a cancellation of debt that precipitated the unrest (29.33).

124. Aratus of Sicyon (b. 273 BCE) was expelled from Sicyon, a Greek town near Corinth, at the age of seven after his father was assassinated. He returned in 251 and enjoyed a successful military and political career until his death, perhaps by poisoning, in 213.

125. Ptolemy II Philadelphus (b. 309/8 BCE) ruled Egypt from 283 until his death in 246.

126. During public auctions, a spear was erected to announce the site of the auction and that it was being held under public authority. Cicero contrasts Aratus's just actions with the auction of property seized during the bloody confiscations first by the supporters of Marius and then during Sulla's proscriptions.

127. Plato, *Laws* 844b.

128. The Greek word *trapeza* can mean both "bank" and "table."

129. For the Greeks, interest on loans was due on the first of day of the month, which coincided with the new moon. The Romans paid interest on the Ides of a month, or the day of the full moon, which fell near the middle of the month.

130. Pericles (ca. 495–429 BCE) was a general and politician who led Athens from 461 to 429 BCE. At his encouragement, Athens rebuilt the temples on the Acropolis that had been destroyed by the Persians.

131. Delphi in Greece had been the site of the most

famous oracle in the ancient Mediterranean, although by Plutarch's time its influence had waned.

132. Plutarch refers to the (ultimately unsuccessful) efforts to save Carthage from the besieging Romans in the Third Punic War (149–146 BCE).

133. The Persian Wars were a series of conflicts between Persia and many cities in Greece (490–479 BCE).

134. The Persians demanded that cities show their submission to their authority by giving symbolic gifts of "earth and water."

135. Solon (ca. 630–560 BCE) was an Athenian lawgiver and poet, who passed numerous economic and social reforms, including the outlawing of debt bondage.

136. Plato, *Republic* 615e.

137. Homer, *Odyssey* 11.578. Tantalus was a mythological king who abused the hospitality of the gods, both by stealing ambrosia, the food of the gods, and by cooking his son, Pelops, and serving him to the gods.

138. Darius (550–487 BCE) was a king of Persia; he sent two generals, Datis and Artaphernes, to invade Eretria and Attica in 490 BCE.

139. Triptolemus was a mythological figure in ancient Greece who was associated with the discovery of agriculture.

140. Plutarch puns on two meanings of the word *tokos*, which can mean both "interest" and "offspring."

141. The aphorism is explained by the geographer Strabo (8.3.7), who says that three towns named Pylos claimed to be the homeland of the Homeric hero Nestor.

142. Herodotus claims that Persians place lying first and debt second (1.138).

143. Homer, *Iliad* 1.154.

144. Crates of Thebes (ca. 365–ca. 285 BCE) was a Cynic philosopher and teacher of Zeno of Citium. The end of the quotation quotes Homer, *Odyssey* 12.257.

145. Cleanthes of Assos (ca. 330–ca. 230 BCE) was a Greek Stoic philosopher and successor of Zeno. When studying with Zeno, he worked nights as a water carrier. Antigonus II Gonatas (ca. 320–ca. 230 BCE) was a ruler of Macedonia.

146. Zeno of Citium (ca. 334–ca. 262 BCE) founded the philosophical school of Stoicism.

147. Empedocles of Acragas (ca. 494–ca. 434 BCE) was an early Greek philosopher who argued that the world was composed of four elements bound by Love and Strife.

148. Homer, *Odyssey* 5.264.

149. Homer, *Odyssey* 5.439.

150. Homer, *Odyssey* 5.291–92.

151. Crates of Thebes (ca. 365–ca. 285 BCE) was a Cynic philosopher, who, like his teacher Diogenes, embraced a life of poverty.

152. Anaxagoras of Clazomenae (ca. 500–428 BCE) was an important pre-Socratic philosopher, who argued that the universe was ordered by *Nous*, or the Cosmic Mind.

153. Philoxenus of Cythera (ca. 435/4–380/79 BCE) was one of the most popular and important musical innovators in ancient Greece.

154. Phineus was a mythological king and prophet in Thrace who was tormented by the Harpies, creatures who were half bird and half woman, because he had dishonored Helios, the sun god.

155. Since the star Arcturus rises in the springtime, the grapes have only just begun to grow.

156. That is, Cumae, a town in Campania, to the south of Rome.

157. Juvenal refers to lawyers, paid to persuade a jury that up was down and wrong was right.

158. The state sold the right to collect urine from the public latrines and resell it to fullers, who used it to clean wool.

159. The Tagus is the longest river in the Iberian Peninsula; it was famous for the gold that washed down in its sands.

160. *Chione*, or "snow-white," was a common name for a foreign sex worker in Rome.

161. Publius Cornelius Scipio Nasica escorted the black meteorite that was symbolic of the goddess Cybele to Rome in 204 BCE.

162. Numa, the second king of Rome, was credited with establishing many of Rome's religious traditions. Lucius Caecilius Metellus was twice consul during the First Punic War. When he was pontifex maximus, Metellus was blinded when he saved the Palladium, a small wooden statue of Minerva, from a fire in the Temple of Vesta in 241 BCE.

163. The island of Samothrace was the site of a major Panhellenic sanctuary to the Greek gods.

164. That is, he is not wealthy enough to deserve her dowry.

165. Owners honored their favorite young slaves through ceremonial offerings of locks of hair and the first clippings of their beard.

166. Since all Roman apartment buildings were walk-ups and smoke from heating and cooking rises, the upper

stories of a building were the least desirable and least expensive.

167. Heavy traffic was allowed into Rome's narrow streets only at night. Drusus likely refers to the emperor Claudius, who was infamous for his frequent napping. The Romans believed that seals experienced deeper sleep than any other animal.

168. The rich man's litter (a covered seat or couch carried by men or animals) seems so large that Juvenal compares it to a warship.

169. When Achilles's friend Patroclus was killed in the Trojan War, he descended into extreme and protracted grief and vowed revenge on his friend's killer, Hector.

170. The Pontine Marshes were a coastal region near Rome. The Gallinarian forest was in western Campania. Both areas were difficult to police and attracted brigands.

Glossary

Album Senatorum (the list of senators). The official list of Roman male citizens who met the qualifications for participating in the senate. Its ranking of seniority—from the consuls-elect to the most junior senator—determined the order of senatorial debates.

Boni (the good guys). Politicians who believe Rome is strongest when there is harmony between the senate and the people. They acknowledge that the senate should be more accountable to the people but will usually oppose reform if it threatens the traditional order, which prevents the rise of their greatest fear: tyranny.

censor. A prestigious magistrate tasked with maintaining the official lists of senators, knights, and citizens; setting property taxes; contracting for major public projects. Unique among magistrates, censors were elected every five years to eighteen-month terms and possessed the power to expel members of the senate for moral transgressions.

client. Roman relationships outside of the family were defined in part by the system of patronage, or *clientela*, which established a complex set of mutual obligations between a patron and his many clients. A patron was expected to protect, mentor, and support his clients. The client was expected to support the patron to the best of his abilities, often by voting for him and his friends. Powerful Romans typically had many clients in inferior classes, but more prominent nobles could also serve as the patrons of other nobles, who would have their own clients in turn. The number of clients a patron had was one manifestation of the social authority, or *dignitas*, wielded by powerful Romans.

consul. The most prestigious and powerful annual political office in Rome. When consuls were in Rome, they were responsible for the legal, political, and diplomatic apparatus of the Roman state; outside of Rome they served as supreme commanders of the Roman army. There were always two consuls, each with the power to block the decisions of the other, an effective check against tyranny.

consulship. *See* consul.

consultum. See *senatus consultum*.

Curia. *See* senate.

cursus honorum (path of offices). The sequence of elected Roman offices that began with the quaestorship and culminated in the consulship. After Sulla's reforms in the late 80s BCE, each office had a minimum age requirement, and candidates had to wait a minimum number of years between elected offices. But these restrictions were often waived in the late Republic.

discessio (separation). The voting method used by the Roman senate (see "Rules and Procedures: The *Mos Maiorum*" in chapter 3).

equites. *See* knights.

hostis (enemy). A public enemy who had taken up arms against the Republic and so was deprived of citizen rights and any protection under the law.

imperium (power to command). The formal authority conveyed on a magistrate to act in the interests of the state within his jurisdiction. Magistrates with *imperium* carried a distinctive ivory baton topped by an eagle and were escorted by lictors, who carried the fasces, or a bundle of rods. Outside of Rome, an axe was added to the fasces to indicate that the magistrate could impose capital punishment.

intercessio (interposition). The right of any magistrate to prevent an action by a colleague of equal rank by calling out "veto" ("I forbid it"). Also, the tribune's right to prevent the action of any magistrate (or another tribune) by interposing his sacrosanct body.

knights (equites). In early Rome, members of the equestrian class served in the cavalry and so had to be wealthy enough to supply their own horses and armor. By the late Republic, knights were part of the Roman elite, along with the senators. Because knights were involved in business and trade, some were as, if not more, wealthy than many members of the senate, but they lacked the full range of political powers enjoyed by members of the senatorial class.

magistrate. Any of the higher Roman political officers (censor, consul, praetor, aedile, and quaestor).

mos maiorum (the way of the ancestors). A general term used to refer to the established customs, behaviors, and traditions of the Roman people. Although it implied traditions of great antiquity, it could refer to any precedents, even those set quite recently.

novus homo (new man). A designation given to the first man from a family to be elected to the quaestorship and consequentially serve in the Roman senate. Also used to refer to the first man in a family to attain the consulship and so reach the pinnacle of Roman political power.

Optimates (the best men). Politicians who sought to preserve or restore the political prerogatives of the senatorial aristocracy; they were often opposed by *Populares*.

patres conscripti (conscript fathers, or enrolled fathers). All the senators, patricians and plebeians alike. In the senate, this is the term senators used when addressing the whole body of the senate.

patricians. Senatorial families who trace their lineage to the time of the kings, before the Republic itself. In the early Republic, they came to monopolize important magistracies and religious offices, although this grip was eventually relaxed. Even in the late Republic, a limited set of (minor) offices and priesthoods could be held only by patricians.

patron; patronage. *See* client.

pedarii (feet-men). Senators who, because of their low status, did not deliver speeches but revealed their opinion "with their feet" by walking to the appointed side of the senate chamber during voting. Technically, pedarii were those who have not yet been entered by the censors in the *Album Senatorum* and so have no vote of their own but could merely signify that they agree with another senator. But the term has come to be applied to those who vote in accordance with their patrons without expressing their own opinion.

perduellio (high treason). According to the Law of the Twelve Tables, a man is treasonous if he stirs up an enemy or betrays a citizen to the enemy. Eventually *perduellio* came to refer to any action by a citizen against the Roman constitution, including attempts to seize tyrannical power and the violation of tribunician sacrosanctity. By the late Republic it was an obsolete law, but it was revived by Gaius Julius Caesar for the prosecution of Rabirius in early 63 BCE.

plebeians (or plebs). All families that are not patricians. One of the consuls and all tribunes needed to be plebeian.

pomerium. The sacred boundary that marked the spiritual division between Rome and the rest of the world. To protect the city from religious pollution, Romans were barred from doing certain things within its confines, like leading troops (with only a few exceptions) and burying the dead.

Populares (favoring the people). Politicians who claimed to support democratic prerogatives and the interests of "the people," including land distribution, cancellation of debt, subsidized distribution of food, and expansion of the vote.

praetor. A magistrate who oversaw the foreign and citizen law courts and assumed the administrative or the military duties of consuls when the consuls were absent.

princeps senatus (chief of the senate). A position of enormous prestige in the Roman senate. Appointed by the censors to a renewable five-year term, the *princeps senatus* was usually an elderly patrician senator who had served as consul and often as censor. His chief duty was to safeguard the traditions of the senate.

promagistrate. A military or administrative post in the provinces filled by a magistrate after his term in elected office is complete; for example, propraetor or proconsul.

proscription. Technically the publication of any written notice, but in reference to Roman history, "proscription" referred to the publication of a list of Roman citizens who had been declared a public enemy (*hostis*) and so deprived of their citizen rights and any protection under the law. Rewards were given to informers who contributed to the death of the proscribed. Anyone who killed a proscribed man was entitled to a share of his property, with the remainder going to the state. During the dictatorship of Sulla (82–81 BCE), hundreds and perhaps thousands of Romans were proscribed and executed without trial, often in the dead of night. This state-sanctioned terror left a deep scar on the Roman psyche.

relatio. A matter presented for formal discussion before the senate.

rex. A king, monarch. A word hateful to the Romans.

senatus consultum. Recommendation of the senate to a magistrate.

senatus consultum ultimum **(SCU).** The final decree of the senate (see "History of the *Senatus Consultum Ultimum*" in chapter 2).

sententia. An opinion delivered in the senate by a senator.

Struggle of the Orders. A centuries-long process through which plebeians won the full rights of citizenship and access to Rome's legal and political system.

tribune (of the plebs). Empowered to protect the life and property of all plebeians against arbitrary abuses by patricians. Because the bodies of tribunes were declared sacrosanct, it was a religious offense to harm a tribune when he exercised his power of *intercessio*, or interposition, on behalf of a pleb.

triumph. A spectacular ceremony that celebrated a great military success, especially the successful conclusion of a foreign war. With the permission of the senate, the triumphator, dressed in a costume to make him look like the statue of Jupiter Optimus Maximus, paraded through the city in a four-horse chariot, followed by his soldiers, captives, and spoils of war. The procession ended at the Temple of Jupiter Optimus Maximus, where the triumphator offered a sacrifice to Jupiter in thanks for his victory.

Bibliography

DIGITAL RESOURCES

Digital Prosopography of the Roman Republic. http://romanrepublic.ac.uk. A comprehensive, searchable database of all known members of the upper strata of Roman society, including information about individual careers, office holdings, personal status, life dates, and family relationships.

Lacus Curtius. http://penelope.uchicago.edu/Thayer /E/Roman/home.html. An extensive collection of texts and resources for the study of the ancient world.

ORBIS: The Stanford Geospatial Network Model of the Roman World. http://orbis.stanford.edu. Reconstructs the time and costs associated with a wide range of different types of travel in antiquity; a fantastic resource for understanding the scope of the Roman Empire and how distance influenced communication before modern technology.

Perseus Project. www.perseus.tufts.edu. The premier open-access, digital collection of Greco-Roman texts; it includes thousands of works in the original languages, translations, commentaries, and reference works. Translations are all drawn from the public domain and so tend to be old (and perhaps difficult at times to understand).

Smith's Dictionary of Greek and Roman Antiquities. https://penelope.uchicago.edu/Thayer/E/Roman /Texts/secondary/SMIGRA/home.html. A treasure trove of information about the ancient world, despite its age (1891).

GENERAL BACKGROUND AND HISTORIES

Beard, Mary. 2015. *SPQR: A History of Rome*. New York: Liveright. See especially chapter 1.

Duncan, M. 2018. *The Storm before the Storm: The Beginning of the End of the Roman Republic*. New York: Hachette. A detailed but quick-paced dive into the period from 146 BCE to 78 BCE, when the generations of the Gracchi, Marius, and Sulla sowed the seeds of the crisis of Catiline; by the creator of the award-winning podcasts *The History of Rome* and *Revolutions*.

Fantham, E. 2005. "Liberty and the People in Republican Rome." *Transactions of the American Philological Association* 135 (2): 209–29. https://www.jstor.org /stable/20054131. Explores the idea of personal liberty or the free condition of adult, male Romans during the Republic and how this differed from the conditions of noncitizens and slaves.

Gruen, E. S. 1974. *The Last Generation of the Roman Republic*. Berkeley: University of California Press. A great survey of the crisis of the late Republic.

Hooper, Finley. 1979. *Roman Realities*. Detroit: Wayne State University Press. See especially chapters 2, 6, and 7.

Levick, B. 2015. *Catiline*. London: Bloomsbury. A lucid, balanced introduction to the crisis.

Millar, F. 1998. *The Crowd in Rome in the Late Republic*. Ann Arbor: University of Michigan Press.

Mitchell, T. 1991. "The Political Ideas behind the Politics of 63." In *Cicero: The Senior Statesman*, 9–62. New Haven, CT: Yale University Press.

Plutarch. *Parallel Lives*. Translated by B. Perrin. Cambridge, MA: Loeb Classical Library. Detailed biographies of several of the key figures in the crisis and its build up, including *Tiberius & Gaius Gracchus, Marius, Sulla, Lucullus, Sertorius, Crassus, Caesar*, and *Cato the Younger*. The latter three biographies extend beyond 63 BCE.

Steel, Catherine. 2013. *The End of the Roman Republic 146 to 44 BC: Conquest and Crisis*. Edinburgh, UK: Edinburgh University Press. See especially chapters 5 and 6.

NOTABLE FICTIONAL ACCOUNTS OF THE CONSPIRACY

Anderson, Paul. 1957. *A Slave of Catiline*. New York: Biblio & Tannen.

Harris, Robert. 2010. *Conspirata*. New York: Simon & Schuster.

McCullough, Colleen. 2008. *Caesar's Women*. New York: Harper Collins.

Roberts, John Maddox. 2001. *The Catiline Conspiracy*. New York: St. Martin's Press.

Saylor, Steven. 2005. "The Consul's Wife;" and "The Cherries of Lucullus." In *A Gladiator Dies Only Once*.

New York: St. Martin's Press. On Sempronia and Lucullus, respectively.

———. 2007. *Catilina's Riddle*. New York: St. Martin's Press.

PHASE 2, SESSION 1: AMNESTY

Alexander, Michael C. 2002. "*In L. Licinium Murenam*." In *The Case for the Prosecution in the Ciceronian Era*, 121–27. Ann Arbor: University of Michigan Press. Explains the reasons for opposing amnesty.

Cicero. *Pro Roscio Amerino*. Cicero's first major speech, in which he defended Roscius on the charge that he murdered his father. Cicero attacks the ease with which weak prosecutions can succeed in convicting an innocent man (35–82) and the perversion of justice for political and economic reasons (122–42).

Flower, Harriet I. 2006. "Punitive Memory Sanctions II: The Republic of Sulla." In *The Art of Forgetting: Disgrace and Oblivion in Roman Political Culture*. Chapel Hill: University of North Carolina Press. https://www.jstor .org/stable/10.5149/9780807877463_flower.9. For Roman social memory and judicial process, with background on the trauma of the proscriptions (especially 98f.) and Catiline's role therein (94–95).

Konstan, David. 2005. "Clemency as a Virtue." *Classical Philology* 100 (4): 337–46. www.jstor.org/stable/10.1086 /500436. Explores how forgiveness was understood as a Roman virtue.

Lintott, Andrew W. 1990. "Electoral Bribery in the Roman Republic." *Journal of Roman Studies* 80:1–16. For context on bribery and other political "bad acts."

Stem, Rex. 2006. "Cicero as Orator and Philosopher: The Value of the *Pro Murena* for Ciceronian Political Thought." *Review of Politics* 68 (2): 206–31. www.jstor .org/stable/20452778. For Roman social memory and its connection to politics during the crisis.

PHASE 2, SESSION 2: LAND REFORM

Cicero. *De Lege Agraria*. Book 1 was delivered to the senate and is interesting for the different approach that Cicero took with that audience; selections from book 2 available in chapter 5; no web resources, sadly.

Hopwood, Keith. 2007. "Smear and Spin: Ciceronian Tactics in *De Lege Agraria II*." In *Cicero on the Attack: Invective and Subversion in the Orations and Beyond*, edited by Joan Booth, 71–103. Swansea, UK: Classical Press of Wales.

Kaplow, L. 2012. "Creating *Popularis* History: Sp. Cassius, Sp. Maelius, and M. Maelius in the Political Discourse of the Late Republic." *Bulletin of the Institute of Classical Studies* 55 (2): 101–9. www.jstor.org/stable/44254113. How earlier politicians were reconfigured in respect to the *Optimates/Populares* opposition in the late Republic.

Sage, Evan T. 1921. "Cicero and the Agrarian Proposals of 63 B.C." *Classical Journal* 16 (4): 230–36. A short summary and discussion.

Sumner, G. V. 1966. "Cicero, Pompeius, and Rullus." *Transactions and Proceedings of the American Philological Association* 97:569–682. www.jstor.com/stable/2936030. Includes a concise summary of Rullus's legislation and Cicero's opposition within the broader political framework of the time.

Virgil. *Eclogues* 1 and 9. Written after 63 BCE but provides a useful source on the discontents of the farmers caused by land confiscations.

PHASE 2, SESSIONS 3: DEBT REFORM

Frederiksen, M. W. 1966. "Caesar, Cicero and the Problem of Debt." *Journal of Roman Studies* 56 (1–2): 128–41. www.jstor.org/stable/300140. On the issue of debt relief.

Frier, B. W. 1983. "Urban Praetors and Rural Violence: The Legal Background of Cicero's *Pro Caecina*." *Transactions of the American Philological Association* 113:221–41. www.jstor.org/stable/284012. Discusses the evolution of the Roman legal system in the 70s and 60s BCE against the background of rural violence during the period.

Shaw, D. B. 1975. "Debt in Sallust." *Latomus* 34:187–96.

Yavetz, Z. 1958. "The Living Conditions of the Urban Plebs in Republican Rome." *Latomus* 17 (3): 500–517. www .jstor.org/stable/41521048. Background about the plight of the urban poor.

PHASE 2, SESSION 4: *SENATUS CONSULTUM ULTIMUM* (SCU)

Cicero. *Pro Rabirio Perduellionis Reo*. A defense of the necessity of the *SCU*—but also the necessity for clemency in the republican system, although it may be difficult for students to extract these points without guidance; note that Cicero wrote two speeches titled *Pro Rabirio*; only this speech refers to events during the crisis.

———. *Third Catilinarian*. Cicero offers evidence that Catiline's accomplices confessed.

Gaughan, Judy E. 2010. "License to Kill." In *Murder Was Not a Crime*, 109-25. Austin: University of Texas Press. www.jstor.org/stable/10.7560/721111.12. An accessible dive into the *SCU* and "sanctioned" political violence in the late Republic.

Lintott, Andrew W. 1999. "The So-Called Final Decree." In *The Constitution of the Roman Republic*, 89-93. New York: Oxford University Press.

———. 1999. *Violence in Republican Rome*. New York: Oxford University Press. See especially chapters 4, 7, and 11.

Price, Jonathan J. 1998. "The Failure of Cicero's *First Catilinarian*." *Studies in Latin Literature and Roman History* 9:106-28.

Tyrrell, Wm. Blake. 1973. "The Trial of C. Rabirius in 63 B.C." *Latomus* 32 (2): 285-300. www.jstor.org/stable /41528650. Most helpful for students who can read Latin.

PHASE 2, SESSION 5: CONSEQUENCES

Batstone, William W. 1988. "The Antithesis of Virtue: Sallust's Synkrisis and the Crisis of the Late Republic." *Classical Antiquity* 7 (1): 1-29. An informative reading of the speeches of Caesar and Cato in Sallust and their connection to the larger issues at play in the crisis.

Bauman, Richard A. B. 1996. *Crime and Punishment in Ancient Rome*. New York: Routledge. Available on Google Books. See especially pages 19-22 and 27-39.

Cicero. *Fourth Catilinarian*. Cicero argues that executing the conspirators is the only way to ensure the safety of the senate and the Republic.

Drummond, Andrew. 1995. *Law, Politics and Power: Sallust and the Execution of the Catilinarian Conspirators*. Stuttgart, Germany: Franz Steiner.

Green, William McAllen. 1929. "An Ancient Debate on Capital Punishment." *Classical Journal* 24 (4): 267-75. www.jstor.org/stable/3289693. Notes the rareness of the judicial death penalty in late Republican Rome and offers an analysis of the debate on the fate of the Catilinarians.

March, Duane A. 1989. "Cicero and the 'Gang of Five.'" *Classical World* 82 (4): 225-34. www.jstor.org/stable /4350381. Discusses why Cicero executed the Catilinarians in the manner that he did.

Ramsay, W. W. 1863. "Punishments Recognized in Roman Criminal Law." In *A Manual of Roman Antiquities*, 309-11. London: Griffin Bohn. Available on Google Books.

Sallust. *Catiline's War* 50-54. The speech by Caesar in favor of indefinite arrest, Cato in favor of execution, and the outcome of the debate.

Printed in the USA
CPSIA information can be obtained
at www.ICGtesting.com
CBHW080303010924
13954CB00011B/391